Eden

An Essay on Arts & Crafts Values, Garden City Ideals, and the 1924 'Wheatley' Housing Act

John Astley

In *Access to Eden*, John Astley explores the influences that shaped the original public sector housing ideals in Britain.

The essay surveys the cultural and legislative strands in a narrative that reveals the origins of public sector housing with company housing (such as Port Sunlight), the Arts and Crafts movement, with architects such as Baillie Scott, the Garden City pioneer Ebenezer Howard, and urban planners such as Raymond Unwin and Barry Parker.

In light of these background perspectives, the author considers (in the aftermath of the 1914-18 War) the impact of the Housing Acts of the 1920s that empowered local authorities of the day to take action on the housing front with a mission to build "Homes for Heroes".

As a case study, the author selects the Merry Oak housing development in Bitterne, Southampton, to examine the practical outcome of the innovative legislation that had been established, and in particular by the 1924 Housing Act of John Wheatley.

The author concludes his essay with a brief look at public sector housing in the present era, and finds a landscape of lost opportunities and a failure to learn from the hard-won lessons of the past. Public sector housing, the author finds, now seems to be seen as social housing as a system of 'distributed Welfare'. . .

Is it really too late, though, for local government to regain the moral high ground and deliver quality public sector housing?

After reading Access to Eden, you will not be able to look at a house - any house - in quite the same way again.

By the same author:

Access to Eden: The Rise and Fall of Public Sector Housing Ideals in Britain (First Edition)

Herbivores and Carnivores:
The Struggle for Democratic Cultural Values
in post-War Britain.

Why Don't We Don't We Do It In The Road?
The Beatles Phenomenon Explained

Liberation and Domestication (Essays 1)
Culture and Creativity (Essays 2)
Professionalism and Practice (Essays 3)

John Astley is a sociologist, lecturer, and writer - and a frequent contributor to journals, conferences, and radio talks. As a sociologist of culture, he is the author of three volumes of collected essays: *Liberation and Domestication*, *Culture and Creativity*, and *Professionalism and Practice* - as well as his well-known monograph on The Beatles phenomenon from a cultural studies perspective *Why Don't We Do It in the Road?*

In recent years, his essay *Herbivores an Carnivores* (2008) looked at the struggle for democratic values in post-War Britain. In 2010, the first edition of *Access to Eden* appeared as an examination of the rise and fall of public sector housing ideals in Britain.

After many years living and working in Oxford, John Astley is now based in Devon.

Access to Eden

An Essay on Arts & Crafts Values, Garden City
ideals, and the 'Wheatley' Housing Act of 1924

John Astley

The 2nd Edition *Revised and Expanded*

IÅ

2012

First Published in the United Kingdom 2012
INFORMATION ÅRCHITECTS
www.IAimprint.com

Worldwide distribution by IngramBook.com

Publication History:
First Paperback Edition 2010
ISBN: 978-0-9556638-3-3
This Second Paperback Edition (2012)
ISBN: 978-0-9556638-6-4
British Library Cataloguing in Publication Data.
A catalogue record for this book is available from the
British Library.

Classification
Non-Fiction:
Humanities/Architecture/Arts & Crafts/
Urban Planning

BIC Codes:
J, AM

03 02 2 0 1 3 – 2
Typeset in Century
Printed by Ingram in the USA and UK

Acknowledgements

I have discussed the development of this study with many people, and had some very encouraging feedback from readers of the first edition. I have also been fortunate in having access to many libraries, and archives, and I would thank all those vital custodians.

I would particularly wish to thank The Bitterne Local History Society for their continued help, and Richard Toye, Professor of Modern History at Exeter University, who was always encouraging about my research and found the time to read my draft manuscript.

John Astley

Foreword

THE DEEPER historical context of *Access to Eden* is revealing. John Astley, the author of the present essay, refers to this perspective as the 'the Past in the Present' - and the past here stretches a long way back in time indeed to find an untold or often forgotten story.

The population of Britain experienced dislocation on a massive scale with the agrarian and industrial revolutions: a span coincident with the various Enclosures Acts (1660-1845). In the aftermath of that exodus from the land to urban centres, the rapidly expanding population had by the end of the eighteenth century placed commensurate demands on food production, such that traditional farming was supplanted by business farming methods on a capitalist model. By the time of the Napoleonic Wars, agricultural production had been intensified to a level that could meet the threat of the European embargo on Britain's food imports.

The rural landscape of Britain had been changed irrevocably to become the recognisable "countryside" of today. As the industrial revolution of the late eighteenth and nineteenth century exploded, the need for extended housing developments for workers eventually drove to innovations in sanitation, architecture, public sector housing, urban planning, and garden cities. Along the way, John Astley suggest, the thinkers and planners of the era established certain ideals.

THE FIRST edition of *Access to Eden* (2010) examined such influences on early public sector housing in Britain, with its roots in company housing schemes, such as Bournville, the sanitation projects of the mid-nineteenth century, and architectural, urban planning and legislative innovations of the early-twentieth century. After the First World War (1914-18), the milestone Housing Acts of 1919, 1923 and 1924 paved the way for "Homes for Heroes". After the horrors of the Great War (as the conflict was called then), the time had come to regain what the author terms 'Access to Eden'. By 1924, he observes, the domestic dwellings of this era were not just 'thrown up' (as they so often seem to be today); there are clear cultural influences at work in these structures, and a particular focus of the essay looked at the impact of the 1924 Wheatley Housing Act under the first Labour government.

THIS SECOND edition of *Access to Eden* (2012) expands and develops these themes, and aims to provide the reader with a more comprehensive overview of the origins of, and influences on, public sector housing ideals in Britain - and what relevance these might have in the present era.

The Editors
Information Årchitects

Preface to the 2nd Edition

THE WRITING of this book began with a memory. I was visiting Port Sunlight in the Wirral and nearly met with Ebenezer Howard, Raymond Unwin, William Morris and Philip Webb. Their influence on this Arts & Crafts-inspired works village, built for the soap manufacturer William Lever, was very evident. Their spirit walked the land, and indeed to a melodious, but challenging, soundtrack by Holst and Vaughan Williams.

These men are all well known as nineteenth and twentieth century thinkers about, and exponents of, architecture, housing and urban planning. In fact, they all knew each other, and if not all were close friends; they were linked by association and commitment. Holst and Vaughan Williams both shared the sentiments of these others, and as we shall see later, drew inspiration from Morris and the Arts & Crafts movement.

My memory was of a late-1920s council housing estate, Merry Oak, in Southampton, my home town. Merry Oak was designed and built at the end of the 1920s and early 1930s as a consequence of the 1924 'Wheatley' Housing Act.

I knew at the outset that whatever I decided to write about Merry Oak would need to draw on the Arts & Crafts and Garden City movements, whose combined influence was so significant in design circles, and in the creation of ideals for better building for more people. A focus on the role of the Arts & Crafts movement raises very interesting issues about reflecting upon a valued past, of a life in England that has apparently been lost due to the impact of early nineteenth century industrial capitalism. Gavin Stamp sums up my concerns well in the Introduction to his book *The English House 1860-1914*:

"Nostalgia can be a creative force."

As Philip Webb once (sadly) remarked: "I can't think the land will ever be grey with old buildings again"- and yet that careful and influential house architect did his best to ensure that new buildings had all the sympathetic qualities of the old, and more. His evocative lament beautifully sums up the Romanticism of nineteenth-century Britain, a Romanticism which inspired much excellent and some great architecture: "A love of the land, of England; a respect for old ways, old traditions and old buildings in the face of the modern industrialism and materialism, which seemed to be destroying both country and society; a reverence for the small house and the cottage, for the roof and the hearth." (Stamp. 1986 p.13.)

There is here an articulation of what Jeremy Seabrook has called "a conserving radicalism", an issue which will receive a good deal of attention in the following pages. (Seabrook, 1993.)

However, the reader will also find in this book an account of some very well articulated ideas about the housing (and other) needs of the working class people, and the manner in which that need could be addressed in a rational and practical way. Morris, like many of his contemporaries, drew on the past in order to inform the present, and set down firm plans for the future.

I SHOULD also add here my agreement with Mark Swenarton, in that there has been far too much focus on 'celebrity architects', while neglecting to emphasise the diverse range of people actually involved in creating and building within a complex set of social, cultural, economic and political contexts. (Swenarton 1980.) Although I do discuss many designers-architects of the nineteenth and twentieth centuries, and acknowledge their contributions to thinking and doing, I hope to have placed them in their appropriate contexts. The Arts & Crafts pioneers discussed in this study were at pains to emphasize their admiration for the anonymous, and invariably un-celebrated craft worker. I hope I have reflected that concern.

As I have suggested in the Introduction, my value orientation stems from a range of concerns of both aesthetic and political value, and while not being either an architect, historian of art or indeed architecture (my role as a sociologist of culture will become apparent), I have tried to bring my knowledge and understanding to this study. As Swenarton has said of the narrow view that "architecture is what architects (alone) do" is just not a satisfactory account of the many-sided cultural processes involved. Indeed, it is precisely because of this many-sided-ness that I have embarked on this study.

There is also something special about the core period of my study, an issue that has been reflected on by others:

"We chose to focus on 1880-1920 because we, as well as others…believe that it is within the shadow of that period, and its meanings, that we still live. Of course, there are many dominant voices in the making of this Englishness." (Collis and Dodd, 1988 in their preface.)

I GREW up in Peartree Avenue, in the parish of Bitterne from the 1940s. My parents had bought a house in the new, private sector development that sat alongside Merry Oak. The house my parents bought was almost certainly built as a consequence of the 1923 Chamberlain housing legislation that encouraged, through subsidy, speculative private development. One of my abiding memories of Merry Oak was that it was an extension of Freemantle Common, which divided the two neighbourhoods, an abundance of trees and park-like open spaces - our playground. It was like a 'green lung' in an otherwise increasingly built-up environment.

So, before launching the reader into this book, let me state very briefly what the core issue is in this study.

Architectural ideas about the form and function of buildings change over time, largely related with the concerns of the day, while meeting the needs of those with wealth and power, and often circumscribed by the materials and practical knowledge available for building. Who builds what, why they do that, and for whom, are always key cultural questions. In some periods of a society's development, certain ideas become more influential, even a paradigm around motivation and design emerges - and dominates building for a period.

A central concern for me is to trace the reasons why the Arts & Crafts and Garden City movements came about, and examine the key messages that they carried regarding the best and most authentic forms of building to be created, while observing that the majority of ordinary people who are usually excluded from sharing in these buildings, are given access to, for example, a good quality, functional and aesthetically valued house, their home.

What physical form housing takes, or should or could take, is constantly open to discussion, if not major disagreements. And while taste is notoriously but inevitably subjective there are - as I shall argue - persuasive cultural paradigms at work. There is also usually debate around authenticity and fakery.

The front cover of this book is a photograph I took of a house in Merry Oak built in 1929. Some people would dismiss this styling as 'Tudorbethan' fakery, while others value this aesthetic. We are here in the realm of 'skiamorphs', shadow shapes, a good example of which would be producing a kitchen worktop laminate that resembles wood. This issue does then raise questions about honesty, and as James Gordon says in his book *Structures*:

"…what are we to think about 'honesty' in design? Honesty compels me to say 'Not much'. If skiamorphs are permissible in Greek temples and steam yachts, what are we to think of the total 'fake'? Is there any reason why we should not dress up suspension bridges as medieval castles, or motor cars to look like stage coaches, or yew-trees to look like peacocks?" (Gordon, 1978 p.372.)

Reader, be warned.

Contents

INTRODUCTION	1
THE ARTS AND CRAFTS MOVEMENT	20
ARTS & CRAFTS ARCHITECTS	55
THE PAST IN THE PRESENT	104
EBENEZER HOWARD AND THE GARDEN CITY MOVEMENT	119
THE ROAD TO THE 1924 HOUSING ACT	146
JOHN WHEATLEY	178
TAWNEY, BEVERIDGE & ASSOCIATES	188
RAYMOND UNWIN AND BARRY PARKER	196
COMMUNITY	237
MERRY OAK	266
CONCLUSION	299
BIBLIOGRAPHY	307
INDEX	318

Illustrations

1. **William Morris (1834-96):** acknowledged as the "leader" of the Arts and Crafts movement in all its diversity.

The Arts and Crafts Architects

2. C.F.C Vosey

3. Richard Norman Shaw

4. Philip Webb

5. Edward Prior

6. William Lethaby

7. **Ebenezer Howard** (1850-1928): his utopian vision led to the birth of the Garden City movement.

8. **The Garden City concept** (1902) by Ebenezer Howard.

9. **Plan for Letchworth:** from the book *Garden Cities of Tomorrow* (1898; 1902) by Ebenezer Howard

10. **John Wheatley:** his 1924 Housing Act was the only major achievement of the Labour Government that year.

11. **R. H. Tawney** (1880-1962): renowned economic historian, social critic and ethical socialist, he was a close associate of Beveridge.

12. **William Beveridge** (1879-1963): economist and social reformer, he remains best known for the 'Beveridge Report' of 1942.

13. **Raymond Unwin & Barry Parker:** pioneers of urban planning.

14. **Southampton antique chart:** the Bitterne area of the city is the location for the Merry Oak case study.

15. **Merry Oak estate** located in the Bitterne suburb of Southampton.

16-20. **Aspects of Merry Oak** *(Author photos)*

Introduction

THE AIM of this book is to show that there were a wide range of cultural influences on the public sector house building developments set in motion by the 1924 Wheatley Housing Act under the first (minority) Labour government of 1924. The nature of these antecedents is central to my wish to show why and how the Act came into being; and what were the direct consequences of that legislation, especially in meeting the housing needs of working class families.

This will require me to consider how the measures in the 1924 Act, following on from the 1919 and 1923 Acts, encouraged local authorities to respond in a variety of ways. I will seek to describe and explain what in my judgement were the important influences that contributed to how the estates and houses actually came to be built in the manner, and styles, that they were. This aim of my book will consider the sets of values that in the early twentieth century helped to shape what, quite literally, the estates and houses looked like on the ground. I will discuss the complex inter-relation between the Arts & Crafts and Garden City movements of the late nineteenth and early twentieth centuries that are of significance. I shall also discuss how certain people came to be the key players in these developments, and the part they contributed in bringing the Act, in its material manifestations, into existence. I am here considering a major shift in the way thinking about design of buildings and interiors was changing away from the largely unselfconscious craft work of the vernacular to the explicit self consciousness of the Arts & Crafts practitioners in their adoption and adaptation of vernacular styling. For the Arts & Crafts and associated movements this was a linked question of aesthetics, functionality, and politics. As we shall see in this study, ideals and motives matter, they mattered a great deal to the many protagonists whose story I attempt to tell in this study. Forms of buildings were important, as always, but why these or those buildings became increasingly important after the mid-eighteenth century and by the mid-nineteenth were crucial. One key factor that changed the culture of design was a whole-ness approach to design, including that of buildings and their interiors.

Many social historians have overlooked architecture (or the design of buildings) as a source of resources to help us understand a society or social change. There is often difficulty for people in bridging what can seem like a daunting gap between the utilitarian role of buildings, their function, and art. Bridging the gap, and exploring and explaining the inter-relationships is exactly what the Arts & Crafts protagonists sought to do. Buildings give off signals; so, what knowledge do we need to read and make sense of these signals?

In the nineteenth and early-twentieth centuries, the thinking about the role, use, and access to housing changed; values were re-assessed and virtue was attributed to a range of ideas and practices that promoted the vernacular, the essential over the ornate in aesthetic terms.

One key aspect in the change in thinking about the role of housing was a very general agreement that access to what was considered as good quality housing (homes) should be broadened to the greatest possible extent. My study is therefore in large part a consideration of change agents, including the role of residents.

Among the key issues that have to be taken into consideration is the sheer weight of population growth. In 1800, the population of Britain was ten million; by 1914 it was forty million or so. In response to this considerable rate of change there was a rapid growth in speculative developers, building firms, architects - and houses. The growing, increasingly 'professionalized', middle classes were the main beneficiaries of this building bonanza. Dwellings, 'sanitary' and otherwise for the working classes changed little, which only added to the growing sense of social injustice felt by many.

I wish therefore to discuss why and how access to good quality housing was denied to most working class families. Access was sought, and political circumstances enabled some significant changes to take place. But the nature and value of the access sought and provided has ebbed and flowed ever since, and now the UK housing crisis is much as it was in 1918. I will return to this contemporary phenomenon in my conclusion.

There is therefore a considerable historical significance in attempting to trace a developing culture; for example, the Arts & Crafts movement that on occasion needs to be revisited, and reconsidered over time to understand these issues of access. If the betterment of people's lives is to be sought in part by access to good quality housing *as a right* we need to have a clear understanding of what has been sought, what has been achieved, and what lost again in these on-going struggles for access to valued resources.

While on the subject of key change contexts, the issue of technological innovation will be addressed. This will range from the experiments in using concrete, for example in the work of Edward Prior, the enthusiasm shown in the 1920s for institutionalised research into improved building techniques, to the considerable impact of the Hoffman Kiln in 1858 that revolutionised brick manufacture. These more recent developments all came after the significant changes to the manufacture of iron and glass, allowing for much more pre-fabrication. These are all aspects of material culture and significant to the constant forward-looking ideas of practitioners over my period of study.

SEVERAL OTHER writers have discussed aspects of my study, but have not usually made the links that I seek to establish here. At a time in the recent history of British society when the provision of public, or social housing, is at a nadir, addressing the issues that I do is of even greater importance. I would argue that the crisis in housing provision we currently face is very similar to that experienced by William Morris and his contemporaries in the nineteenth century through to Ebenezer Howard and Raymond Unwin in the early twentieth.

The Arts & Crafts movement was primarily a reaction to the crisis caused by the full-blooded impact of industrial capitalism, with rapid and unprecedented urbanisation as a key issue. The response of the Movement was to put these concerns, this revulsion, into an historical perspective. Life in many ways, and certainly house design and building, had been better in the past, and the Arts & Crafts devotees argued that life could be better, and sought to inform, educate, cajole, campaign, reform and revolutionise societal thinking and doing. A clear aim was to challenge the *status quo* and recast the values that should dominate social action.

However, I should add here a word of caution. Using a term like 'Movement' might suggest that all those involved in the diverse aspects of Arts & Crafts were united in a collective response to the travails of everyday life. This was certainly not the case, and although the Movement may look a homogeneous culture group from the outside, it never was, or sought to be. Of course there were many groups of like-minded people in the late nineteenth and early twentieth centuries that were focused on a particular set of interests and concerns - social, cultural and political. But, many of the contributors to the Arts & Crafts 'Movement', and certainly so among the architects, were self-conscious individualists; indeed, so much of the period under scrutiny here could be described as an era beset by the politics of creative individualism. For better or for worse, the creative tensions of the period make it all the more stimulating and remarkable.

It should also be said that *my* sense of 'movement' is derived from a general sociological understanding of 'social movement' as an analytical concept. This widely used concept emphasises the collective, organised, sustained and non-institutional challenge to authority(ies), power-holders, or as a challenge to cultural beliefs and practices. It is often the case that all these sets of criteria are so inter-twined that a challenge to them is holistic. (See Goodwin and Jasper 2003.) Most of the 'movements' that I will discuss in this book embrace all these criteria at some point, and did so either as a deliberate aim from the outset, or as a consequence of the ideas expressed, and social action taken, and often the reaction to this engagement with a change agenda.

THERE IS also here the sense of a general movement in societal shifts in belief and values that are discernible; either at the time or in retrospect, these result in significant changes over time and space. The rise, role and influence of the physical, natural and social sciences during the course of the nineteenth century are a good example. I will suggest in this study that the period of English history from the mid-nineteenth century for a hundred years could be characterised as a concerted drive to improve the everyday quality of life for all people regardless of their income and status. There was the general belief among reformers that the times *were* right for fundamental shifts in values, and that there was a political will to take action in pursuit of these changing values and beliefs.

This also leads to a key feature of my study, namely the on-going tension between a focus on the traditions of the past, for example a wide interest in vernacular building design, and the value of the authentic 'un-professionalized' craft worker, *and* a genuine and widespread desire to grasp promise of modernity in, for example, ideas about democracy, design, and building techniques.

I shall argue throughout the book that the late-nineteenth and early-twentieth centuries were replete with outstanding thinkers and activists, all focused on the key issue of a planned and socially just environment. Without exception, they all grappled with the complexities, contradictions and tensions outlined above. I will seek to describe and discuss the debates and arguments that took place throughout British society in the late-nineteenth and early-twentieth centuries. What was being said and written about housing need, and especially the role of the State, national and local, in meeting housing need? How were aesthetic values being shaped, and a series of design benchmarks created that would shape the way estates and houses looked for a generation and more?

I also have to acknowledge that for many members of the liberal elite, and intelligentsia, my period of focus was marked by a deep melancholy and pessimism about the very future of 'civilisation'. (Overy, 2009.) I will argue that those who strove to improve housing opportunities and resources for the working classes had a more optimistic outlook, based in part on their socialist values. It should be added that many of the leading enthusiasts for housing reform were not Socialists, for example, Cecil Harmsworth, a key Letchworth protagonist.

A part of my endeavour is to ask whether as a society 'we' have actually learnt very much from the period that I am exploring.

Arthur Edwards, in his book, *The Design of Suburbia* (1981) raises the same issue:

"This book is a history, and, like any history, it is a selective account of past events and situations. The basis of selection is the belief that suburbia will be built in the future as in the past, and that we cannot expect to do better than our forbears if we do not understand the influences which led them to build as they did." (Edwards p.2.)

I would add 'ideas' to events and situations, and suggest that doing as well, let alone better, would be a good start from a very low base.

Is a new start feasible? Where do we start? Understanding what actually happened is, surely, one way of addressing these issues?

Is it the case that in the last hundred years the dominant values of British society have changed to an extent that the foundations laid in the late-nineteenth and early-twentieth century have been 'built over' drawing on a very different way of thinking about housing, and other needs? The 'learning' I query is not just about design values, but essentially concerned with arguments that a society that considered itself to be civilised should promote policies and practices that sought to create a socially just access to decent housing, a safe and secure home for all regardless of their social class, status and locality.

RAYMOND UNWIN (1863-1940) the architect and planner, epitomises the crucial contribution that was made by particular people in the realization of the aims for good quality public sector housing that was enabled by the 1919, 1923, and 1924 Acts. I will show how Unwin, and many of his contemporaries, influenced the attitudes and behaviour, and helped stimulate the imaginations of a generation of planners and builders. Unwin's role within the newly created (1919) Ministry of Health will be discussed, focusing on his contribution to these policy making measures both before and after the 1924 Act. Wheatley's Act did not proscribe or describe the form the estates or houses should take beyond some concerns about room sizes, general amenities, and advice on styling. However, Unwin and many of his associates did write extensively on planning matters like estate and house design, and the Ministry certainly did publish exemplars, which were taken up by many of those working in local authorities. It is my suspicion that at a national, and particularly at a local level, those responsible for planning, designing and building public sector estates - and even private sector ones- would have read Unwin, *et al.* In the rapidly expanding housing and planning related literature there are regular references to Unwin-like values emphasising and reinforcing *via* repetition the creation of a new paradigm, that is, an emergent culture. These aesthetic influences were also located within a wider culture of design values that were by their very nature political. For example, there were still unresolved tensions between a Continental European Modernism, and the domestic traditions invariably understood as Arts & Crafts. Even by 1932, these tensions were still evident as voiced by the painter Paul Nash: "Whether it is possible to 'go modern' and still 'be British' is a question vexing quite a few people today." (Quoted in Harris 2010.) Alexandra Harris adds in comment on Nash & co.: "A machine age with old-fashioned doorbells: it was an unusually elastic idea of modernity, but by the late-1930s it could claim a great deal of support.' (Harris p. 37.)

It would be fair to add that the core influences of the Arts & Crafts and Garden City movements became embedded in an aesthetic design culture that is still very familiar today, but failed to develop an appetite for a continuation of the theoretical arguments of William Morris' day. That particular radicalising baton was passed to continental Europe (especially so Scandinavia and Germany) and North America.

One of many really significant consequences of this loss of

focus in Britain can be witnessed in the need for a regular 'reinvention' of a design aesthetic linked to practical building solutions. The legacy of Unwin was still alive in 1944 when the Labour Party housing and planning policy swung behind a report by Charles Reilly, committing it to a very Arts & Crafts and Garden Suburb approach for integrated and cohesive neighbourhoods.

Unfortunately, developments did not turn out that way, and the landscape, and working class lives were blighted by sub-modernist gimcrack systems-technology high-rise. This was an astonishing aesthetic and social failure that has taken a considerable toll on imaginative and empathetic public sector housing ideas.

THIS BOOK includes a case study, the purpose of which is to demonstrate the realization of these influences in one particular estate: Merry Oak in Bitterne, a suburb of Southampton. The processes that were involved in the planning and building of that public sector estate epitomise for me the manner in which the vision of many people, individually and collectively, came together to create a material reality with lasting value.

"So everything, in its ruin, seems in England to live a new life; and it is only this second life, this cottage built in the fallen stronghold, that is English." (George Santayana from his *Soliloquies in England* 1922.)

THE METHODOLOGY that will be used is cultural materialism, whose aim is to go beyond a study of isolated artefacts of 'culture', like a house, to investigate the material processes, relations and institutions of culture as well. I wish to acknowledge the idea that everyday life for all people is a complex amalgam of being socialized into cultural groups, with all the consequences of that, while also being the creators of culture over periods of time. The cultures that we belong to, that help inform our understanding of identity and role, are in certain relations to other cultures that affect our place in society. Conflicts caused by differing perceptions of 'who' we are can be seen as sites of struggle over the ownership of identity. There are certainly hegemonic issues to be addressed here. As Stuart Hall has argued, we need now to move on to focus on the 'how' and not just the 'what' of cultural systems. (Mulhearn, 2000.) In the 1980s, I sought to do this in my study of the cultural phenomenon that was and is (now a brand) The Beatles. The 'what' has been discussed a good deal, and I wanted to consider how it was that a Rock band like The Beatles could come to occupy the cultural and social status that they did. (Astley, 2006.)

Questions need to be asked about our human labour, mental and physical, within society, and how the nature and value of this labour can and does change over time, an historical as well as a materialist process. Also as a *materialist* I look at cultures in a particular way, in that the experience of people, and their reflections upon that experience, are crucial to the actions people take. I wish to explore the complex ways economic reality shapes the imagination. This most certainly embraces both the imagination of those who design and build, and of those who come to engage in an educative process by being residents of a particular place at a particular time. For both 'groups' this can be an enlightening process that involves both reflection upon the immediate social reality of everyday life, the quotidian, but also, crucially, utopian ideals about an alienation-free life in the 'good society'. A society in which our personal labour is given to benefit all those in the community, and not just meet our own particular needs. 'Society' does exist, but requires us all to play a full part in the care and promotion of that collective, and designing and building good quality housing to meet the needs of everyone is good place to start. The people discussed in this study knew that, and took action accordingly.

I should also acknowledge my intellectual debt to Critical Theory (CT), which was initially the outcome of debates among members of The Frankfurt School in 1920s Germany. There are, for me, key aspects to Critical Theory (CT) that have guided my intellectual work. In essence, those who adopt CT:

- ❏ accept the necessity of interpretative categories in social science;

- ❏ are aware that many actions that people perform are constructed by social conditions and through social processes. People are 'objectified', and their agency limited;

- ❏ seek to uncover those structures of social relations which direct the actions of individuals, including the unanticipated, though not accidental consequences of these actions;

- ❏ seeks an explicit recognition of the inter-connections between social theory and social practice, and that theory is essential to examining, and exposing, the unexplained and misunderstood.

THERE IS also an important general methodological point to be made here. I would argue that for any period - say 1918 to 1929 - we can comprehend that time *through* the culture of the day, rather than see cultural activity as a by-product of 'society'. Raymond Williams conceptualised this sense of social life as 'structures of feeling'. (Williams, 1977.) Like Williams, I see this approach as going beyond a discussion about ideological influences, important though they are, and acting as a 'bridge' between a materialist conception of social relations and a more idealist notion of people's active engagement with ideas.

Just one random example I would cite is how did the new house dwellers respond to actually having a separate and proper kitchen, an important design aspect of 'Wheatley' estates? Well, in the 1920s there was a growth in information and publications on cooking in small kitchens and the use gardens and estate allotments for growing food. These were ideas that sought to change the material conditions of people's lives.

As in most things, my starting place is informed by addressing the complex inter-relation between social structures, culture, and biography. The first is the changing (or developing), but unaltered in fundamental terms, context to people's class-based life; *i.e.,* it may look as if change is taking place in society and the relationship between classes (and ideological rhetoric may assert such) but this is in fact epiphenomena. Second, a life receiving and making cultures, re- and pro-active, defensive and offensive; and, third, the story of a person, a group, or class. The unfolding narrative of those lives, which are commonplace - the quotidian –– and yet unique in that no other person has lived/lives *our* life.

I, we, often complain that what is written in the name of Sociology or Social History seems to miss some key point or other about *real* life - although, what can I write that is better? I am not certain and certainly need to interrogate my own approach. Some life does not give in to the researcher's point of view. It ought to be possible to take a rearguard approach, to look for drama in the concept of retrenchment, to find grit in the life of Brenda or Bill: something several hundred thousand people would be glad to read with a nice cup of tea and a biscuit, something that draws the weave of 'lived life' together. It is what is next that I have to work on, though in the end this is all I, as a researcher and writer, ask for. To participate briefly in the lives of others, to speak in a plain truth-telling voice, not taking my own achievements too seriously, and then to have done with it. Since after all it is one thing to research and write, but another thing entirely to live a life. However, it is still possible for the most surprising things to happen in the interfaces between sitting down to write like a Sociologist or Social Historian, and then standing up to get a better perspective on social reality.

EVERY ONCE in a while we can locate a door in someone, an opening into their life, through which one can achieve a glimpse of what things are like, have been like, for them. Sometimes this happens in a real-life face to face way. However, this is not so easy when discussing the lives of people who lived some time ago, and who are only revealed to us through their own or others' words or pictures. This is in large measure my dilemma in drawing together evidence, data, information, images and so on from the period of my study. Like all researchers I am, at a considerable distance, drawing on contemporaneous archives of many forms, and making judgements about the lives, ideas and actions of those people. Of course, I am informed, encouraged, and guided by what other researchers and writers have said. I am not completely alone in this or that quest.

This in turn raises questions about agency and the extent to which any person, group or class has the opportunity to exercise choice. To what extent do the social structures and the cultures of which we are a part determine the degree and nature of agency we have? One key aspect of this kind of discussion touches on the roles we inhabit; by choice or otherwise; and the sets of rules that are associated with every role. What opportunity do any of us have to re-negotiate those rules in order to perform the role in a way more to our liking? In these circumstances, which we all face in everyday life, cultural creativity plays a crucial part.

I would argue that cultural creativity, almost certainly related to place, class, generation and so on, can be seen as an antidote to alienation, invariably being an imaginative route out of those socialization and social control strangleholds. This embedded, or grounded, aesthetic opposes the view often espoused by 'community historians' that 'place' does not matter, that it is not a significant influence on people. (See Astley, 2006.) It is essential here to distinguish a history from 'the bottom up', *i.e.,* a version of history from the perspective of the working classes, as distinct from a history of the 'bottom', i.e., a somewhat abstract, and even patronising, account of the lower orders. I have an interest in the former, while being very aware of the dominant influence of the latter even among well-meaning liberals.

Over time the meanings placed on buildings, real ones and those of the imagination only, can change. For example, Andrew Ballantyne argues that: "The stones have not moved. It is the culture that has shifted. Architecture is not an attribute of a building in itself, but of a building that is experienced in a culture - and we all bring some culture or other to bear on a building when we experience it." (Ballantyne, 2002 p.31.)

An instance I would cite is the way English Gothic cathedrals have been secularised over the past century, culturally shifting from the Christian response to pagan classicism, to their present status as essentially a major tourist attraction on the heritage industry trail.

On the meanings we all place upon houses in particular, I do of course have to acknowledge that many people may not articulate their thoughts, feelings and expectations in the way I have outlined a tendency to cultural creativity, but it is my contention that the very experience of being involved with these housing realities can illuminate such matters as a central part of everyday life. For example, there is the crucial question of ownership. When most people talk about houses they use the word *property*, which is most often used in an un-self-conscious way, but is wholly appropriate because who owns this or that house is important in such a status-obsessed society. It is the epitome of possessive individualism. One of the aspects of stigma that has been increasingly attached to the tenants of council and other social housing is that they are not owners unlike those who are owner-occupiers. This is important because what we have seen in the last forty years or so is an outpouring of propaganda from politicians and others downgrading and denigrating the council house and its occupiers. Of course, the forces of capital accumulation and the role of 'fictitious' capital (mortgages, and so on) have played a major part in this process of using ideology to shift values and attitudes in society away from the appropriateness of public sector housing for working and middle class families (and this was certainly the case in the 1920s) and towards a private sector finance solution for housing need.

"Economic exchange creates value. Value is embodied in commodities [like a house] that are exchanged. Focusing on things that are exchanged, rather than simply on the forms or functions of exchange, makes it possible to argue that what creates the link between exchange and value is *politics.*" (Appadurai, 1986 p3.)

A further dilemma in dealing with methodology for the researcher is that of the double hermeneutic, the researcher's interpretation of the researched subject's interpretation of life.

I also acknowledge the idea that all cultural production can involve the creation of ideologies that seek to inform people of how they should think and behave. For example: are all people, regardless of their particular circumstances, entitled to be housed in a way that adequately meets their needs, individually and collectively? We are once again caught up in the rhetoric about the deserving and the undeserving poor.

One of the abiding ideas that informed the two movements I focus on - the Arts & Crafts and Garden City movements - was that planning and building houses in convivial and aesthetically pleasing environments was not just about bricks and mortar and the standardisation of techniques. Ideas were developed from the late-eighteenth century that emphasised the value of a craft-based approach to building, coupled with a concern for a spiritually uplifting setting for all people to make a home and live a fulfilling life. Architecture is essentially about ideas, and not just concerned with the processes we call building.

The 1924 Housing Act did not just come about as one of many legislative ideas concerning the Labour government of the day. Many diverse ideas and practices over many decades contributed in a dialectical way to how the Act was fashioned, and administered into existence, and then developed at a local level.

The importance of values will feature widely in my argument because my experience as a Sociologist has taught me that the values that people hold, individually and collectively, do have a fundamental affect on their social action.

Of course, this begs the question of whether the values of planners, architects, and so on, are shared by the users of housing? Are the users ever asked? If the prime goal of the user is to be well housed at an affordable cost, are they bothered about aesthetic considerations? Should they be? Perhaps this is an educational process for all involved, allowing people to see (quite literally) why this or that particular environment is regarded as important, that is, of *value*.

One further dimension to a discussion on values is that many of the key players in the period covered by my study espoused socialist values in their myriad forms, essentially the idea that a shared, socialised economy democratically controlled is better than one driven by the private ownership and use of capital.

I have no doubt at all that the diverse range of people involved in the development of Garden Cities and of those who helped create the Arts & Crafts movement learned a great deal from each other. I also believe that these activists wished that many more people could share that knowledge: the insights into alternative ways of living, and witness a rise in expectations. A rise in this 'new' knowledge as a key aspect of power in the struggle over resources and identity - or to put this in sociological terms, is the agency of people increased and enhanced?

A major aspect of the context to my study inevitably concerns the dominant values at the end of the nineteenth century. Harrison in his book on late Victorian Britain begins his chapter on 'Certainties' by quoting T.E. Hulme, the critic, poet and early modernist from 1924, who asserts that values are eventually taken for granted by people as 'the truth'. Enshrined doctrines dominated the mind of the elites and rulers of the late-nineteenth century, not the least of these being the doctrines of economic liberalism (*laissez faire*), the belief in supply and demand as the law of social action. Any alternatives to these paradigms and conventional wisdoms were usually ignored, or often seen as impractical and dangerous. Science was to become a major influence in discussions about progress, and an increasingly high value was placed on Science as a rational activity with the potential as salvation for every problem worth considering. However, the great strength of Science, then and now, is that of uncertainty, a lasting commitment to enquiry, reflection and change. So, the twins of economics and religion were central to much thinking at the time, with scientific versions of reality regularly challenging people's faith.

In his following chapter, 'Doubts and Anxieties', J.F.C. Harrison suggests that this fixed orthodoxy was seriously challenged in 1880-1890 by the rise of (scientific) socialism and the labour movement. (A spectre is haunting Europe!) (Harrison, 1991.) One major 'doubt' that prevailed in the face of progress was the actual or potential loss of the past, and the values that were central to that actual or mythical time: lamenting of things passed, reflections on a 'golden age' that was just slipping from grasp was a constant theme in the late-nineteenth century. (Walvin, 1987.)

The educative dimension to public sector housing development will also be a focus of concern in my study. It is a key aspect of *my* value orientation, the reasons why I am doing this research. I wish to show how the quotidian, the everyday life of people, contains, or could contain, important ideas about access to housing and a socially just life. There is also an important discussion to be had about the actual or potential co-operative nature of the working classes. In view of their commonplace circumstances, they are much closer to ways of life, *their* quotidian, that reflect the ideology of nineteenth century communism. Most working people, especially the poorest, relied heavily on a social network of mutual support, a co-operative infrastructure created and maintained out of necessity. This was, essentially, a practical orientation rather than an intellectual one, unlike, for example, the theoretical world of Marx and Engels, who wrote the first communist manifesto in 1848, drawing extensively on Saint-Simon, Fourier and Owen among others, which influenced much 'socialist' (including social reformist) thought in the mid- to late-nineteenth century. William Morris certainly understood this, and demonstrates a fundamental grasp of pre-industrial 'communism' in his epic poems, his talks and many articles, and then later in his evocation of a communist future in his 1880s novel *News from Nowhere*. My argument will be that the direct, practical and everyday experience of working class families, within their communities, had the potential and/or actually realised a degree of co-operation that was quasi-communist. This was an *educational* phenomenon, experiential and experimental.

WHAT I have outlined above emphasises the complexity of my study, an account of inter-relationships that I cannot tell fully in one neat paragraph. What follows are a series of chapters which discuss the various aspects of my enquiry, but are, of course, each dependent on the others in developing a full understanding of the subject matter. As the reader progresses through this study, I hope that a picture will unfold that informs, educates and entertains. I also hope that what I have to say will encourage the reader to question, to read more, and to discuss; not just the issues focused on here regarding the late-nineteenth and early-twentieth centuries, but also on the situation of the here and now.

The Arts and Crafts movement

The Arts & Crafts movement in the nineteenth century expressed many or most of the values identified in my Introduction (with Aims) chapter, and gave these values an aesthetic and 'green' twist. William Morris (1834-96), for example, had realised that it was only through socialism that all could enjoy the immense benefit of 'the arts' routinely reserved for the privileged few. I should add here a note of guidance for the reader in that I shall use this now well-known name 'Arts & Crafts', although this title for the nature of myriad activities thus bracketed was only 'officially' given a collective identity in 1884, and - typical of the day - *via* an exhibition.

Even before this, in a Birmingham talk of 1879, Morris argued that his peer group all loved good architecture, but, sadly, that the tide of current civilization mainly produced ugliness and inconvenience.

In his 1884 article, 'The Housing of the Poor' Morris links together his concern with labour as a commodity, to be bought and sold only in the interests of making profit, with the unhealthy and ugly environments in to which most people in such a vulnerable position are condemned. He, like many of his contemporaries, emphasises the complete 'anarchy' of rapidly expanding industrial capitalism, and the dominance of machine-age values. Not surprising, then, that Morris defined art as 'the expression by man of his pleasure in labour', and that a goal should be for art to again become a pleasure for maker and user.

Krishan Kumar in his book *Prophecy and Progress* (1978) underlines the nature of the contradictions to be found in these industrial developments. Kumar emphasizes that by using the word 'progress' all manner of changes could be enacted on the basis of who, in all reason, would want to stand in the way of progress?

1. William Morris (1834-96): acknowledged as the "leader" of the Arts and Crafts movement in all its diversity.

I will discuss this core issue several times in this study in different contexts, and address - for example - what has often been described as a 'radical nostalgia' at the heart of the critique of industrial capitalism - critiques that increasingly moved from a Romantic and utopian socialism, to a revolutionary one.

We should also recall that the second-half of the nineteenth century was a period of intense and growing interest in science. Many Scientists of the time were widely and liberally educated people, and saw themselves as agents of change. First and foremost all science regardless of the object under scrutiny is a social activity. Science is essentially about human need and desire, and the meanings placed on these practices became influential. Of course, the *pursuance* of responses to needs that are articulated as the criteria, or reasons, for *pursuing* science can result in harm to many people. This is a key issue that was argued at length in the nineteenth century, and most people involved realised that their practice was largely focused on providing knowledge for people in that society. Whatever the science, even where the objects under scrutiny are rocks, or plants or animals, the audience is made up of human beings, and that knowledge is in the social domain. Most members of the Arts & Crafts fraternity understood this very well.

For example, there is the small matter of the 1851 Great Exhibition in Paxton's Crystal Palace. The vast array of exhibits from the Empire was of interest to many visitors that summer, but the event was primarily a showcase for the products of the rapidly expanding industrial might of Britain. This was indeed 'prophecy' of the great times that lay ahead. However, William Morris and his contemporaries were not impressed by what they saw, especially the increasingly apparent factory-based mass production to flood the market with goods.

As Morris once remarked: "Shoddy is King."

John Gloag raised these concerns in his 1947 *The English Tradition in Design* where he comments on the eventual effects of the English aristocracy taking the 'grand tour' and returning with all manner of stylistic notions; and, before long:

"Art had become a specialised, aristocratic study; the craftsman, who was also the designer in the Middle Ages, was becoming the artisan, the workman whose skilled hands obeyed directions that were dictated by fashionable taste. He was losing his independence and his right to initiate ideas…(English) design was in eclipse." (p.10, Gloag.)

The role of the 'Picturesque' movement is important here as well. As David Watkin argues in his 1982 book:

"The title of the present book derives from the assumption that the theory and practice of the Picturesque constitute the major English contribution to European aesthetics. Deeply rooted in the country house, the Picturesque became the leading building type in post-Reformation England and has long been recognised as the nation's principal contribution to the arts. Between 1730 and 1830 English poets, painters, travellers, gardeners, architects, connoisseurs and dilettanti, were united in their emphasis on the primacy of pictorial values. The Picturesque became the universal mode of vision for the educated classes. Thus for Horace Walpole in 1770 landscape gardening meant that 'every journey is made through a succession of pictures.' " (Watkin p.vii.)

Watkin adds that the development of the Picturesque is related to the green-ness and small-scale landscape. There is also here a clear sense of the English obsession with 'the Past', especially so a mythologized one, where patterns of behaviour and the aesthetics artefacts of everyday life reflect this perpetuation of myth, for example, *via* garden ornament and ritual. This was a growing desire to create the simulacrum; the cult of the ruin.

Ruskin described the Picturesque as 'parasitical sublimity', and he and his associates were to preside over a transformation of values and taste well away from the Picturesque. This is not to suggest that vestiges of the Picturesque did not live on in the work of Lutyens and others, it did, and should be acknowledged.

Gloag also comments on the Great Exhibition of 1851, and takes up Morris' theme of distaste for much of what was inside Paxton's "great greenhouse":

"…inside that building the depth and breadth of Victorian ignorance were shamelessly apparent, though nearly everybody was delighted with the contents. Nearly every exhibit produced in England showed that as the Victorians had mistaken 'comfort for civilisation' they had also mistaken ornament for design." (p.23, Gloag.)

Indeed, a key issue to recount here for Morris and his emerging *modern* Socialist contemporaries is the nature of civilization. The general view among even the *liberal* middle classes was that civilization had been achieved, and was now in the process of further adornment. Morris challenged this view:

"Apart from the desire to produce beautiful things, the leading passion of my life has been and is hatred of modern civilization…What shall I say concerning its mastery of, and its waste of mechanical power, its commonwealth so poor." (From Morris' *How I became a Socialist* 1894.)

Morris was very consistent in his critique of 'civilization';

the Arts & Crafts movement was essentially the embodiment of a protest movement. Morris and his associates were 'against the age', as can be seen in their negative response to the 1851 Great Exhibition.

And to repeat what many previous writers have said of Ruskin and Morris, they strove to make society fit for art to flourish; such that, if 'society' could not accommodate this, then society must be *changed*. This is a difficult idea when posed in abstract terms, but, essentially Morris was discussing the stranglehold that alienated labour has on the workingman and woman. Little time or inclination can be directed to aesthetic matters, to help lift the human spirit; for example, through creativity, but for most the very idea of an immersion in aesthetic sentiments as the dominant focus of life is out of the question. He, like many others then and since, feared that when the opportunity did come for working people to have some 'leisure' time, that time would be circumscribed by a limited aesthetic horizon, and increasingly oriented to a 'bread and circuses' popular culture that merely developed and sustained a new consumerism. Hegemony by any means.

A moral and moralising agenda is very commonplace in Arts & Crafts thinking:

"The Arts and Crafts movement was inspired by a crisis of conscience. Its motivations were social and moral and its aesthetic values derived from a conviction that society produces the art and architecture it deserves" (Naylor 1971 p7.)

Naylor goes on to cite Ashbee in 1908: "The Arts and Crafts movement means standards, whether of work or life; the protection of standards, whether in the product or the producer, and it means that these things must be taken together."

It is certainly true that a large part of the Arts & Crafts, and Garden City activity - in word and in deed - was a response to a crisis of reaction to the impact of industrial capitalism, rapid urbanisation, and secularisation, a loss of spirituality, for example, in relation to nature. One of the targets of Ruskin, Morris, Howard, *et. al.*, was the dominant idea of progress *and* civilization.

In the writing on planning, the arts and in architecture throughout the nineteenth and early-twentieth centuries, there is a growing understanding of the disjuncture between what 'seems' and what 'is' in this 'strange new today', a disjuncture between rhetoric and reality.

After 1918 there was a growing crisis in society due to the rhetoric of reform, such as "Homes for heroes to live in" while not addressing the reality of an acute lack of adequate good quality housing, the continuing growth of slums, and the lack of a coherent strategy and policies to deal with this.

The 1919, 1923 and 1924 Housing Acts are all part of the response to this 'crisis'. The ideas and actions of the Arts & Crafts and Garden City activists foreshadowed this post-1918 crisis because their work created a paradigm shift in thinking about social life in the future if 'society' maintained the current disastrous trajectory.

In this chapter in particular, I shall address fundamental aspects of the Arts & Crafts response to this situation of chaotic social change. The main thrust here was to evoke and build on a version of a past value system that privileged the craft worker and emphasized the vernacular in design, linked to a call for a fair, socially just and democratic process of reform. A characteristic of writing in this period of intense speculation was a 'calling up' of selective memories to support an understanding of, a position to, current changes. An aspect of this paradigm shift was a recognition that many questions about the future could not be asked until certain real changes were in place, an understanding of the dialectical nature of social and personal change.

Gombrich is one writer who emphasizes what was for many people in the nineteenth century (and since) the contradictory nature of linking civilization and culture in the same breath. Highly valued aspects of culture, especially cultural objects, are invariably seen to be central to a civilization. This is what civilizations do: they are cultured, people are acculturated. However, as I have said this was not a view shared by all. (Gombrich, 1969.)

As I have said elsewhere in this book, Morris knew his Marx, and although he would not have been able to read what we now call Marx's *Economic and Philosophical Manuscripts,* I am sure Morris would have fully endorsed what Marx said there:

"We have seen what significance, given socialism, the *wealth* of human need has, and what significance, therefore, both a *new mode of production* and a new *object* of production have: a new manifestation of the forces of *human* nature and a new enrichment of *human* nature. Under private property their significance is reversed: every person speculates on creating a *new* need in another, so as to drive him to a fresh sacrifice, place him in a new dependence and to seduce him into a new mode of *gratification* and therefore economic ruin…The increase in the quantity of objects is accompanied by an extension of the realm of the alien powers to which man is subjected, and every new product represents a new possibility of mutual swindling and mutual plundering. Man becomes ever poorer as man, his need for *money* becomes ever greater if he wants to overpower hostile beings…his neediness grows as the *power* of money increases.' (Quoted in Heller 1976 p.147.)

Stephen Yeo in his essay, 'Socialism, the State, and some oppositional Englishness' points to Morris as a key player is this advocacy of oppositional values. Yeo argues that Morris saw two opposing roads of socialist politics. One was to work within Parliamentary institutions, the other - Morris' preferred option - was to work outside of these institutions and build-up, through education and organisation, a great Labour Combination that would effectively be a parallel 'Labour Parliament', where democratic relationships would prevail. Morris realised that when it came to the processes 'needed' for the production and distribution of wealth the State would be the organising apparatus on behalf of, and at the behest of, the ruling class.

William Morris' fear was that theories of reform, which already had a stronghold, and which were based on the enlargement and extension of the existing State, were concerned [with what] would come to dominate and to define Socialism. He knew how necessary such theories were for capitalism's survival, how inevitable their multiplication was, and what an available mould for counterfeiting socialism they provided.' (Yeo in Colls and Dodd, 1988 p.349.) Morris understood that the parliamentary politics of socialism would in fact be controlled, be circumscribed, by the State apparatus. Given that many of these 'socialists' were very uncomfortable with the idea of a democratic working class movement, they would always side with the State apparatus, and as a consequence reinforce the shadowy controllers in the background. Morris knew; as Marx had argued, that the State was the 'political' agent of the capitalist class and essentially existed to do their bidding, while keeping the struggle for social justice and equality at bay.

For a key exposition of the limitations of Parliamentary Socialism in the UK, Ralph Miliband's *Parliamentary Socialism: A Study of the Politics of Labour*' 1961 is one place to start a discussion of these always topical issues.

In his essay, Yeo makes the valid point that Morris did not 'need' Marx to inform him about the radical English tradition of opposition to abstract, absent and illegitimate authority. Morris was steeped in this literature, which drew on this 'past' to inform his ideas about the present and the future. This is why the communist society that Morris describes in *News from Nowhere* is a localised, post-State society, where the Houses of Parliament are used to store manure! This 'English road to Socialism' was the core of Morris' developing understanding of what was wrong with society (so called 'civilization') and what was needed to be done. His grasp on the everyday realities of cultural materialism, on the relations of production, distribution and exchange was a core part of his life as a designer, and as a human being.

In their 1988 book *Englishness: Politics and Culture 1880-1920* Colls and Dodd argue that the period was one where an understanding of what it was to be English was created and embedded for good or for ill in the cultural consciousness of the people. Morris and others associated with the Garden City and Arts & Crafts movements *knew this,* and worked very hard to make their voice and their images heard and seen. How else can we really understand the enthusiasm for vernacular architecture, say, without linking it to an aesthetic and political project to make this design style a *leitmotif* of Englishness?

Chris Stephens in his chapter 'Ben Nicholson: Modernism, Craft and the English Vernacular (in *The Geographies of Englishness* 2002), argues that: "The idea that modernism's international focus demanded a transcendence of national cultural identity from those who would have been associated with it seems to persist." (p.225.)

The 'return' to landscape by Piper and Sutherland, say, is an important factor in a general concern that English artists had with an authentic cultural identity. Stephens suggests that to couple 'landscape and Englishness' is reductive, and one thinks here that many Continental European painters chose landscape as a theme to explore their national identity. Stephens draws in the craft issue by emphasising the 'handmade' nature of Nicholson's works, which applies to so many others. For example, in the three-dimensional work of Henry Moore or Barbara Hepworth there is a clear reference to landscape, including, obviously, the location of these objects in a particular, usually outdoor, space.

Among others, Stephens cites Gertrude Jekyll's enthusiasm for the domestic craft tradition, for instance, ceramics, and he believed that this was being lost. Stephens also discusses Herbert Read's *The English Vision* (1933) where Read sought to define 'The English Ideal' to distinguish this culture from the Teutonic hegemony, and as he saw it the eventual Continental European lurch into totalitarianism. The same was true, of course, of the Italian fascist version of Futurism and Modernism.

These early-twentieth century issues may seem someway distant from Morris and his contemporaries in the later nineteenth century, but they are in fact very closely linked. Just as Morris and his associates drew a good deal of their 'modern' ideas from Ruskin (often seen as an anti-modernist) the generation of Read drew on Morris, *et al.* The desire to identify, develop and promote a distinctive Englishness was then, and is still today, a key cultural issue. But just evoking the central influence of landscape is not enough, and important though it clearly is, there has to be more, not the least of which is the Arts & Crafts focus on who worked on and in the landscape - and why.

Morris did not need to get into politics to make his name, to become famous. By the time he did engage with the Democratic Federation in 1883 (coincidentally, the year of Marx's death) he was already well known as a poet, designer, successful business man, and educationalist. It was his values and deep-seated sense of social injustice that drove him across "the river of fire", as he described it, into active political life. This was a 'crossing a border' experience taken out of necessity and desire. In his 1950s book on Morris, Edward Thompson argued that this transformation was characteristic of Morris' practical and whole-hearted solutions to problems he faced in all aspects of his life. When there was no viable or acceptable alternative to hand, he engaged in 'making a revolution'. It is also vital to emphasise the educational dimension of those 'modern' Socialists, in the Democratic Federation and elsewhere. They understood the nature of hegemony, the power of the ruling elite to shape and control ideas about self and society; and sought to change people's awareness and understanding through education. (For more on these issues, see Astley 2006.)

I have already said a good deal about the Arts & Crafts *movement,* and before going further a word of caution is necessary.

"All movements in architecture, like movements in art, literature and politics, are created by theorists rather than practitioners. Inevitably, for such persons the present seems complicated and multivalent, the past easily dealt with in sweeping generalisations. That is why few movements are disinterred retrospectively." (Pawley, 1986.)

Pawley alerts us to the dangers of retrospectively attributing coherence and cultural homogeneity, and the reader should understand early on that my assertions about the eclectic nature of Arts & Crafts is one way for me to deal with the presumptive way I have discussed these phenomena.

For example, it is important to recall here that Morris is often bracketed with The Aesthetic Movement, which developed from around 1860, and was focused on 'Arts for art's sake'. Oscar Wilde was certainly a leading member of this fraternity, as was

Walter Pater, the author of the very influential 1880s study of Renaissance aesthetic life. Ned Burne-Jones, Morris' life-long friend and co-designer, was always closely associated with this grouping. However, Morris was to part with this increasingly dilettante and hedonistic movement because he realised that without transforming society along socialist lines the aim of giving access to beauty for all people was not going to happen. He transcended *his* romanticism for revolutionary politics. The key figures in the Aesthetic Movement were at best apolitical and in many ways prefigured the increasingly individualistic outlook on the life of the arts.

So, if for some of his contemporaries, these engagements with the aesthetic 'lifestyle' were 'the new civilization' this was not so for Morris who, as I have already argued, increasingly saw civilization as a contested concept for understanding the actual and potential development of modernity and the plight of the individual in a God-less world.

These fundamental moral issues were to continue into the early-twentieth century, of course, and the debates around the emergence of a Marxist cultural intelligentsia in the 1920s and 1930s have occasioned much debate.

Steve Buckler in his discussion of this phenomenon says:

"In the 1920s, intellectual and artistic life had, to a large extent, been orientated towards disengaged reflection and a singular aestheticism, which did not readily lend themselves to moral or political interrogation and which, in the new politically charged situation, seemed to symbolize only a sense of irrelevance and powerlessness. A new image of the place of intellectuals was required if they were to be capable of addressing the questions that the political situation posed for them." (Buckler in Navari 1996 p.87)

For many intellectuals and radicals of the day, Marxism was

the answer, and the practical example of the Soviet Union only served to reinforce this, even if a good deal of this thinking by the intelligentsia was 'philosophy before food'.

The sentiments discussed above, crucial to radical thinking during and after Morris' time, are also linked with his account of the revival of architecture, left behind in the mad rush of this highly suspect progress. For him, the ideas of Pugin (1812-52) and Ruskin (1819-1900) set the tone for a 'getting back to basics' perspective on planning, design and building.

However, as in all things, Morris went well beyond the scope and critique of both men. Here is Morris writing on 'The Revival of Architecture' in 1888:

"In short we must answer the question with which this paper began by saying that the architectural revival though not a mere piece of artificial nonsense, is too limited in its scope, too much confined to an educated group, to be a vital growth capable of true development. The important fact in it is that it is founded on the sympathy for history and the art of historical generalization, which, as aforesaid, is a gift of our epoch, but unhappily a gift which few as yet have a share. Among populations where this gift is absent, not even scattered attempts at beauty in architecture are now possible, and in such places generations may live and die, if society as at present constituted endures, without feeling any craving for beauty in their daily lives; and even under the most favourable circumstances there is no general impulse born out of necessity towards beauty, which impulse alone can produce a universal architectural style, that is to say, a habit of elevating and beautifying the houses, furniture, and other material surroundings of our life."

(Quoted in Chris Miele 'William Morris on Architecture' 1996.)

As Miele argues in the introduction to his book of Morris readings, the latter had a very broad view of 'architecture', seeing it 'as a kind of shorthand for the totality of the man-made environment' and Morris' general values about art are intrinsically tied up with this perspective on building design. (Miele p.4)

I will re-visit this key issue later when focusing my attention on a select number of Arts & Crafts architectural designers.

In many ways, this also reflects the diverse nature of Morris' interests and accomplishments. This is reflected by Christine Poulson when she quotes from his *The Aims of Art*: "…for Morris 'the true secret of happiness lies in taking a genuine interest in all the details of daily life.' (Poulson, 1996. p.2.)She adds that for Morris: "The way one's house is furnished can never…be a morally neutral choice." (Poulson, p.2.)

She also emphasises the educational dimension to Morris' daily life; for example, his regular talks around the country:

"The audiences were overwhelmingly male and consisted of men with a professional interest in the arts, often on the artisan level. They reflect the longing of working class men for education and the consequent proliferation of institutes and evening classes from the mid-nineteenth century onwards."

(Poulson, p.2.)

Onwards, indeed, to the foundation of the Workers' Educational Association (WEA) in 1905, among many other initiatives aimed at the autodidact. [Jonathan Rose's 2001 book *The Intellectual Life of the British Working Class* is a valuable source here.]

The advent of the Arts & Crafts movement was clearly just such a fresh start across the board. In architecture, there was a reassessment of *why* we are building, for whom, and with what consequences? This was a time when 'new' ideas were coming to the fore, with alternative versions and visions of the past, present and future - for people of all classes to engage with, and often be enlightened and liberated by.

There was also a considerable growth in the writing of fictions of Utopia and Dystopia, and even Cacotopia, renditions of dystopias where life was *really* bad! These accounts often portray the working class as the dangerous, 'mob-ish' agents of change, for instance, in H. G. Wells' *The Time Machine* (1895). In his book *Utopia Ltd.*, Matthew Beaumont discusses the Utopian literature of the 1870-1900 period, carrying as it often did, ideologies of social dreaming. Beaumont reflects on the enormous popularity of these fictions, coming as they did around the mid-1890s, when the single volume novel became established as the publication norm.

It should be noted that the rise of secularism, and the growing influence of the National Secularist Society from the 1860s, had a profound influence on thinking about social change. Discussions centred on the nature of change agents, and a diverse range of thinking, individually and collectively, radically challenged religious ideas about the nature of future life. There was, for example, a considerable appeal of the secular utopian visions, that extolled the virtues of socialistic and communistic societies, as well established, harmonious, fair and just - and, importantly, where the nasty transformation struggles had already been transcended. As Beaumont adds, these years saw an increase in contradiction, fracture and mutation within classes, and shifts in consciousness fed by critical social dreaming. (Beaumont 2005).

Morris added to this phenomenon by publishing his particular example of social dreaming, *News from Nowhere: or an epoch of rest* (1890).

The Arts & Crafts architects/designers insisted on putting

function before form; houses for everyone should be designed from the inside-out, and should be healthy, comfortable and habitable.

Pugin had set down three basic rules:

❑   Structural honesty
❑   Originality of design
❑   Use of regional materials or character.

The assertion that the way any site was used was crucial here, and is constantly reflected in Arts & Crafts work. What is also important to take on board is that the best of twentieth century architecture (especially so domestic) has adhered to these rules. It is also appropriate to note that Pugin is usually credited with what has become a commonplace idea (if not necessarily understood by all its advocates) that the art and architecture of a particular period is directly inter-related with the ways of life, or culture, of that time. Pugin's insistence that a Gothic Revival must go hand-in-hand with a revival of the Catholicism of the original Gothic was not always acceptable to other enthusiasts for 'the Gothic'. In his *Contrasts* (1836), Pugin argued for a clear line of connection between society and its architecture, and he struck a heavy moral tone. (See David Watkin *Morality and Architecture* 1977 on this.)

Pugin took the discussion of Gothic away from associationism and back to arguments about the intrinsic value of the buildings themselves. This was Pugin's version of cultural materialism with its insistence on the dignity and value of labour, creativity and the nature of materials, honestly and authentically used. Truth to materials was, of course, to become an Arts & Crafts credo. Considering the real problems of a moral narrowness in Pugin's *Contrasts*, there is a general issue here to be addressed about insisting on a particular style for the reason that it is 'good for people', one of the reasons why Morris thought it was too limited in its appeal.

In his book on *The Gothic Revival* (2002) Michael Lewis discusses Gothic literature and argues that for *Gothic* to be seen as valued it had to have a focus other than beauty. This was to be 'associationism': ". . .according to this doctrine, a work of art should be judged not by such intrinsic qualities as proportion or form, but by the mental sensations they conjure in the minds of viewers" (p.14.).

Lewis suggests that this idea goes back to Locke's *Essay Concerning Human Understanding* (1689), which treated sensory experience as the source of human knowledge. Richard Payne Knight (1750-1824) developed this idea, arguing that the "real richness of a work of art was not in the opulence of its materials or elegance of its form but in its limitless capacity to induce thoughts and impressions." (p.14.) The associations in mind are with a wood, a childhood picnic, or whatever. Eighteenth century picturesque gardens were a direct expression of this idea. The paintings of this 'school', where melancholy was a key feature with, for instance, ruined Gothic buildings. This motif became very fashionable in the landscaped gardens of the gentry. In his chapter on 'Literature', Lewis suggests that an increasing emphasis on Gothic was also a British (mainly Protestant) response to the Catholic Baroque, and used as a nationalist symbol.

Kent was the favourite eighteenth century medieval-minded landscaper for the Whigs. Increasingly Gothic theorists like Langley, in the mid-eighteenth century, drew analogies with the influential Vitruvian 'five orders' of architecture. Vitruvius Pollio was the most well known Roman architect and theorist who became very influential from the early Renaissance onwards, and remained a point of reference well in to the nineteenth century.

By the end of the eighteenth century, and after a good deal of Gothic writing and theorising, a clear notion of Gothic architecture as having a high value of morality had grown. However, it has to be said that it is clear that many designers were unaffected by this architectural fashion, and I shall return to this issue later.

Ruskin certainly wished to win Gothic for the Protestants, while Morris objected to Pugin's lack of concern with the life of ordinary working people.

It is also worth emphasizing that Ruskin, like the (Cambridge) Camden Society "had been forced back from the merits of a building to the merits of the men who built it. . . so Ruskin's (infinitely more) profound theory of Gothic ornament changed him from a critic of architecture into a critic of society.' (Clark 1964 p.186.) I would add that this critique applied equally to the men who commissioned the work, and the many anonymous craftsmen who actually did the building work. Ruskin had issued a challenge to contemporary thinking, and like many of his contemporaries, was greatly influenced by Thomas Carlyle (1795-1881), who was one of the earliest 'modern' critics to set down a clear marker on the nature of social change in his *Signs of the Times* (1829):

"Knowledge, and education are opening the eyes of the humblest; are increasing the number of thinking minds without limit. This is as it should be; for not in turning back, not in resisting, but only in resolutely struggling forward, does our life consist."

This is as radical shift in perspective towards a critique of 'Society'. As I have already indicated above, this also applies to Morris, who in his 'crossing the river of fire' epiphany came to a realisation that 'art' could only be enjoyed by all (making and using) in a socialist society: "The chief accusation I have to bring against the modern state of society is that it is founded on the art-lacking or unhappy labour of the great part of men." (From his 1883 essay 'Art under Plutocracy'). And, he added: 'Art is the expression by man of his pleasure in labour."

This is a very clear statement from Morris on the threat of alienation, the idea that once people lose control over their own creative and necessary labour, their sense of identity and self-worth is diminished. But there is also a sense here that human labour is limited to profit-making, or at best personal acquisitiveness, and fails to contribute to the general well being or the welfare of people.

These sentiments prevailed long after Morris' own epiphany; for example, in 1937 Edgell Rickword could write:

"For the Marxist, culture is not a mass of works of art, of philosophical ideas, of political concepts accumulated at the top of the social pyramid by specially-gifted individuals, but the inherited solution of problems of vital importance to society. The breaking-down of the specialisation of class-divided society brings the past into contact with the lives of the people, so transforming their consciousness and giving a new significance to these past achievements themselves." (In *The Mind in Chains: Socialism and the Cultural Revolution* edited by C. Day Lewis, 1937 p.254.)

As I have said elsewhere, Morris was to link his socialism to the work of Karl Marx, commenting that: "Marx is on our side." There is a sense here of the 'distance' of Marx from many movements and activists, even though he spent most of his adult life in England. Eric Hobsbawm has recently reminded us that until the late 1860s very little was known of Marx and Engels and their writings *in* England. (Hobsbawm, 2011.) This was especially so for those who relied on an English translation. There was not a great deal to read of Marx on the art and aesthetics, even for the ardent Socialists in the Arts & Crafts movement, and even for those with sufficient interest in the issues of the relations of production and labour value.

Ruskin and Morris and their associates had placed a considerable emphasis on the artisan role, the craft worker, in contrast with the idealist notion of the isolated artist. Morris first read Ruskin's seminal *The Stones of Venice'* in 1853, while an undergraduate at Exeter College, Oxford. Most Arts & Crafts designers and architects were focusing their attention on the framework and fabric of the everyday life experienced by most people - a way of life that was constantly fractured by the possessive individualising anarchy of industrial capitalism. There was a widely shared view that 'the arts' should not be the sole province of the bourgeoisie, or conform just to a commodity set of relations, or that ordinary people should be excluded from beauty in most spheres of everyday life. This is one reason why planning, housing and the home featured so much in the aesthetics of the Arts & Crafts movement. The Home increasingly came to symbolise the domain where the private and public self met. So meeting the collective as well as personal need for a place where people could be 'at home' rather than merely satisfying individuals in the market place featured centrally in Arts & Crafts values.

It must be acknowledged, of course, that not everyone has been optimistic about the influence that Morris and his contemporaries could have to change attitudes towards art and artistic practice. Graham Hough, writing in the 1940s, proffered a pessimistic view about the public in general ever aspiring to 'art' beyond the mass-produced and fashionably popular. William Morris, he argues, produced for a wealthy clientele, and in his promotion of handicrafts ensured that labour costs would keep prices high and exclude most people. However, Hough also acknowledges that Morris sought to educate the growing middle class, and pro-active members of the working class in matters of good, honest design, which is clearly a moral agenda. (Hough, 1961.)

It is certainly the case, then and now, that what is popular among the middle class will influence mass production tastes, and the subsequent exploitation and commodification of those tastes. However, Morris also argued that everyone should be a *producer* as well as a *consumer* of aesthetically valuable objects. The vernacular would be a realistic route for people to take if they had the time and means - even at a grounded community level - to do crafts for themselves, The division of labour in the nineteenth century (and since) precludes most people from craft work in their own and other's interests. However, people do it everyday as they work in their gardens and allotments, or on community projects. Despite their day-jobs many demonstrate through their leisure based practices (an epoch of rest?), hobbies, and so on, that they have valued skills in craft work; this is work that certainly has an intrinsic as well as an extrinsic value.

One reason why Socialists then, as now, look to the public sector as a provider of services to meet needs (like housing) lays in the belief that profit making is not, nor should be, the prime motive for social action. Even some Liberals, and many liberally minded people of the day, found themselves drawn towards at least a social democratic ideology given the logic of their values. William Morris, with some others, did read Marx and were especially attracted to the latter's historical analysis of a dialectical social change through the transformation of the relations of production. There was a core of ideas in the Arts & Crafts movement that did indeed understand that a radical aesthetics could have an educative and consciousness-raising value. As has been said above, Morris understood that the daily experience of beauty could not be enjoyed by all, until a Socialist, and then Communist, transformation of social and cultural relations had happened. As I have said above, it is easy to see what motivated Morris to elaborate these ideas in his utopian novel *News From Nowhere: or an epoch of rest.*

However, to recap on the issues raised above, we should not assume that Ruskin and Carlyle were embryonic Socialists, or even advocated the development of Socialist theory and practice. They offered a critique of *laissez-faire* society, the dominance of market place and labour as a 'free-floating' commodity, but they did this from their position of advocates for the old order, of everyone in their fixed class position. As I have argued in my chapter on 'Community', and elsewhere in this study, a good deal of writing on the question of 're-creating' social order and stability of values amid the carnage of industrial capitalism was really quite conservative.

J.M. Richards in his book *Modern Architecture* first published in 1940, reflects on this legacy of social critique, and asserts that Morris, Richard Norman Shaw (1831-1912) and their contemporaries let a "...new light into the practice of architecture." (p.64.)

Richards singles-out Charles Voysey (1857-1941) as a designer who revelled in the originality of his work, while drawing on the traditions that the Arts & Crafts movement had fostered, and offered as a basis for new work. Richards emphasises that for these, and subsequent architects, a belief in *modern* architecture was not incompatible with an admiration for what was designed and built in the past. I shall say more about Shaw, Voysey and some of their contemporaries in a later section of this book.

Robert Furneaux Jordan in *Victorian Architecture* (1966) adds that: "It was this marriage between a simple vernacular and the elaborate ritual of late-Victorian family life that was the basis of Shaw's best work." (p. 226).

It is also worth remembering that Morris once commented: "We are all moderns now."

Michael Saler picks up this issue in his book on the English *avant-garde* in the inter-war years (1918-39), where he distinguishes the 'romantic medievalism' of the late-nineteenth century and the emerging 'medieval modernism' after 1918. Saler's argument is that the concept of 'design' became much more apparent in the early-twentieth century with the linking of fine art with the applied arts. (Saler, 1999.) These developments were signalled by the Arts & Crafts protagonists themselves in their demand for an holistic approach to the arts, and ending the elitist distinction between art and craft, artists and craftsmen. William Morris spoke and wrote at great length about these particular issues; one of my favourite of his essays being 'The Lesser Arts', based on an 1877 talk where he insists that the so-called lesser, or decorative arts, should not have a low value attached to them. They should be seen as the potentially joyous expression of our labour. I have always argued that people's engagement in creative cultures, which are often also oppositional ones, can be seen as an antidote to alienation. I enumerated this in my book *Culture & Creativity*:

- ❑ It is to be welcomed that the UK is a more multi-cultural society, but there are continuity as well as change issues here;
- ❑ Human action creates culture, contributing to the personal and social expressions of identity;
- ❑ Culture reflects the diversity and semi-autonomy of 'us';

- ❏ However, contradictions and conflicts arise. People's aspirations *versus* forces of control. Struggles occur, often located in particular sites.
- ❏ People invariably feel that their needs can only be met by engaging in these struggles;
- ❏ Culture, as articulated opposition to exclusion, and these marginal cultures as an antidote to alienation and oppression. (Astley 2006 p.13/14.)

It is also important here to emphasise that the focus on nature that imbued so much of Arts & Crafts thinking is often about spirituality. This view of nature is also true in the Marxist sense, too, of human beings *reaching up* to embrace nature, not descend to it from the lofty position of civilisation. A good deal of writing on the new Socialist Social Being, from Marx to Morris to Marcuse and beyond emphasises that people can and will think differently in a future 'communist' society.

There were many Christian Socialists active at this time, but there were an increasing number who felt religion no longer had the answers, let alone asked the right questions. This increasingly contested empty-ness in spirituality was often filled by a re-focus on Nature, and these ideas came to assume a significant dimension in the arguments about everyday life, including all the 'back to Eden' debates.

However, we should also recall that the organised Christian Church has tended to be on the side of 'civilisation', even rationalisation, in contrast to brutish and often uncontrollable 'Nature'. Man and Nature are cast as separate and opposed forces, which perhaps only an appeal to some utopia could alleviate? Indeed, most of the Genesis stories emphasise that until The Fall, Adam and Eve were actually a part of Nature, not separate from it.

English literature from Oliver Goldsmith in the late-eighteenth century (for example, in his well known poem 'The Deserted Village') to the evocative poetry of John Betjeman and beyond, in our own era, is replete with references to a lost 'golden age', a way of life that has just been lost, just slipped from our grasp, and for which we mourn.

The loss of the pastoral idyll overcome by *modern* and *urban* life is one explicit domain for such symbolism. There are important cross-references here with my discussion of the Gothic revival. There were eighteenth century examples of these sentiments, and Richard Reid in his book on *Cottages* reminds us of influential sources: "The cottage today represents that other dream, Virgil's myth of a Golden Age in which man lived on the fruits of the earth, peacefully, piously and with primitive simplicity." (Reid 1977 p.11.) We should, of course, remember that:

"By the 1740s, rural life had begun to change rapidly. The wealthier landowners had already started enclosing their estates, evicting tenants and destroying their homes. The Parliamentary Enclosure Acts of 1761-1845 accelerated this process, which created the hedgerows of the typical English countryside. Evicted farmers began to establish themselves on the less fertile moors, hills and mountains, while the landless labourer began weaving, spinning, basket-making and other home crafts to earn a little extra.' (Reid p.17/18.)

Between the mid-eighteenth century and the 1860s the Acts of Enclosure had enclosed seven million acres of common land. Cottagers were deprived of their grazing rights and had the land that they could work reduced eight-fold to half-an-acre. The compensation of a few thousand acres in allotment land was not likely to adequately or fairly replace the millions of acres enclosed in the official ideology of a more efficient farming regime, the rapid growth of agricultural capitalism.

So in these respects the characteristics of the 'pastoral', what mattered culturally, are a key and complex issue here, and we need to understand why at a time of increasing urbanisation so many people reacted as they did to 'the loss' and the despoliation of the countryside. Did the rapid loss of access to land represent, at the time and in the next century or so, much more than 'just' the countryside?

IN HIS 2004 book *A New England,* G.R. Searle suggests that after the 1880s the very specific local identity of places, counties and towns had undergone a transformation, not least by the new forms of communication. Even many of the growing middle classes who had a huge stake in the development of industrial capitalism, and certainly enjoyed many of its benefits, abandoned the inner city and town centre for the leafy suburbs. (Indeed, I am sat writing this in one such suburb laid-out in 1908).

By the end of the nineteenth century, the Arts & Crafts architects and designers could ride the crest of a wave of reaction to industrial and urban change. There was a considerable weight of ideas, theories (on clothes and food, for example) and everyday practice that promoted the general beneficial effects of rural life.

Many books, often of the nostalgic and even melancholic 'golden age' variety, promoted the value of such simplicity and authenticity. Of course, there are clear references to Thoreau and his contemporaries here. Many critics of the industrialising and urbanization processes saw one clear consequence in the destruction of the countryside, and had already feasted their imaginations on the pictures of Samuel Palmer and of the Pre-Raphaelites.

While talking about Palmer, I should mention Suzy Gablik,

who in her 1988 book *Has Modernism Failed?* castigated contemporary art for selling its soul to market capitalism and celebrity, and for abandoning more appropriate values:

"For nearly all of human history, the world was enchanted. As material and rationalist values have gained in pre-eminence, however, spiritual values have declined in direct proportion. Once uprooted from the world of symbols, art lost its links with myth and sacramental vision. The kind of sacramental vision to which I am referring is not that of routine church-going or religious dogma as such, but a mode of perception which converges on the power of the divine…the spiritual in the material." (Woodcock, 2001.)

Leigh Wilson in his 2007 book *Modernism* emphasises the radical nature of these modern ideas by essentially asking 'What is the world like, now, and how do people experience it?' Again, the rise of Theosophy and the like is not surprising. The mix of the cultural with the technological is always close at hand, and the transformative role of new technologies was constantly addressed. For example, it was Lenin who declared that "Communism = electricity plus the soviets!" Given that the world was being turned upside down, and the nineteenth century present was a complex set of contradictions, a search for the spiritual, especially so perhaps in the bonds between nature and human beings, is such a focus for the Arts & Crafts protagonists.

In tune with these thoughts, E.M. Forster [author, of course, of *Howard's End* (1910)] once famously suggested that the countryside represented civilization's only safeguard against the creeping 'red dust' of suburbanization and the intrusions of the motor vehicle.

It should also be noted that The Design and Industries Association (DIA) was set up in 1915, an attempt by a diverse range of people (including Lethaby) to bridge the gap between good design, craftsmanship, and industry and commerce. This was seen as a practical, and not overly 'arty', road to incorporating the desire for good quality design into a saleable form, and shopkeepers like Heal were in the forefront. Most associates of the DIA were much closer to the commercial sentiments of Henry Cole and his group in the mid-century. This overtly commercial and mass production-oriented approach was always a tricky area for Arts & Crafts people, who although they invariably saw themselves as 'Modernists', were aware of the dangers of compromising their progressive design principles for commercial success. As Fiona MacCarthy put it in *A History of British Design 1830-1970*: "The DIA had settled for a life of common-sense, urging its designers to talk man-to-man to industry: in the interests of appeasement, never mention Art." (MacCarthy, 1972.)

Another important voice in the discussion on tradition *versus* the commercial version of modernity was A.L.Morton, who in his *The English Utopia* (1952) discusses the ancient and magical land of Cokaigne, a utopia, where 'communism', peace, plenty and rest prevail for all, an escape from the brutal realities of life:

"Medieval man was…strongly aware of his struggle against his environment. He felt deeply the hostility of the world, the briefness and uncertainty of life. Man was a stranger and a sojourner, passing from darkness to twilight and thence into darkness again, a darkness only slightly alleviated by the church's promises of heaven and rendered even more impenetrable and horrifying by its threats of hell." (p44.)

I would also mention that Morton's use of Cokaigne is in part shared by Edward Elgar in his 1901 orchestral piece

Cokaignei, which says much more about the Elgar of the Malvern Hills than it does of all that pomp and imperialism stuff that his legacy is often dogged by. The idea of Arcadia is regularly recycled because it evokes the land of plenty; it is another version of utopia. But because 'Arcadia' has so frequently been written about, and painted, it is not 'no place', but definitely 'some place', and thinking about the Greek words forming the origin of 'utopia' it is both 'a good place' *and* 'nowhere'!

That said, we should recall that in most depictions of Arcadia there is a seed of doubt, famously in Poussin's *Et in Arcadia Ego,* translated as *Even in Arcadia, I (i.e.* Death) am present.'

Simon Schama in his book *Landscape and Memory* (1995) reminds us this and the wider issues, the topography of our cultural identity, and explores this terrain as the "garden of the western landscape imagination."

Dennis Hardy and Colin Ward also had a somewhat more positive tilt at these issues in their 1980s book *Arcadia for All: The Legacy of a Makeshift Landscape,* which considers the multitude of shanty self-builds in the countryside and by the sea. These 'anarchic' developments gave many urban families the opportunity to enjoy these out-of-town environments in an economical and idiosyncratic way. First, or second homes, with a difference. On the cusp of the estuary and docks in the south-east Devon coastal town where I live, there was one such place, now gone, and replaced by a 'marina' with very expensive apartment blocks, mainly owned by wealthy week-enders. Poussin could have painted a picture here.

As I have argued above, William Morris and many of his contemporaries were inspired by 'Nature', by organic forms. Their fundamental concern with the inter-relationship between the 'natural' and design, including the design of the built environment is evident in all their work. Indeed, Morris tried to persuade anyone who would listen that their teachers should be 'history and nature'. He also insisted that nature should not be imitated but interpreted as a treasured resource in an appropriate design context. As I shall explore further in this study, the Arts & Crafts architects were committed to the idea that houses should look as if they had grown up, organically, from the land about them. Morris set the tone here with his comments on the beloved Kelmscott Manor: "A house that I love with a reasonable love, I think…so much has the old house grown up out of the soil and the lives of those that lived on it."

I am reminded here of a range of well-known Batsford books from the 1930s: *English Village Homes, The English Countryside* and *The Legacy of England*, among others. One distinctive characteristic of all these books is an acknowledgement that the old England is passing, urbanisation and neglect are taking their toll, and the ancient landscape is being transformed, yet again. Plenty of room for nostalgia here; for example, the evocative Brian Cook picture covers; and, as I have suggested elsewhere in this study, an often conservative melancholy haunts these pages. However, that is not to say that the diverse range of authors of these books is unrealistic about the forms and consequences of change: far from it; for example, in their reflections on the cultural materialistic realities of the landscape and the buildings within it. These authors consistently discuss the way the landscape bears all the hallmarks of creative human labour. The landscape has been and is, *worked*, to be lived in, and lived with. And of course these books are usually received in a different way now than when they were published. Again, I am reminded of Thomas Hardy and his understanding of everyday life in the countryside of his day.

AT THIS point, it is relevant to mention the creation in 1877 of the Society for the Protection of Ancient Buildings (SPAB).

This was another Morris-led development, which has expanded over the years to become the very active and influential organization it is today. In the words of SPAB itself, the Society was set up to "counteract the highly destructive 'restoration' of medieval buildings being practised by many Victorian architects," and among these was G.E. Street, with whom a young Morris and Philip Webb were apprenticed. The founding members of SPAB were particularly concerned with the tendency to scrape away the surfaces of ancient buildings, an over-zealous cleaning-them-up process. This approach led to the SPAB nickname of 'Anti-Scrape'. The original members were an illustrious band of Arts & Crafts devotees who felt passionately about the casual destruction of English heritage.

One of the main irritations for SPAB members was George Gilbert Scott, an ardent neo-Gothicist, who during the nineteenth century 'tidied up' many cathedrals and other significant buildings, often obliterating original Gothic features. This work, and some of his designs for new buildings, for example churches and State buildings, seriously upset Morris and his associates. Scott was very much a man of the big scale public building arena, some distance from the domestic architecture that I have concentrated on in this study. Scott was caught up in the big mid-nineteenth debate between the Gothicists and those still embracing the Classical style (the French version or otherwise). One can see the outcomes of all these activities in major cities in Britain (usually the political elites in those cities competing with their contemporaries in other cities nearby - go and compare Liverpool, Manchester and Leeds, for example), and in the main these buildings were much frowned on by the devotees of Arts & Crafts.

The SPAB also supported the creation of the National Trust in 1896, and has continued to promote the development of craft and conservation skills, and the passing-on of those skills to others. This continuing aspect of SPAB's work clearly reflects the enduring values of the Arts & Crafts movement and of the issues discussed in this book. It is also worth mentioning that Thomas Hardy was a very active member and caseworker for SPAB. Hardy, an architect himself, and the member of an architectural family, was particularly involved in protecting churches in his beloved Wessex.

It is also worth noting that in 1865, several years before the SPAG, Morris, Ruskin, J.S. Mill, T.H. Huxley and others had formed the Society to Protect Commons, Open Spaces and Footpaths. The saving, protection and public use of Hampstead Heath was one of their successful campaigns.

BY THEIR very nature, the issues addressed above are political and invariably oppositional, then and now, not the least reason for this being because of values and status issues. This is also a result of the exercise of power in the control of the essential resources for a good life; for instance, the fundamental need for housing.

So, it has remained central to these arguments that *if* the People's government was going to further the interests of all in a fair, socially just and practical way, the People's need for good quality and affordable housing, within an aesthetically pleasing environment, needs to be satisfied.

In view of the nature of the Arts & Crafts values I have discussed, it is important to place the design and delivery of estates like Merry Oak in to a further context.

At their heart, Arts & Crafts values are enlightening and democratising, and the building of estates like Merry Oak is no exception. I would argue that the creation of Merry Oak was *educational*, in particular for the residents, but also for other observers of the development. It was educational in the sense that most education can be a social and cultural process, which demonstrates to people the necessity and appropriateness of something that they did not even know they needed; and, even something they considered impossible for them to access. The educative value of life in an 'ideal' house and environment is certainly not a new idea; Richard Reiss was expressing this view in 1924, and I will return to this issue in my chapter on Merry Oak. (Reiss 1924.)

Arts & Crafts design has always had the potential to be transformative, taking the residual, or traditional forms of culture and creating an emergent culture; and by demonstrating through its many diverse forms an alternative way of seeing and living, a lingering influence on our day, like a palimpsest, an impression lasting beyond its original formation. Many of the key players in the Arts & Crafts movement *were* proselytisers, often echoing the passion of William Blake: "Those who restrain desire do so because their [own desire] is weak enough to be restrained." The vision of creating better places for people to live, like Merry Oak, is one such example, and demonstrates leadership given by activists like the designer Walter Crane (1845-1915). He was closely associated with the 1888 Arts & Crafts Exhibition Society event that fixed (as cited earlier in this book) the movement's name, and argued that the mission of the Society was "to turn our artists into craftsmen and our craftsmen into artists."

One further important aspect of Arts & Crafts values is the desire to reflect an Englishness in both theory and practice. Nikolaus Pevsner comments on this in his 1955 book *The Englishness of English Art* by emphasising the vernacular style of most Arts & Crafts buildings, which drew a clear distinction between the utilitarian and the ornamental. He says that there was, usually in nineteenth century England, buildings wrapped up "'in clothes not made for them but for buildings of other ages and purposes" (p.29) and "...It is no accident that this architectural historicism started in England; for in England there existed…a disposition in favour of narrative, and the thatched Old English cottages as against the Italianate villas tells a story by their very costumes. Their effect is evocative, not strictly aesthetic." (p.29)

Pevsner echoes Morris in seeing these Arts & Crafts values as a move towards a more explicit modern style: "The revolution which led to the establishment of modern architecture was prepared step by step in England, first by Morris in theory and design, then by such architects as Voysey, but the revolution itself had to be made abroad." (p.61.)

This was to be in the USA (Frank Lloyd Wright and Gustav Stickley) and in continental Europe, especially so Germany. Michael Collins makes the point in his history of design from 1851 that the inter-relationship between Britain and the USA was very strong and fruitful. (Collins, 1994.) I will expand on this issue below. It is no accident that the design and architectural baton was passed to the new generation in Germany in the 1920s, with Bauhaus. Nor is it a surprise that so many of those designers then came to Britain as refugees from the Nazis. The parallel development of The Frankfurt School of Marxist-oriented Social Scientists was to have a profound affect on debates about the true path of Modernism and Aesthetics.

Arts & Crafts Architects

At this point, I wish to turn the focus of my attention on the architects and designers of 'the movement', and to help my argument I shall pay more attention to certain practitioners. I will therefore say much more about five of the key architects associated with the Arts & Crafts movement. They are Mackay Baillie Scott, Edward Prior, Richard Norman Shaw, Charles Voysey and Philip Webb. I shall also offer an extensive account of the work of William Lethaby, *the* designer, writer and administrator polymath of his generation. Of course, I have been selective here in a way that reflects my own valuation of the protagonists, and have inevitably made reference to many other architects, while realising that some writers would have a slightly different list of the people whose contribution they valued. These designers with many associates created what is usually referred to as the early phase of the English Domestic Revival. I also need to say something about 'the vernacular'. Arts & Crafts pioneers, especially so the designers/architects, embraced the vernacular to a greater or lesser extent. They celebrated, and placed a high value on, all the key characteristics of vernacular in building; for example, local responses to particular (and often culturally specific) needs, the use of local materials, and regional design traditions. Style is by definition a dimension of the emergence in a dialectical ways of solutions to specific need. The vernacular is also characterised by the role of the local craftsman tradition, no abstract theory, no professionals, just a focus on buildings that are fit for purpose and created in time-honoured ways. From the late eighteenth century onward, more Continental European styles were employed by professional 'architects' in building for the wealthy, relegating the vernacular of that particular locale to the same 'dustbin of history' as a pre-factory system of economic and social relations. The circulation of patterns of 'universal' designs *via* pattern books, magazines and the like, added to a sense of a wider perspective for the growing number of 'professionalising' architects and builders. This was an important generalising and standardizing process and an aspect of a further division of labour that led to the emergence of people who saw themselves, and were seen by others, as professional architects. Also at this time, the costs of transporting building material around the country began to decrease with better roads, the canals and, eventually, railways. The Public Health Act of 1870, and subsequent attempts by the Local Government Board and the new Ministry of Health in 1919, added to a tendency to uniformity that many architects and planners resisted. The rise in influence of the Gothic revival from the early-nineteenth century added to and complemented by the 'Old English' style, while the Vernacular and Arts & Crafts movements restored the value of the vernacular characteristics cited above. The aesthetic informed embrace of the Arts & Crafts architect-designers only enhanced the enthusiasm for, and value of, the vernacular. That said, I should cite the argument on style of Geoffrey Scott in his 1914 book *The Architecture of Humanism: A study in the history of taste.* Scott's book was quite influential at the time, and in a 1999 reprint Henry Hope Reed wrote a foreword in which he states that the book was hailed as the finest on architecture since Ruskin: "The book's fascination stems largely from the fact that Geoffrey Scott offers the clearest analysis of the theories and ideas behind much of the nineteenth and twentieth century architecture theories and ideas...held today...the heart of the book: a discussion of the classical tradition as reflected in the architecture of Renaissance and Baroque Italy and the role given the human body in contributing to that tradition." (p.vii)

Reed argues that Scott considered the dominant ideas about architecture to be fallacies, because they were not defined by aesthetic standards but by moral, philosophical, or scientific ideas. He suggests that the advocates of styles opposed to classicism were in fact using a discussion of architecture to address other issues, *e.g.*, social relationships and social inequality, or modes of production and so on. Scott, born in Hampstead in 1884, reflects the general tenor of arguments in the Aesthetic Movement, and as I have said elsewhere in this study the role of Walter Pater and his associates was a regular focus of criticism in the 'style wars' that carried on well in to the twentieth century.

(Richard) Norman Shaw and Philip Webb were both born in 1831 on the eve of the first Reform Act (1832), and three years before Morris. Charles Voysey was born in 1857. Mackay Hugh Baillie Scott was born in 1864. Shaw died in 1912, and Webb in 1915; they both lived through extraordinary changes in English society, and to see the coming of 'Edwardian' society that in itself was the harbinger of the European *fin de siècle*. Voysey lived until 1941, and Baillie Scott died in 1945. A good many of those pioneers that I discuss in this book straddled the nineteenth and twentieth centuries. They were all in vital ways the personification of the cultural and social conditions of their time, *and* the creators of a *zeitgeist;* there were other, non-Arts & Crafts voices of course, but nothing to match this paradigm. A great deal has been written about these designers, and it is not my intention to compete with such accounts. There could have been many more *dramatis personae* here for there was a genuine symbiotic relationship between these designers. My aim here is to say something of their contribution to the inter-linked issues that are the focus of this study, and the people they connected with during their lifetimes.

2. Charles F. C. Vosey
   (1857-1941)

3. Richard Norman Shaw
   (1831-1912)

2- 6. Arts and Crafts Architects

4. Philip Webb (1831-1915

5. Edward Prior
(1857-1932)

6. William Lethaby (1857-1931)

On the windowsill by my desk is a photograph of The Red House in Bexleyheath, Kent, designed by Philip Webb for William Morris and his wife Jane, and where the Morris family lived from 1859 to 1865, when they decided to move back to London. Webb and Morris chose the site, ten miles from central London, for several reasons as explained by Fiona MacCarthy:

"Morris needed the vista of the river or the hill to offset the claustrophobia that easily attacked him. . . .Historic association was another of his cravings, and at nearby Abbey Farm were the remains of an Augustinian priory which Cardinal Wolsey had suppressed. Red House was also close to the ancient Watling Street, the pilgrims' route to Canterbury: Morris, the devoted Chaucerian, referred to the squat and cosy garden porch at Red House as 'the Pilgrims Rest'. He continued to curse the iniquities of railways, but he was to make good use of Abbey Wood, his local station, only three miles away on the newly opened North Kent line." (p.154)

Edward (Ned) Burne-Jones the painter and Morris' close friend since Oxford, once described The Red House as "the beautifullest place on Earth" It should also be said that later in life Webb reflected that his younger-self had not made all the right decisions about the house, its position and layout, but he *had* made those decisions.

It is important to note that The Red House dates from 1859, at the height of the Gothic revival. It is possible to see in Webb's work the influence of Street, Butterfield and others associated with the Gothic revival. Webb has invariably been seen as a puritan of style; honest, plain and workmanlike. Robert Macleod in his 1971 book *Style and Society: architectural ideology in Britain 1835-1914* emphasizes the influence of Butterfield's 'secular vernacular', and the role played by the

Ecclesiological Group I have discussed elsewhere in this book. Macleod also comments on the close working and creative relationship of Webb and Morris, much like that of Holst and Vaughan Williams. Macleod adds: "Philip Webb begat William Richard Lethaby. Of all the links in Victorian architectural genealogy, none is more clearly established or of more interest in its results than this one.' (Macleod p.55.) And Lethaby's biography of Webb has been the much admired and remains the standard work since its first publication in the early-twentieth century.

Morris and Webb had met in the architectural offices of George Street in Beaumont Street, Oxford, in 1856 when Morris had decided to become an architect. The young and flamboyant Morris had been placed under Webb's wing, and in their subsequent life-long relationship Webb remained the guiding hand even though Morris was usually providing much of the artistic stimulus and opportunities. Webb would often provide key parts of Morris' designs for textiles and wallpaper, for example, drawing birds. Norman Shaw, a pupil of Street's, then mentored Lethaby, Sidney Barnsley and Edward Prior among others. John Sedding (1838-1891) was also a pupil of Street, who went on to mentor the two influential Ernests, Barnsley and Gimson, along with many of the 'Wandering Architects' like Detmar Blow. (See Michael Drury 2000 on the *Wandering Architects*; the group of influential peripatetic designers and builders.) So among this generation of architects there were several associated with Street in one way or another. Incidentally, Street was famous in his time for church building (indeed I lived opposite one, SS Philip & James in Oxford).

Shaw was very much for the independence and separate-ness of architecture, but others like Lethaby argued for much more integration of the arts and crafts. The Devonian William Lethaby (1857-1931) was to become one of the key thinkers and theorists of the Arts & Crafts movement. "Architecture was for Lethaby the quintessential art, the ultimate expression and sum of civilized man's social organization; it was "human skill and feeling shown in the great necessary activity of building.'" (Rubens 1986 p.247.)

Lethaby was in his late thirties by the time he embraced the rising radical Arts & Crafts socialism, in response to, argues Rubens, his raised consciousness of the gulf between designer and artisan. Lethaby argued that only through a thorough knowledge of, and experience with, the raw materials of designing buildings could anyone be a progressive influence. He also advocated that the architect-designer should be a group player. This led Lethaby to be an enthusiast for the building unions and for a Guild-style approach to fellowship and the mentoring of the next generation. In the 1920s:

"Lethaby argued that architecture should be a national
service and the architect a public servant, concerned primarily
with the construction of humane and efficient towns, public
buildings and housing. But behind these beliefs can be sensed
something else: the idea of the architect not just as a member of
an exclusive profession, but as something far greater, the
archetype of man himself - man, the designer and creator, who
in making his world makes himself." (Rubens p.258.)

I have always thought that the extensive and influential groups of post-1945 architects who chose to practice in the public sector had inherited Lethaby's values. This public service ethos meant that many talented architects eschewed private practice in favour of working in local government, school building programmes and town planning projects. Unwin was also a significant influence here on the practical application of knowledge and skills to public sector housing. (For a very interesting account of these trends, see Andrew Saint's 1987 book *Towards a Social Architecture: The Role of School Building in Post-War England* .

It is also important to recognise the increasing influence of magazines and journals like George Godwin's *The Builder*, singled-out by Pevsner as an early vehicle for building information, and key debates like that on "copyism versus originality." (See Pevsner 1972.)

Lethaby, like Morris, considered himself to be a modernist, but he questioned the technocratic approach of architects like Le Corbusier, who he thought put the functioning of 'the machine' before the 'living in'. Lethaby was also a very practical man in respect of design education (as I outline below) and in the links between craft and commerce leading to his association with the Design and Industries Association.

In addition to his design practice, he was also very influential in his role as educator and proselytiser for design education. He assumed, like William Morris, that the most important aspect of education, like life, was art. He had no time for education of any kind that did not have working practice or 'craft work' at its core.[1] Lethaby was empowered by the London County Council to set up the Central School of Arts & Crafts in 1896. His educational zeal could be summed up in his comment: "It is a difficult world to live in! It makes one long for a sort of balcony to the world, so that one could go outside and get a breath of fresh air." (Ward, 1991 p.97.)

Like Lethaby, I have always believed that a well-rounded education can be that 'balcony'. Lethaby thought that the likes

---

[1] It is interesting to note how these specific concerns with a practice-centred education should re-surface in the guise of 'reflective practice' for professionals in the 1970s and 1980s in the work of Argyris, Schon and Richard Sennett (see Astley 2006).

of Matthew Arnold and his ideas about the centrality of 'culture' was all very well but Lethaby's view of culture was much more diverse, and multi-cultural. In the 'real' world of ordinary people's everyday life where there should be a high value placed on the poetic nature of common things:

"..the world of labour, adventure, and invention, a very different type of education is needed from that which the 'humanities' are identified with dreaming and divorced from doing…Education should be an apprenticeship to life and service, and workers will have to educate their would-be instructors to the knowledge that there are diversities of culture by the very nature of things." (Rubens, p.262.)

On first reading this I was reminded of Raymond Williams' comments on working in Adult Education in the 1950s, and being "brought down to earth" by his students!

Lethaby shared a conviction with Morris (and Williams, of course) that art was for everyone, but access to the joys of art were deliberately denied to the many in order for the few to gain privilege. Indeed Lethaby's outlook chimes very well with the title of Wendy Kaplan's book *The Art that is Life* (1987), her study of the emergence and development of the American Arts & Crafts movement. In her introduction, 'The Lamp of British Precedent', Kaplan says of the Arts & Crafts practitioners that they were: "Passionately committed to righting social ills, (these) groups of English and American reformers chose art as their medium" (Kaplan, p.52.) and, while acknowledging the differing routes to realising their ideals, there was a unity of purpose: "The Arts & Crafts ideal was not so much a style as an approach, an attitude toward the making of objects."(p.52.)

So, as Alan Crawford says in his 1985 book on Ashbee, it was in the 1880s that this cohort of people became aware of themselves "as a group, and named themselves." This fits with the first Arts & Crafts exhibitions in the mid- to late-1880s. It is worth mentioning here that Charles Robert Ashbee (1863-1942) was another fan of Whitman, and did actually do some work in the USA. In one of my books on Arts & Crafts, there is a photograph of Ashbee taken by Frank Lloyd Wright in 1910. Ashbee was also a major influence on Gustav Stickley the American Arts & Crafts designer and publisher of *The Craftsman* journal from 1901. It is worth noting that many British designers and architects of the later nineteenth century were first attracted to Arts & Crafts *via* their access to American publications carrying examples of English Arts & Crafts ideas and designs; this is testimony to the importance of the spread of magazines and other practice-oriented literature at this time.

I should also add that one of Ashbee's mentors was Edward Carpenter (1844-1929), the author and poet often called 'the English Whitman'. I will have more to say about Carpenter in my chapter on Raymond Unwin. Ashbee, like Unwin, was passionate about the role of practice education, and here again we can see the hand of Lethaby. Ashbee's creation of the Guild of Handicraft in 1888 was one more dimension to the literally hands-on approach of the Arts & Crafts ideology, that is, theory and (practice) knowledge leading to action (praxis). Ashbee was also involved with Toynbee Hall, whose influence I discuss below, and although Morris was not convinced that Ashbee's idealistic approach to a syndicalist solution to a socialistic transformation of society would work, their values consistently overlap.

Godfrey Rubens in his 1975 introduction to a reprint of Lethaby's 1891 *Architecture, Mysticism and Myth*, emphasised the latter's theoretical concerns: 'Like Vitruvius, Lethaby proposed 'three ultimate facts behind all architecture', and the first two of these correspond to those originally offered by

Vitruvius, who wrote that there were three things to be considered in any building: utility or commodity, durability and beauty. Lethaby's third is "style/nature" and though "beauty" may be the outcome of "style" it is here implicitly a relative quality.' (p.x.)

Lethaby posed what was for him the big question on architecture: "What, then, I want to ask is, Are there ultimate facts behind all architecture which has given it form? Mainly, three: First, the similar needs and desires of men; second, on the side of structure, the necessities imposed by materials, and physical laws of their erection and combination; and, third, on the side of style, nature." (p.3.)

I should re-emphasise the ideological nature of the historical interpretation of the past that brought about the successive influential movements in architecture at this time. The various protagonists for Gothic, Queen Anne, Vernacular, Arts & Crafts in general, and even later for Classicism, were all making a case, expressing their values very clearly and visually in the form of buildings of many kinds. Often, as I have already said: 'The bigger and grander the better!"

THIS IS an issue taken up by Reyner Banham in his book *Theory and Design in the First Machine Age* (1960), where he draws a distinction between Lethaby and Geoffrey Scott on this matter. Scott's book *A Study in the History of Taste* was published in 1914, which argued in favour of Classicism and against most of what Lethaby and his associates valued. Banham emphasises the importance of early-twentieth century developments in Germany and especially the creation of the Deutscher Werkbund in 1907. By 1915, Lethaby had formed the view that pioneering English architecture was in decline and that 'We' in England should look to Germany for inspiration. Banham suggests that Lethaby *et. al.* were over-looking developments in Art Nouveau, especially so in Scotland with Mackmurdo and the Mackintoshs. Banham argues that from 1904-5 there was a distinct shift in England (back) towards Classicism. Scott, close to Pater and the Aesthetic movement, was a key player in this critical shift. These variants of design were antithetical to Arts & Crafts, and Banham suggests that Lethaby, like Ruskin and Morris before him, was not a 'systematic thinker' (*i.e.,* a Rationalist in design terms) but a man of feeling, a devotee of the 'free style' in architecture.

As I have mentioned elsewhere in this study, the advent of Art Nouveau at the end of the nineteenth century marked a distinctive, but complicated, split between those admirers of Arts & Crafts and 'Aesthetics'. Increasing numbers of designers and entrepreneurs diverted their energies in to an explicitly decorated style, an 'arts for art's sake' approach that took the naturalistic styling of Arts & Crafts in to a much more sensuous line. However, there were contradictions in the 'purity' of the Aesthetic advocates; for instance, the contributions of Wilde and the young illustrator Aubrey Beardsley (1872-1898) led to a 're-branding' for a much more commercial market, with Arthur Liberty (1843-1917) opening his shop in London in 1875, and employing a variety of designers like Archibald Knox (1864-1933), he of the 'Celtic revival'. Edward William Godwin (1833-1886) should also be mentioned here as another eclectic designer whose Japanese-style creations could be found in Liberty's shop, and in 1877 designed a house for James Whistler, having begun his architectural career designing 'Ruskinian Gothic'.

In this study I also mention Christopher Dresser and Walter Crane as key contributors to these developments, who along with the craft work of Ashbee, for example, if seen out of its Arts & Crafts specific context, could be assumed to be Art Nouveau. So, even among the 'Anti-Rationalists' there were inevitable overlaps in these design developments, and they took varying forms in different countries.

What is clear here is that when the German Arts & Crafts devotees took on the movement they did systemise it much more, and developed a rational and often utilitarian approach that created Bauhaus and beyond. Banham cites Voysey as a key member of those practising the 'free style' that Lethaby warned was being lost due to focus and neglect.

The builders of high-rise in the 1960s were Rationalists, systematisers, offering their utilitarian version of the 'moderne' for general consumption. Perhaps the late-1920s and early-1930s Arts & Crafts suburbs were the last throw of the dice for *that* tradition, soon to be lost in the Depression, and afterwards, with a few honourable exceptions, into an era of lowest common denominator 'mass' housing?

There is also considerable common ground on these issues between Banham and Pevsner (for example. as expressed in the latter's *Pioneers of Modern Design*). They come close to agreeing that the prominent 'modern' architects of the post-1918 period were all schooled in the Arts & Crafts movement and the theoretical debates of the late nineteenth and early twentieth centuries. Pevsner in particular argues that after 1914 Arts & Crafts in England was finished as *the* leading theory, and architects, increasingly professionalised, went off down many stylistic *cul-de-sacs*, for example with Futurism.

In his essay 'Nine Swallows - no summer' published in 1973, Pevsner expands on this assessment. He poses the question of what was happening in British architecture between 1900 and 1925.

Pevsner suggests three dominant themes at work:

- ❑ 'Tudor traditionalism', and here he cites Dawber, Voysey and Ballie-Scott as the lead figures.

❑   An official style of 'Edwardian Imperial', an eclectic
       styling of neo-classicism, *beaux arts* and English
       Palladian, and used for many 'official' and
       Establishment buildings.

❑   He then cites Ernest Newton (1856-1922), an apprentice
       of Shaw, and the growth of the neo-Georgian, which in
       fact is more Queen Anne in the way of William Nesfield
       (1835-88), Webb and Shaw. (Pevsner in *The Anti-
       Rationalists* 1973, but see also Sharp, Dennis in the
       Bibliography).

I would also argue that there was a residual culture of Arts &
Crafts design values that was carried forward to the post-1918
period. Unwin, *et. al.* seem to have had *the* lasting influence in
contrast to emerging styles. It could be argued that the
architectural and planning design choices made after 1918,
including Merry Oak, perpetuated the Arts & Crafts aesthetic
almost despite the increasing diversity. Given the more diverse
design palette, was the continued use of an Arts & Crafts
aesthetic a conservative choice and/or preservative choice? It is
certainly the case that given the mix of complex values that I am
discussing in this study there was an overwhelming choice of
the Arts & Crafts and vernacular aesthetic, and that for Unwin
and his associates saw this as a democratising choice.

So, there was 'a battle of the styles' in the late-nineteenth and
early-twentieth centuries, and there was certainly in
consequence the development of a creative eclecticism. Michael
Collins underlines the very importance and value of this
eclecticism in his book on the history of design, which I have
already cited. (Collins, 1994). There was also a general call for
architects/ designers to 'come down of their theoretical
pedestals' and *build*. There was here, quite literally, a 'grounded

aesthetics', a common culture, that was often at odds with the pressure to 'professionalise' architecture, and this brought about fixed standards, exams, certification, and so on. Sedding was one prominent architect/ designer who saw his role as more akin to an expressive artist rather than (just) a competent master artisan. There would be increasing pressure for 'profession-alisation'; and often, for example, in the laudable aim of giving public service.

Raymond Unwin is an example of these trends that comes to mind because he was certainly agnostic about the value of professional status, and my chapter on him, and Barry Parker, addresses this issue.

Rubens has also emphasised the manner of Lethaby's commitment to a life of service to society: "Service is, first of all and of greatest necessity, common productive work," a clear statement of a 'grounded aesthetic'. Like so many other voices in the Arts & Crafts movement, he sought to emphasise that human labour is, or certainly should be, art. The influence of Ruskin and Morris on these sentiments is clear, and remained with Lethaby throughout his life.

Lethaby was one of the Arts & Crafts luminaries criticised by David Watkin is his 1977 book *Morality and Architecture*. Watkin accuses Lethaby of a Romantic populism, in that the latter overlooks the complex set of inter-actions that actually bring about changes in ideas about buildings and style.

Watkin argues that Lethaby is one of the heirs to a view of the Gothic espoused by Pugin and his contemporary Viollet-le-duc, that there was an unbroken heritage from the 'organic' Gothic past to the mid- nineteenth century.

Watkin argues that this is a taking of the moral high ground in building design that is unjustified in its over-simplistic account of change.

Watkin accuses Lethaby of attempting to take consideration

of style preferences out of the ideological realm, and to claim what modern architecture must be:

"The Romantic populistic view, developed in the early-nineteenth century, was that anonymous people, labouring silently in confrontation with the hard tasks of life, produce works which no one has deliberately designed but which are products of the unconscious wisdom, the adaptive resourcefulness, of the 'folk-soul'.

"This idea seems to pervade several of the interpretations of architecture...for example, the religious and social determination, and the argument from technological necessity. It also relates to the all-pervasive collectivist belief that the architect has no will or imagination of his own, but is simply the 'expression' of something lying in the 'collective unconscious'. He must ever respond to collective needs and must act as the collectivity demands." (Watkin, p.37.)

Watkins deplores the tendency towards social engineering factored into the role of design and architecture. On the basis of the discontinuous nature of social change, Watkin can see no justification for the historicism that he argues is evident in the ideas of Lethaby and others.

In his argument, Watkin clearly distrusts the way in which Lethaby and most of his contemporaries make their judgements about the way in which architecture can, and should, contribute to the 'good society'. Watkin believes that this organic and/or holistic approach to style, based even at a level of generality on the Gothic, is highly selective and misses the inconvenient truths about 'the past'. Watkin accuses Lethaby of assuming that a Gothic-derived organicism is a natural outcome of the social conditions of the day, an inevitable material culture given the social conditions. The fact that Lethaby and others derided the Renaissance because it was based on 'knowledge, taste and

connoisseurship' is seen as both ideological and simplistic by
Watkin - who is, however, less vocal in acknowledging his own
right-of-centre ideology and politics.

While I do not share Watkin's criticism of the ideas of
Lethaby, he does raise a relevant general issue that should be
addressed. Just because someone, for whatever reason, believes
that this or that truth about the connections between social and
cultural phenomenon points us in a particular architectural
direction, this does not guarantee that they are right. Nor does
this mean that the subjects of these chosen approaches can
deliver, for the majority of people, appropriate solutions to their
needs. For example, a good deal of uninformed commentary
suggests that the 'International' *Moderne* style of architecture
never really developed in Britain.

However, the opposite is true with regard to social or council
housing. A considerable amount of post-1945 housing for 'the
labouring classes' was, stylistically, and ideologically, derived
from the Continental Modernists, drawing extensively on the
ideas of Le Corbusier and his contemporaries. This approach
was not a 'pure' architectural choice based on appropriate style
criteria, but often a political and economic set of choices based
on a systems building approach that was seen as quick and
cheap(er). Many local authorities travelled down the high-rise
road commissioning versions of the *moderne* without consulting
their existing or future tenants. This *was* indeed social
engineering on a considerable scale, where the top-down
approach was compounded by the very inadequate quality
controls exercised over the building processes, the lack of
money spent on long-term maintenance, and the total disregard
for tenant security that would have been completely
unacceptable for a middle-class clientele. Like or loath the
moderne style, this approach to architectural solutions to
housing need was not even given a fair chance of success

because of the class politics at the heart of decision making. These phenomena can be seen as even more contradictory given the public service ethic of many post-1945 architects (a point I made earlier). Perhaps it is also a basic fact of the matter that middle- and upper-middle class people seeking housing were more likely to be beguiled by the Arts & Crafts-style private estates of Metroland and elsewhere? They had more choice, and *these* were the choices they made based in part on a shrewd strategy by developers opting for what they saw as a conservative aesthetic.

It should also be said that the key relationship between techniques, materials innovation and building features strongly here. It is somewhat ironic that the many innovative architectural ideas of the *moderne,* when translated into real buildings, used - out of necessity at the time - materials that were just not up to the task. Designers and builders of a *moderne* style today can use materials for roofs, windows, waterproofing, and so on, that make these designs actually viable. As I have said above many of the public sector high-rise and other large scale 'systems' design estates, where the parts of buildings were pre-fabricated in a factory and assembled on site, were prone to materials and assembly faults that very soon led to a degradation of these buildings. In my chapter on Raymond Unwin, I will be returning to these design and delivery issues.

Lethaby was anxious about the impact of Modernism. Just before his death in 1931, he was increasingly aware of the pressures from Modernists in architecture to press for the rational over the romantic, or even the pressure on staying with the 'progressive eclecticism' of the Arts & Crafts. The Modernists - Le Corbusier, Lubetkin, Chermayeff, *et. al.* - called for an end to 'style', *i.e.*, 'progressive eclecticism', and sought a dominating machine aesthetic. Lethaby feared that the imposition of Modernism in architecture would eradicate the organic qualities that he and others of the Arts & Crafts had witnessed and promoted. Lethaby, like Ruskin before him, argued that beauty was independent of utility, which was anathema to the Modernists. Lethaby's response to the advocates and practitioners of the 'Brutalism' of the 1950s onward (some critics would see this development as the logical extension of the Modernists' values) would surely have been that a mean society makes for mean architecture!

This issue is taken up and developed by J. Morduant Crook in his excellent book *The Dilemma of Style: architectural ideas from the picturesque to the post-modern*. Crook quotes Lethaby in regard to Philip Webb and the issue of style: "Webb in building, like Browning in poetry and Maddox Brown in painting, was first of all a realist; but then he sought for the romantic and the poetic in the real." (Crook 1987 p. 173.)

I would have added Thomas Hardy to Crook's list. Crook makes the key point that since the Renaissance, which left us with the notion of the 'artist' creating an individual style, architects have often been perplexed by the two-fold nature of their calling: building as service and building as art; the eternal tension between form and function. It is his belief that the Picturesque merely confused matters *via* Pugin, Ruskin and Violet-le-Duc, by arguing a moral case. Crook raises many of the issues on style and a moral agenda for the architect that I have raised above and elsewhere in this book. Given their diversity the motives of the Arts & Crafts devotees was complex and often confusing, as Crook says: "The Arts and Crafts house - child of the Gothic revival, unwilling ancestor of the Modern Movement - summed- up an eternal ambivalence in English aesthetics: puritan instincts and romantic yearnings' (Crook p.231.)

So while the early impact of Modernism was felt in the early-twentieth century, I would argue that this was not the case with the majority of housing developments after 1918. Admittedly, there were considerable problems caused by some local authorities 'just' building to meet need (including political need) but then 'washing their hands' of issues with infrastructure development and democratic rights for the tenant.

In these fundamental concerns, we are back to the key issue of function and form, an issue discussed by Thomas Markus in his book on *Buildings and Power*:

'Whilst what a building looks like, whether the roof leaks and what it costs are matters of great concern, for most people the first question is: "Is it good to use?" The answer to this depends on owners, designers, institutions of all kinds, and occupants, so this must be a question about society...I take the stand that buildings are not primarily art, technical or investment objects, but social objects.' (Markus 1993 p.xix)

Markus argues that relations between people are shaped by buildings, and crucially the spaces around and between buildings, and this if often to do with access and with control, for example, with schools. In his argument, Markus enters into discourse theory here by emphasising the inter-relation between language and meaning, where the inner and outer person meet. As culture in general changes, with residual and emergent forms, then so language is a key aspect of this in that what we talk about with regard to buildings, in all aspects of the role and process of a building, is a central part of everyday life. The differing meanings of House and Home would be an example; a distinction that Unwin went out of his way to emphasise. There is also the matter of housing issues; in general, but usually in the particular; entering the public domain, and consciousness, to be discussed, debated, argued over. After 1918, the housing situation required a public and political response. Once Lloyd

George and others had opened this particular Pandora's Box there was no going back.

I do consider these often moral and ethical issues elsewhere in this book in slightly different contexts, but in discussing the role of the designers and architects of the Arts & Crafts we are never far away from these core concerns.

For now, though, let me return specifically to the Arts & Crafts architects I mentioned at the opening of this chapter, and begin with the role of Webb, who would eventually be seen as a leading force in the Arts & Crafts architectural movement. He was to remain a lifelong friend and business partner of Morris (Morris & Co. was created in 1861) and Webb, like Voysey and their contemporaries, he was a multi-skilled designer of interiors and exteriors - although Webb actually disliked the term 'designer' because it separated thinking from doing. Webb was also to follow Morris in to The Socialist League. Sheila Kirk in her 2005 biography of Webb refers to him in the book's title as a "pioneer of arts and crafts architecture", and many people then and now would share that view of Webb's importance in the movement. Andrew Saint quite rightly points out that Kirk's well illustrated book on Webb complements Lethaby's biography of the architect. (Saint, 2005.)

And, yes, the Red House *is* red; it is red brick with red tile roofing. The aim of the design, outside and in, was to 'return' to a rustic simplicity that in fact incorporates all of the Arts & Crafts criteria I listed earlier, and embraces its core values. Webb set the tone by insisting on designing houses from the inside-out, with function determining form.

It has often been emphasised that Webb sought to take architectural design out of the office and in to the builder's yard. Like several of his contemporaries, he sought to build what were considered to be honest and localised houses, concentrating on traditional materials and craft skills.

Like Morris in his work, Webb also suffered discomfort from the reality of building houses for the wealthy. He did tend to build for self-made businessmen and professionals, rather than the gentry, but it was still an issue. As Saint points out: "The question which Webb and his contemporaries faced was how in a deracinated society they could root their houses and their owner - how could they make them real." (Saint, 2005).

FOR WEBB, Voysey and many of their contemporaries the answer lay in developing an authenticity in relation to the vernacular, a realist's (rather than a Romantic's or Fantasist's) approach to building. Webb had ideas, but they were always eminently practical and 'hands-on' ones.

In the late-nineteenth and early-twentieth centuries there were, generally speaking, skilled craftsmen available, and materials and labour costs were still relatively low. There were also examples of architects becoming somewhat pedantic in their pursuit of the vernacular, which raises questions about authenticity and fakery.

I have discussed above issues raised about the moral role of architecture, and of architects, and the unease that many practitioners have had regarding authenticity in aesthetic matters. Again, as suggested earlier in this chapter, and other parts of this study, there was quite understandably some adverse reaction to the spread of 'Tuderbethan' private sector suburbs in the 1930s. I would just add here that Webb and his associates would not have looked favourably on any attempts to create fake antiquity purely to satisfy aesthetic fashions, or the culturally conservative assumptions made by speculative developers. It has been argued, by Pevsner, for example, that there was an historicism at work here, that the power of influence that is attributed to an earlier era has totally dominated thinking about the present. This line of argument could be cited in favour of the influence of Arts & Crafts, and/or the Vernacular, in a negative or positive way. (Watkin, 1977.)

It needs to be emphasised that by the end of the war in 1918, there was much talk about, as it were, the 'virtues and values of the old country'. I have discussed this cultural phenomenon from a number of contextual perspectives in this book, but the influence of this sentimental reference point *was* influential, especially so among decision-makers in, or close to, the Establishment.

I suspect that anyone interested in the Arts & Crafts movement and the development of modern architecture in Britain will have their own list of houses, and other buildings, to visit and enjoy. Over several years, I have visited many of the splendid creative products of these designers, but I do keep adding to my list. For example, it took me until 2008 to visit the beautiful Blackwell at Bowness on Windermere, designed inside and out by Baillie Scott at the very end of the nineteenth century. The work of these and other Arts & Crafts-oriented designers was, and still is, profound; their ideas continually crop up in contemporary designs, and often without any acknowledgement of their Arts & Crafts heritage.

As I have already mentioned, Voysey was quite different from most of his Arts & Crafts associates in that he was essentially an old-style Tory radical. He was in fact much closer to Ruskin in sentiment. He did join the Art Workers' Guild soon after its formation in 1884 and remained an active member throughout his life, valuing the 'networking opportunities' (as they would say now) that Guilds offered members. However, he was not a left-leaning, collectively minded designer. He was also a religious person, which was not that unusual for the time, but this probably contributed to his sense of separate-ness at a time when the Free-thought and Secularist Movements were at their height. (see Astley, 1969.) It seems that Voysey's approach to *his* religious faith was similar to his approach to design, direct and simple, a no-frills practice. For example in his 1911 essay 'The English Home' these criteria were moral qualities to be looked for in architecture as in people.

Voysey's architectural work is invariably cottage oriented, and even his larger buildings do still reflect this design characteristic. He was, essentially, *the* great enthusiast for the vernacular. He said that his aim was to create a tranquil domesticity where traditional values could be fostered. He was though in tune with many of the core values of Arts & Crafts architecture. 'The lines of his houses were long and horizontal with deep eaves and roof planes sloping low towards the ground. The elevations were enlivened by gables projecting from hipped roofs. The horizontality was emphasised by the long lines of small windows with leaded lights just below the eaves' (Brunskill, 2004 p.187)

When I look at a house designed by Frank Lloyd Wright, the leading American Arts & Crafts architect, I see the influence of Voysey. Brunskill interestingly suggests that Voysey was close to the young Lutyens (1869-1944) in design temperament.

Apparently, Voysey was often disappointed by his clients in that his enthusiasms for the vernacular styling were not always shared. Voysey also worked loosely with the emerging firm of Arthur Sanderson and Sons (est.1860) creating many interior design items for them, and also designing the new Sanderson factory in Chiswick in 1902-3. One of Voysey's more appreciative clients was H.G. Wells for whom Voysey designed Spade House in Sandgate in Kent *c.* 1899.

In her comprehensive book on Voysey, Wendy Hitchmough (1995) emphasizes the former's debt to Morris, with Voysey commenting in 1896:

"It is he who prepared the public mind and educated it, and who has done for me what I might not have been able to do for myself - made it possible for me to live." (p.18. Hitchmough.)

Voysey had read Morris' books, but in later life he stated his dislike of Morris the political activist and atheist. This is clearly a reflection of Voysey's Tory and religious sentiments coming to the fore. However, Voysey's dogged commitment to the vernacular is echoed by Christopher Alexander in his 1979 book *The Timeless Way of Building*. Alexander argues that the essence of the vernacular is that this is an ego-less design and building. This fits well with most Arts & Crafts practice of Voysey's time; for example, in the consistent resistance to the 'professionalisation of architecture'. The Arts & Crafts is in this sense a culture group that has within it a language that expresses a traditional, residual set of values about the way skills and therefore knowledge is both practice-based and transmitted personally to the next generation. In his 'leadership' role, Morris had set down some clear guidelines for architects:

"Be careful to eschew all vagueness. It is better to be caught out in going wrong when you have had a definite purpose, than to shuffle and slur so that people can't blame you because they don't know what you are at. Hold fast to distinct form in art...Always think your design out in your head before you begin to get it on paper...You must see it before you can draw it."

John Gloag (mentioned above) makes a good point here in that Morris was able to create a space for the return of the artist-craftsman. Gloag cites Ernest Gimson (1864-1919) as the best example of this phenomenon, and links Gimson with Barnsley. There is also yet another fascinating link in the twenty-year-old

Gimson going along to a meeting in his hometown of Leicester to hear Morris speak on 'Art and Socialism'. While being quite happy to promote the work of these two (and I would have wished to say much more here), it seems to me that Voysey is also an ideal example of the artist-craftsman.

By the 1930s, Voysey was talked about by Pevsner, Betjeman and others (and, much later, by Richards) as one of the pioneers of modern architecture. It is quite clear that his influence in Europe, North America and elsewhere was significant, despite the fact that Voysey had always argued against the importation of foreign styles into England, this being one dimension of his reaction to the eighteenth century styles. His influence embraced his holistic sense of design, his artistic style, and as suggested above his commitment to creating buildings that 'worked' for the inhabitants.

Hermann Muthesius in his influential survey *The English House* (1904; but not translated in to English until 1979!) singled-out Voysey as a pioneer in the creation of the 'whole house' experience.

A pioneer Voysey may have been, but he acknowledged his debt to Arthur Mackmurdo (1851-1942), who was perhaps the most eclectic of the Arts & Crafts luminaries, a true 'total design' practitioner.

Mackmurdo knew Morris, travelled to Italy with Ruskin, and had a significant influence on the development of Voysey's approach to designing the *complete* house. By general agreement, then, and since it was Mackmurdo who opened up a branch line to Art Nouveau, this was a journey that Voysey did not take with him. Neither did Voysey share Mackmurdo's increasing use of mechanisation in design development practice.

However, Voysey was not pleased by the status afforded him over the years and resisted the idea that he was a pioneer of modern architecture, seeing himself as a quintessential late-nineteenth century English Vernacular revivalist, and more broadly, an Arts & Crafts practitioner.

I should add that on his travels around English housing sites Port Sunlight particularly impressed Muthesius. He saw connections with Shaw's work at Bedford Park: "In both places the architects drew upon early vernacular architecture, the motifs of which offered the best source for the design of the houses and the layout of the streets." (Quoted in Stamp 1986 p.225.) He also understood very well the expressed and explicit aim of Morris and his associates and disciples to extend a middle class housing ideal to everyone.

Indeed, he lived in Hammersmith, not far from Morris, and had a clear understanding of the attachment the English had to living in houses, rather than apartments, and to their house *as a home*. He commented on the fact that England was almost unique among advanced industrial societies in this respect. He added that the English would never be happy in 'tower blocks', and would certainly not be able to rear their children in such places!

Stamp adds that Muthesius embraced the old in the new that he saw: "...a fresh breath of naturalness wafts through the house and a sound down-to-earth quality is combined with a sure feeling for suitability." (Stamp p.16.)

Muthesius also approved of the traditional layout of contemporary houses, where an emphasis was placed on either a central living space, and/or the use of discrete rooms leading off a hall that provided privacy and comfort. As I have said elsewhere in this study, the design of the all-purpose, multi-class house was a significant development that he saw and approved. Essentially the privatised, multi-purpose middle class house/home was coming to dominate the architectural and planning discourse. This is what can be seen in the Merry Oak estate - my case study.

Stamp adds that Muthesius, in tune with the Arts & Crafts luminaries of the day, did not like *Art Nouveau* because of the decent into an 'art for art's sake' ornamentation. We cannot be surprised that the adventurous banner of Arts & Crafts building design soon passed to Germany and the USA, where practitioners in those nations maintained and creatively developed the pioneering work done by Morris and his associates. What is tragic here is that the great potential of Modernist building design, developed to great effect in Germany, was first ignored in Britain, and then introduced in the mid-twentieth century by philistine and penny-pinching politicians, who would not have lived in the sub-standard housing they were happy to foist on working class families.

Stamp adds that the late-nineteenth century saw this surge of interest in the vernacular; often dubbed 'the domestic revival', such that by 1900 there were several illustrated books published on cottages and farmhouses that promoted even more reasons to value the national and regional styling. Architects like Guy Dawber were in the forefront of promoting the vernacular in their own work, and as I mentioned earlier this underlines the importance of books and magazines in spreading the word and pictures to a growing following. *Country Life* first published in 1897 (the same year Architectural Review was first published) became increasingly influential on matters of taste. This was all very aspirational and 'lifestyle'-oriented, and often took this emergent neo-vernacular design culture well beyond the scope of Arts & Crafts.

Baillie Scott was close in his tastes to Voysey, and shared similar sentiments. He was adamant that those many middle class people who lived in urban stucco villas were missing out on the benefits of sound and solid vernacular inspired buildings.

Writers on Baillie Scott, for example, James Kornwolf (1972), have emphasised the homogeneity of style and unity of purpose of the architect's work. It is clear that Baillie Scott owed a great deal to Voysey, while having less of a public profile than the latter. Baillie Scott also shared admiration for the work of Philip Webb and greatly admired The Red House. For a short period of time around 1901 Baillie Scott fell out with Unwin and Parker following the publication of their *The Art of Building*; since this was mainly as a result of their use of the 'popular press' to promote their architectural style ideas. But there was some rapprochement by the time of Letchworth. Towards the end of his career, in the early-twentieth century, Baillie Scott was often criticised for his 'Romanticism', but Kornwolf, with others, suggests that Baillie Scott was a considerable influence on the next generation of modernist architects both in Europe and the USA. One reason for this is discussed in the introduction to Baillie Scott's book *Houses and Gardens: Arts & Crafts Interiors* (1906). In this, he argues that a house should be designed around the occupants (once again, we see that function drives form) and that as a consequence he is adverse to the smaller house experienced by working class families merely being a scaled-down version of the middle class home. This is why he does not like to see a separate parlour, the 'best room' which rarely gets used. He preferred the large open and uncluttered living room with its multi-use possibilities. I have always found it interesting that in the late-twentieth century when the embourgeoisment of what were essentially artisans' houses led to the new occupants removing as many interior walls as possible to create more light and usable space. I shall return to this parlour *versus* non-parlour debate in my chapter on Unwin and Parker.

This central concern with styling, the layout of houses, and use of rooms is echoed in Alan Calder's 2003 book on another Arts & Crafts architect James Maclaren (1853-1890):

"The Arts & Crafts architects believed intensely in the importance of place; but the need to respect the vernacular did not entail the slavish imitation of regional features and resorting to pastiche. Instead, they called for the progression and development of the local style and the devising of new forms of expression which were in sympathy with the established order but respected the past in spirit only." (Calder, p.108.)

It is clear that by embracing so much of the value of the vernacular, whether in town or countryside, the Arts & Crafts movement promoted this stylistic paradigm as the best model for living, a reaction against the ways of life that were being lost in the burgeoning and over-crowded metropolis of industrial capitalism.

This sense of the organic, functional approach to design for the house and home, set within the neighbourhood of shared everyday life and away from the uncontrolled and sprawling metropolis became an important issue for Ebenezer Howard and his associates. (I will take up this issue again in my chapter on Howard.)

However, it is necessary to add that Ruskin and Morris led the way in arguing that the Arts & Crafts architects and designers could not just abandon the town and city. A much more scaled-down and even development of towns may have been desirable, but urbanisation had to be addressed in a practical way that embodied as many core values as possible. Shaw's involvement in the design of Bedford Park in London is one such example. Shaw was called-in by the landowner and developer Jonathan T. Carr. The design here reflected the 1870-80 vogue for the Queen Anne style of red brick and white woodwork, with characteristic 'classical' motifs like gable ends. Shaw was also responsible for the church and the Tabard Inn in Bedford Park with decorative tiles by Walter Crane and William de Morgan, the latter closely associated with Morris & Co.

However, as Adrian Tinniswood in his 1999 book The Arts & Crafts House reminds us the end result was a mixed bag:

"Bedford Park was, as Carr proclaimed, 'the most conspicuous effort yet made to break the dull dreariness of the ordinary suburban villa.' It attracted a progressive set of occupants…Yet charming though it was, there was something irredeemably unreal about Bedford Park, with all its aesthetes and anarchists and Anglo-Catholics playing tennis together or discussing dress reform in the Tabard, its pretty Kate Greenaway children bowling their hoops down its meticulously swept streets, and - let's be honest - its air of smug superiority." (p.128.)

So while Bedford Park may have been a progressive design that most of those associated with Arts & Crafts could agree with, it hardly dealt with the major issue of adequately housing the vast majority of people. Nor can we ignore the fact that the design model used for most of the 'country cottage vernacular' styling was derived from the estate re-building programmes of a few benign members of the eighteenth century gentry.

While discussing Shaw, I should mention one of his famous pupils, Edward Schroeder Prior (1857-1932) who was articled to Shaw in 1874. In 1880, Prior set up his own practice from which base he speculated and theorised; for example, on the use of concrete in building within the Arts & Crafts paradigm. In 1870, he published *A History of Gothic Art in England*, and later on became Slade Professor of Art at Cambridge University, where he established the Cambridge School of Architectural Studies. My house is fifteen minutes walk from The Barn in Exmouth, Devon, a house Prior designed in 1896, which is generally regarded as a mature masterpiece. The house was so well regarded that it featured in Muthesius' book. Indeed, most books published today on Arts & Crafts architecture in Britain will have a reference to The Barn. While still articled to Shaw, Prior became aware of the generations of creative and building skills located within the sphere of contemporary builder-craftsmen. (So, yet another designer who enjoyed rummaging around in builders' yards.) Throughout his long career Prior continued to be seen as the ideal builder-designer in the Ruskin sense.

For a while in the 1890s, Prior lived next door to Voysey in the way of 'two Tories together'. As with many of his contemporaries, especially Lethaby who was a friend despite their different politics, Prior was very interested in practice education. This concern of Prior's created a further set of links with his part in the inauguration in 1884 of the Art Workers' Guild. This grouping of artists - note the medieval title - was unhappy with the narrow fine art focus of the Royal Academy (RA), and the Guild sought full integration of the arts. The Guild also opposed the drive of the Royal Institute of British Architecture (RIBA) for increasing the 'professionalisation' of architecture. The first concern was summed-up in the Guild's slogan 'Art is Unity', while the second issue chimed with Prior's awakening to the hands-on skills of craftsmen. This issue was directly linked to the crucial 'architecture as profession or art' debate of the day. The Guild members were a diverse group, and they tried to steer clear of political activity. So while Morris, among others, was in general supportive, he did not really involve himself. Morris was, however, elected in 1892 to the annual position of Guild Master.

Pevsner also reminds us the Art Workers' Guild was not unique:

"It is extremely significant that between 1880 and 1890 five societies for the promotion of artistic craftsmanship were started: in 1882 Arthur H. Mackmurdo's Guild…in 1884 the Art

Workers' Guild, In the same year the Home Arts and Industries Association, particularly interested in rural crafts, in 1888 Ashbee's Guild and School of Handicraft, and also in 1888 the Arts and Crafts Exhibition Society." (Pevsner, 1960 p.54.)

I wish to return to the issue of Guilds and their role in a while; for now, though, it is worth emphasising that 1884 was an interesting year in another respect as the Fabian Society was founded, and with the passage of the Third Reform Act which enfranchised most adult males.

It will be evident to the reader that I have mainly discussed the men at the heart of Arts & Crafts, especially so with regard to my focus on architecture. The were many women practicing crafts within the movement, as Fiona MacCarthy has said:

"…it is now becoming recognised that some of the most original and marvellous craftworks of the period were made by artistically pioneering women. Georgie Gaskin's jewellery, Katherine Adams' bookbinding, Wilhelmina Geddes' stained glass, Margaret Mackintosh Macdonald's textiles, the glowing enamelled metalwork and murals of brilliantly versatile Edinburgh-based designer Phoebe Traquair.' (MacCarthy, 2005.)

One of the many architects who were part of the Arts & Crafts movement not discussed above in some detail is Clough William-Ellis (1883-1978). (Yes, 1978 is correct and not a typing error!) If people have heard about this man at all it will certainly be because of Portmeirion, his community/hotel/village built over fifty years in north Wales. Clough knew 'everybody' and was very influential in his own rather eccentric way. He first met Frank Lloyd Wright on one of his trips to Russia. He was well regarded enough to be recruited as the post-1945 chairman of the first new town corporation at Stevenage. Clough soon realised that politicians were not to be trusted. His most well known publication is *England and the Octopus*. First published in 1928 (but re-published as recently 1996; see Rattenbury 1997), this is a polemic against shoddy commercial building and the ruination of the environment, which develops his Arts & Crafts, Socialist and vernacular values. He was influential in the cottage-building aspects of the 'vernacular movement', and advocated a focus on building small, functional, comfortable, good quality and yet in-expensive housing. This was all part of his belief in the absolute necessity to create the social and material infrastructure for the improvement of people's lives, and to raise expectations. His enthusiasm for the vernacular focused on the use of local materials, what was to hand, and had been used for centuries to good effect. For example, he was an advocate of Rammed Earth methods.

While considering building techniques, and the use of certain materials, it is necessary here to say something of craft skills, and the place that this key issue has in my understanding of the role of the Arts & Crafts and Garden City movements in the development of housing policy and building practice.

An early introduction for me in to the issue of craft skills was through reading one of my Sociological heroes Charles (Chuck) Wright Mills. In his 1959 classic text *The Sociological Imagination,* there is an extensive appendix 'On Intellectual Craftsmanship' which sets out the kind of 'apprenticeship' that any budding Sociologist should serve. A key point that Mills makes is that this 'apprenticeship' cannot be rushed; careful observation, self-reflection, and a sceptical outlook are crucial characteristics for developing the skills of this particular craft.

This is also an issue addressed by another American Sociologist, Richard Sennett, in his recent book *The Craftsman* (2008). Sennett suggests that there is a range of skills to be learnt and developed through experience of dealing with material factors, until these skills become 'capabilities'. He says of these: "To deploy these capabilities the brain needs to process visual, aural, tactile and language-symbol information simultaneously."

The self-respect that people can earn by being good craftsmen does not come easily. To develop skill requires a good measure of experiment and questioning; mechanical practice seldom enables people to improve their skills. Too often we imagine good work itself as success built, economically and efficiently, on success. Developing skill is more arduous and erratic than this.

But most people have it in them to become good craftsmen. They have the capacity to become better at, and more involved in, what they do - with the abilities to localise, question and open up problems that can result, eventually, in good work. Even if society does not reward people who have made this effort as much as it should, in the end, they can achieve a sense of self-worth - which is reward enough." (Sennett; from a *Guardian* piece on his book 2 Feb. 2008.)

There are echoes here of the ideas of the French Anthropologist Claude Levi-Strauss, who died in 2009. In his 'structuralist' theories he placed great emphasis on the interactive nature of the brain, and the key role played here in holding and developing symbols. These symbols are in themselves a corner stone of all human cultures. Sennett and his associates also remind me of much twentieth century work done on reflective practice (also mentioned elsewhere in this study), the idea that as practitioners we should be constantly assessing the learning we take from our encounters, which informs our future actions.

The forms of discourse on art and on craft described above have never gone away since the Arts & Crafts practitioners of the late-nineteenth century set out their criteria. This is especially so in discussions about the artist-craftsman. Howard Becker, the American Sociologist, shares other issues with the likes of Morris and Lethaby when he says:

"By accepting beauty as a criterion, participants in craft activities take on a concern characteristic of the folk definition of art. That definition includes an emphasis on beauty as typified in the tradition of some particular art, on the traditions and concerns of the art world itself as the source of value, on expression of someone's thoughts and feelings, and on the relative freedom of the artist from outside interference with the work." (Becker, 1982 p.275/6.)

He then addresses the relationship of craft worker to artist-craftsman, always a hot topic for the Arts & Crafts movement;

"We might imagine the differentiation of craftsmen and artist-craftsmen as a typical historical sequence. A craft world, whose aesthetic emphasizes utility and virtuoso skill and whose members produce works according to the dictates of clients or employers operating in some extra-craft world, develops a new segment. The new segment members add to the basic aesthetic an emphasis on beauty and develop some additional organizations, which free them of the need to satisfy employers so completely." (Becker p.277/8.)

To return here to my discussion of the nature and role of Guilds and their associates, I should mention Arnold Dolmetsch (1858-1940), the single most important person in the early music revival at this time. Dolmetsch came from a continental family of musical instrument makers, and on coming to England became a pro-active enthusiast for Tudor and Elizabethan music.

As an increasingly accomplished instrument maker, he was eventually drawn into Morris' orbit around the 'medieval'. Ned Burne-Jones, who was a friend of Dolmetsch, introduced him to Morris in 1894. Morris, not renowned for his interest in music, attended a concert of Dowland's music performed by Dolmetsch, and was very impressed. With his usual gusto, Morris joined with Burne-Jones in a scheme to publish some Tudor music, but it was Dolmetsch's craft base that most intrigued Morris. The latter recognised a kindred spirit, not the least of reasons being the value of researching the past and making it available to a contemporary audience. Around 1896, Dolmetsch decided to make a harpsichord:

"It is not known exactly when Dolmetsch started work on the harpsichord that he intended to display at the Arts & Crafts Exhibition Society's Show at the New Gallery in October (1896), but the fact that it was started at all was due to William Morris, who suggested that he should complete it for the exhibition." (Campbell, 1975 p.100.)

Despite my own obvious enthusiasm for Arts & Crafts, and the value I place on this aesthetic, I have to acknowledge that there are many doubters who have written-off the Arts & Crafts movement as a hopelessly romanticised account of life, in the countryside or in the town. There are certainly traces of the early- nineteenth century continental Romantic movement in the work of all the architects and designers discussed above. However, I would argue that most Arts & Crafts devotees were not blind to the inadequacy of potentially progressive ideas, which were based on what could be seen as a reactionary and one-dimensional Wordsworthian account of Nature and our relationship with it.

The majority of Arts & Crafts practitioners were fairly 'hardheaded' in their practice values, of what should and could be achieved. For example, in relation to designing and actually building houses and estates there is a consistently advocated view that put authenticity, beauty, and quality before shortsighted policies to house people of all classes on a lowest common denominator basis. Of course, there are those critics who have continued to see the Arts & Crafts movement, including the architecture, as a home for lost causes. That, however, misses the point of whether Arts & Crafts values and ideals are still as relevant now as they were invariably recognised as being then. Even the critics of Arts & Crafts design usually, if begrudgingly, acknowledge that - idealistic or not - the movement had, and continues to have, a profound influence at home and abroad:

"Thus by 1900 the Arts and Crafts architects had produced one resounding collective success: a new vitality and new standards for domestic work." (Service, 1977.)

A further context can be added, as explained by Wendy Hitchmough in her 2000 book *The Arts & Crafts Home*:

"The Arts & Crafts period coincided with a building boom in Britain and America as home ownership became available for the first time for a growing number of unskilled and semi-skilled workers and the ideal of a second home in the country became a reality for the more affluent middle classes." (Hitchmough p.12/13.)

Many architects made their designs available through mail order catalogues, newspapers and magazines like *The Studio*, *The Craftsman*, *Country Life*, and *Homes and Gardens*. In one sense, all this activity reflected a democratising of Arts & Crafts design. However, let us not overstate this when a hopelessly narrow and patronising middle class journal like *Country Life* rode the golden age 'Olde England' bandwagon. But there were inevitable connections made with the resurrection of country mores, as identified by Roy Strong in his book on *Country Life*, suitably subtitled 'The English Arcadia':

"Such a folk revival fitted in exactly with the tenets of the Arts and Crafts Movement which reacted against industrialisation and the city. The Movement's practitioners, among them C.R. Asbee, W.R. Lethaby and Ernest Gimson, fled capitalist centres of commerce and set up workshops in the Cotswolds to produce handicrafts." (Strong, 1996 p. 43.)

Strong over-simplifies the Arts & Crafts values, but the general drift of his point is fair. He also comments on the magazine's (*Country Life*) support for and coverage of the SPAB, the passing of the Ancient Monuments Protection Act in 1882, and the creation of The National Trust.

By the end of the nineteenth and early twentieth centuries, retailers like Liberty and Heal in their commodification of 'the home' were opening up access to an increasing number of Arts & Craft-style artefacts. This trend in 'home making' led Wendy Hitchmough to argue that another of the contradictions inherent within the popularising of Arts & Crafts was to enshrine woman's place in the home. I would also acknowledge that the spread of the Arts & Crafts aesthetic influenced the private sector and middle class suburbs in the 1920s and 30s (think of John Betjeman's documentary *Metroland*) to reinforce the woman's role as homemaker. Most working class women could not afford such focused domestic bliss.

As I have argued above, one significant extension of Arts & Crafts architectural and design influence was in the

'International Style' central to twentieth century Modernism. In the 1930s, Pevsner could show the significant influence of Arts & Crafts values on the likes of Gropius, Le Corbusier and the Bauhaus designers among many practitioners. There were many poor imitations, and certainly many commercial mass production spin-offs to be purchased at the likes of Heals or Habitat. We should, however, not indiscriminately decry the attempts of such commercially oriented organizations to popularise Arts & Crafts design and provide access to people with an eye for these timeless qualities. Terence Conran, the founder of Habitat, had a craft- based education, and always expressed a desire to see function, authenticity in materials and good design, as key criteria for the products available in his shops.

What I have said in this chapter raises several key issues about the designing of houses and the role of the builder-architect, confronted with the physical reality of building. David Pye in his 1960s book *The Nature of Design* argues that: "A painter can choose any imaginable shape. A designer cannot."

As a consequence of this fundamental issue, we are immediately cast into another debate about the inter-relation between form and function. While I suspect that most Arts & Crafts architects would have balked at Le Corbusier's idea that "a house is a machine for living in" they were very focused on these issues, and the inter-connection of form and function remains a *physical* problem to be solved. Modernists like Le Corbusier consistently insisted that function was the dominant partner, hence the machine designed to meet life's essential needs without any unnecessary ornament. Their position was invariably struck in opposition to Art Nouveau, which often overwhelmed sensibilities at the turn of the century. Architects in general, regardless of whether they were designing for the private or public sector, were aware of social and demographic trends. Smaller families, less or no servants for the middle classes (the 'daily' was the 'modern' trend), less clutter, more open plan and so on. People's circumstances, attitudes and sensibilities were changing in the 1920s and 1930s, and architects and interior designers were reflecting this. Burnett argues: "People did not want 'a machine for living in' so much as a vehicle for living out a fantasy". (Burnett p.261.)

Morris had created shock waves with his bare white walls and naturalistic designing, and some early-twentieth century designers were no different in their ability to shock. Certainly in the 'new' century this was invariably linked to a further reassessment of aesthetic values, but with a growing focus on 'life-style' and conspicuous consumption.

I am sure that many of us have endured modernist buildings that look heroic on the skyline, but just do not 'work', the triumph of form over function! So while Arts & Crafts designers were invariably multi-skilled and had an extremely good eye for decoration, they were essentially creating buildings for people to live and work in and to feel 'at home' there. The scale of building can be a factor; for example, the domestic houses discussed in my Merry Oak case study are on a small scale, and as mentioned above, Baillie Scott among other perceptive designers, gave due consideration to layout, decoration, and the role of furniture; for example, in his essay on 'An Ideal Suburban House' from 1895:

"It is a common belief that to build an artistic house a large sum of money is required. Art and ornament are often understood as synonymous terms, and the house that possesses the largest amount of ornament is often held to be the most artistic. It will therefore be necessary to state that the reverse of this is very often the case, and that a house is artistic in proportion to the amount of skill and thought displayed in its design, and not in the proportion to the amount of decoration it possesses...what is really required is that we should spend more thought on our houses rather than more money." (Quoted in Benton, Benton and Sharp, 1975 p.9.)

We encounter these realities on a daily basis. For instance, most of the furniture in my early-twentieth century house would simply not fit into most houses built since then (almost regardless of cost). Arts & Crafts designers were faced with such realities and often came up with solutions; for example, window seats, that were decorative, cushion covers and the like, conserved space, and as *solutions* to design problems were certainly functional.

Reyner Banham is one among many observers of the period who has emphasised the practical outlook of the architects, especially so from his perspective with respect to solving problems with the essential working parts of a house, that is, the mechanical services. (Banham, 1969.) He argues that when most people consider the strengths and weaknesses of a building they usually consider the structure, *i.e.*, what the building looks like. Little attention is paid to what goes on behind the façade, the 'guts' of the people, the practical essentials that can determine the degree to which any building actually functions efficiently and effectively. This is further confirmation of how so many Arts & Crafts architects combined enthusiasm with common sense.

As I have also said, several Arts & Crafts architects were pioneers in construction techniques, and as mentioned above Edward Prior's experiments with concrete are one such example. Contrary to the accounts of some critics of Arts & Crafts, these designers were constantly planning ahead and being innovative, and were certainly not *living* in the past. I would also cite the progress made in the manufacture and use of ironwork as a further example of innovation within the context of the Arts & Crafts aesthetic context.

When considering their building designs and how the exterior and interior decoration was to be realised, Arts & Crafts practitioners did keep essentially to the criteria of function and form as discussed, but always added context. Arts & Crafts architects were fanatical about fitting a building into the landscape; and, wherever possible, using local materials in ways that chimed with traditional local and regional values. So in addition to all of the appropriate and necessary function and form considerations, Arts & Crafts designers embraced a value around the aesthetic expression that signifies the cultural ethos:

"Vernacular architecture incorporated symbolic associations in its buildings, of course, but the most important, such as the Church, were expressed by monumental architecture…vernacular architecture borrowed motifs from the palaces and churches of the high culture. But the main symbolic expression of vernacular architecture was in expressing the continuing identity of the community. Architecture is a reminder of the continuity of existence; buildings and towns provide visible evidence of the past." (Benton and Baker p.35.)

Most people have (and still do) distinguish architecture from 'just' building, and usually use a shorthand like 'building + art = architecture'. This formula is very Ruskin-esque, but once again it has to be said that many Arts & Crafts architects were more focused on the physical process of *building* rather than on a practice that dealt with house design in an abstract theoretical way. In this respect, they are of course echoing the folk craft tradition of the master builder and stonemason, handing on their skills and know-how from one generation to the next.

Architecture as a separate theory and ideas-based practice

came later, and as I suggested above was hotly debated throughout the Arts & Crafts movement. Many of the well-known people I have already discussed, along with numerous others, considered themselves to be designers. Of course, all such designer/architects had a theory, or theories, personal and shared, on design; and I have expressed these values many times in this study starting with Pugin's criteria. Just because Arts & Crafts practitioners elevated the organic over the mechanical or formal does not mean they ignored mechanics and technique, far from it.

I WOULD therefore argue that in the second-half of the nineteenth and early-twentieth century a movement was begun and developed that not only had a dominant and significant influence at the time, but has continued to this day, *i.e.*, a real and significant *movement,* promoting significant change, while seeing that process through:

"Architecture is never entirely of its own period. Constantly, it draws on the past, feeding information of various kinds in a constantly evolutionary process. Climatic, psychological, social, cultural, ritual, economic and physical factors, all play a part in determining house form, which represents a complex interplay of forces. But although house form is modified by many factors…what ultimately decides the form of a dwelling, and moulds the spaces and their relationships, is the vision people have of the ideal life." (Benton and Baker, p.35.)

This is certainly 'Access to Eden'!

There is no doubt in my mind that the design of a 'Wheatley' estate like Merry Oak was directly influenced by the legacy of Arts & Crafts design, and which reiterated the foundation values on which these creative imaginations built. After all, several of the 'pioneers' I have mentioned were still alive when Merry Oak was planned.

While arguing that the Arts & Crafts designer/architects have had a lasting legacy, I need to acknowledge that the *crafts* side of Arts and Crafts was less successful commercially, while the architecture and decorative arts side of 'the movement' prospered. One significant exception was William Benson (1854-1924), who became a good friend of Burne-Jones, his *entrée* to the Arts & Crafts fraternity. After completing his university studies in Classics and Philosophy he moved in to architecture, but then soon developed his design and manufacturing skills with domestic objects of great diversity. He founded his own business in 1880, had a leading role in the Arts & Crafts Exhibition Society in 1886, and became chairman of Morris & Co. in 1896, the year of Morris' death.

One reason why the architects and interior designers *did* succeed is through the advantage of their values and practical ideas chiming well with the growing reaction to the over-bearing stuffiness of middle class Victorian life. Morris once commented that he had rarely been in to a wealthy man's house that would not benefit from nine tenths of the contents being taken out and burnt in the front garden! Webb and his associates soon parted company with the 'heavy' Edwardian Baroque of Shaw and others, and sought out a more vernacular and pastoral styling and scale.

Over Webb's red brick fireplace in the main sitting room at Red House is the inscription *Ars Longa Vita Brevis* - art is long, life is short. However, while emphasising this lasting value of Arts & Crafts design, I do need to comment again on the semi-demoralising side to the influence of these designers, a point made by Pamela Todd in her excellent *The Arts & Crafts Companion*:

"Ironically, the Arts and Crafts tradition survived longest - though vulgarised and watered-down - in suburban housing schemes, in which thousands of semi-detached houses with half-timbered gables, lean-to porches, tile-hanging, and hipped roofs were put up by speculative builders in the inter-war period. Such houses still line arterial roads in and out of British cities, leading Nikolaus Pevsner to complain bitterly of being 'haunted by miles of semi-detached houses mocking Voysey's work.' " (Todd 2004 p.114.)

In this way, John Betjeman's "...various bogus Tudor bars" in Maidenhead appears to unite these two, often opposed, critics.

One final comment here must be to emphasise that despite the many innovations of the Arts & Crafts designers, they did not in any fundamental way alter the conventional layout and room function within the houses they designed. There were also some well-observed aesthetic 'rules' about what furniture and fittings should be placed, so radical in many ways, but socially conservative in others. Do not dare to put a sink in the kitchen; that must go in to the scullery along with the skivvy responsible for its use!

As I have said above, my coverage of the designers and architects of this period is selective, and there are many books written of the period and individuals that go well beyond my brief study. Many of these books have been cited here, but I would add Alastair Services' Introduction to *Edwardian Architecture* (Thames and Hudson, 1977) with good coverage of the diverse range of design and building styles and their creators, plus plenty of illustrations. In these two chapters on Arts & Crafts, I have made a case for placing a high value on the ideas, producers and products associated with the 'Movement'. As I have indicated above, I have joined a long list of 'fans', and what I have offered will certainly not be the last word on the subject matter. However, I do have to ask the question whether my advocacy for seeing Arts & Crafts in such exalted terms is justified. For example, Peter Davey in his book on Arts & Crafts architecture said:

"Was Arts & Crafts architecture any more than a fashion of the rich: rich architects and designers toying with idealism and rich clients in search of a grand, yet undemonstrative, setting for their lives?" (Davey, 1995 p.244.)

Davey remarks that the life of most building and decorating workers was untouched by the Arts & Crafts Movement, and even those who did work on Arts & Crafts contracts did not always have a better life. Davey argues that of all the Arts & Crafts architects only Ashbee made serious and consistent attempts to improve the lot of workmen; and even then Ashbee found this difficult given the level of costs in relation to the finished price. Ashbee, like others, could have used more machinery to replace handicrafts, but this would have run contrary to his principles. Such are the problems inherent in any syndicalist solution of managing an island of socialism in a sea of capitalism. Davey reminds us that eventually Arts & Crafts production was squeezed out by the cheaper 'Classicists' with their standardisation and greater use of machinery. Are Arts & Crafts design values merely a surface, a veneer on the 'real thing', whatever that might be? While Morris and his Socialist contemporaries could see the answer lay in a revolutionary transformation of society, as described in *News From Nowhere*, the majority of Arts & Crafts architects were not inclined to follow this path. Morris had *his* epiphany, crossed his 'river of fire' to the realisation that only through a complete change in social relations could everyone enjoy art. His particular version of Marx's dictum that 'freedom for all is freedom for each' did not persuade everyone, then, since and even now.

"If the Arts & Crafts movement had any coherence at all, it was concerned with the quality of life…The Arts & Crafts people know that quality of life depends on all five senses, and that it is to do with the experience of making and using artefacts…Thinking and making should be brought closer together." (Davey, p.245.)

We also have to acknowledge that even where machinery can be used to reduce the burden of many tiresome tasks (and Morris argued this) the end result is invariably more unemployment, more people surplus to requirements. Davey shares my view that there was always more to the Arts & Crafts than a few nice houses and other attractively designed artefacts. I have, and will, argue here that what is *lasting* are the Arts & Crafts values central to working and production, leisure and life.

I have already suggested that the movement did seek to educate people of all classes; and I develop a link to this in my chapter on Merry Oak. Baillie Scott was one among many advocating the need to educate the public taste away from the cheap and flashy. These people were proselytisers, and were in their diverse ways living what was later argued by Herbert Marcuse: "…the truth of art lies in its power to break the monopoly of established reality to define what *is* real." And in an effort to demonstrate their democratising credentials many Arts & Crafts people would join with Eric Gill in asserting that "…the artist is not a special kind of man, every man is a special kind of artist."

This is not to say that 'the artist' is not special, or the artistic temperament of value, but to argue that all can strive to bring an imaginative and creative dimension to their everyday life and labour.

The Past in the Present

Before moving on to discuss the Garden City movement, and the pioneering role of Ebenezer Howard, I should discuss what I would call 'The Past in the Present'.

The obvious fact that England is an 'old country' is constantly reflected in the sentiments that permeate our cultures and set values. Most English values relate to a rural-ness, and ideas about 'the countryside', that are definitely of a *gemeinschaft* kind (as outlined above). Of course, many of these sentiments today are in fact sentimental, a nostalgia for a 'golden age' of aesthetically and morally pleasing community life that does no really match up to most of historical reality. Indeed, I suspect that most English people are woefully ignorant of the history of rural life, and are, as a consequence, easily duped by the glossy values of the 'heritage industries', television and cinema. Even the well-meaning National Trust can reinforce sentimental and unrealistic notions of 'the Past', as well as the present.

Herbert Read's 1933 anthology *The English Vision* fits in to this 'golden age' format, with 300 pages of extracts from a variety of English writers that he feels goes some way towards understanding the links between 'their blood and with the soil to which they belonged', which was, he argues, a core aspect of their character, and sense of identity, of self. As I discuss elsewhere, there are also plenty of painters and musicians at this time that produced work aligned with this outlook on life.

Raymond Williams in his 1973 book *The Country and the City* makes the point that both town and country are changed places, and are being transformed before our eyes, such that it is increasingly difficult to maintain a clear sense of separate-ness. Indeed, it is a false dichotomy. They are, as Ebenezer Howard and others in the late-nineteenth century saw, one and the same problem. The fact that a certain value is placed on the understood face-to-face-ness, the knowing-ness of the rural situation is usually due to fiction more than fact. Williams reminds us that the narratives in common usage and exchange, oral and literary, of different kinds tend to perpetuate the fixedness of 'old style life' in the countryside. As I suggested above, this has often led to an idealisation of the rural life that is far from accurate, either in the past or now. As outsiders to these localised cultures, we invariably give life a value that suits us, fits how we would wish it to be, and as a contrast to the rapidly changing and increasingly hostile town or city. How we talk about the countryside can obscure the reality of social relations and the demands of everyday life. In our own day 'townies' are happy to be in the countryside so long as they have all their urban mod cons with them, especially cars to make journeys in minutes that would otherwise take hours to walk. This is another example of 'urbs in the rure', and a vast opportunity for further commodification of 'the countryside' representations.

Williams reminds us that while admiring the glories of the English country house we should pause to consider the nature of these *worked* realities; whose labour actually built these houses, serviced the house and gardens, and worked the land so as to maintain such an admirable 'lifestyle' for the gentry.

Over twenty years ago, there was (as suggested earlier) a heated debate between those assessing the nature of heritage, and the 'heritage industries'. My references to Raphael Samuel, among others, are significant in this respect. It is also worth mentioning the proliferation of undergraduate courses in Heritage Studies, with an assumption of employment in those industries to follow.

David Gervais has been one among several writers reflecting on the way ideas about the loss of 'Olde England' became fixed in the cultural consciousness of the middle class in the early-twentieth century. He argues that after the 1914-18 watershed most thinking about Englishness was characterised by nostalgia, (and I would add) even to the extent of creating, or emphasising, a melancholia among the forlorn observers of undesirable change. In view of the complex cultural currents swirling around 'the modern world', these responses are far too complex and problematic for any simple definition. He suggests that what emerged from the late-nineteenth century was a set of parallel 'Englands', where particular class and culture groups knew little of each other, and were often not very interested. Gervais cites Charles Dickens as an insightful contributor here, and singles-out *Bleak House* as a novel that deals extensively with the key issue of parallel worlds.

I also cite below Dickens' *Hard Times*, his tirade against the unplanned and chaotic growth of industrial urbanism. There is there as well the sense of a fear of a machine-age future run by functionaries in a totalitarian manner. I cannot help thinking that Mr Gradgrind in *Hard Times* would have been an enthusiastic advocate of the top-down imposition of 'Brutalism' in design matters.

It is true, of course, that one of the aims of the more political participants in the Arts & Crafts movement, certainly Morris, was to provoke discussion about these divergent cultures. A major aspect of their *raison d'être* was to argue for a convergence of experience, and to bring an end the exclusiveness of so much that was considered aesthetically valuable. Social reformers of many persuasions were also busy to expose the unfairness of these separate Englands, and I discuss many such protagonists in these pages. However, we should not forget that then, as now, many middle class people saw the lives of the lower orders as shocking but exotically compellingly (*e.g.*, slum tourism). There was, and is, an element of voyeurism involved. Gervais cites Ruskin as one critic who understood just how hard life was in the countryside, and distanced himself from the 'daffodil'-oriented poetic movement. (Gervais, 1993.)

Gervais also makes the important point that, by the time Hardy had stopped writing novels, the English countryside was for most people a work of the imagination. A point raised by Raymond Williams in his writings, especially so in *The Country and the City.*

In his review of Gervais' book, Terry Eagleton emphasised the reactionary aspect to much speculation about the portrayal 'Englishness'.

"Literary Englishness proved a powerful inoculation against the virus of modernism, an art of the metropolis rather than the maypole. The tenaciousness of the rural is surprising given that we are the world's oldest industrial nation; but we also had the most powerful landed gentry in Europe, which was able to wrest the cultural initiative from the industrial middle class."
(Eagleton, 1993.)

We should not forget the somewhat demeaning name given to the emerging middle class: the "the middling lot".

Patrick Wright led the way in these cultural heritage debates with his book *On Living in an Old Country* (1985), where he argues that the heritage industries seem to offer-up a utopian view of the value of the past, a vision of possibilities. However, this vision is separated from the realities of the present, as if preserved in a glass case in the museum with a sign saying DO NOT TOUCH.

The potential for radicalising people's ideas *via* what they see, for placing meanings on this 'history' that might promote a desire and demand for change, is lost in the commodification of this 'past' and the selling back to the envious viewer a sanitised version of the *status quo*. At the end of the 1980s, Alan Bennett reflected on what he saw as a rapidly encroaching menace of the heritage phenomenon:

"The village in Yorkshire where I spend all too little of my time now sports one of those DoE brown Heritage signposts declaring it a 'Dales Village' and its only a matter of time before the inhabitants start playing it up as 'Dales Folk'. We're fortunate not to be in 'Herriot Country' or the temptation to act the part might be even greater. But it's toy-town now on every hand, dignified and stately barns converted into bijoux residences with bottle glass windows and carriage lamps that bring with them a view of the countryside that is equally folksy. The village shop becomes The Village Shop, the confectioners The Village Bakery; it won't be long before some well-meaning parish council will be employing some of those turfed out of psychiatric hospitals as Village Idiots.' (Bennett, 1989.)

I would also add that, for a correction of our illusions about the countryside, we would all be better off reading Thomas Hardy! A recurring theme in the stories of Hardy is the countryside, and market towns, under considerable pressure of change and transformation. One key feature in his writing was the increasing gap between the customary life of the countryside, and the educated consciousness of people both within the countryside, and beyond it. Changes in thought and feeling were brought about that were often complex, and difficult to resolve to everyone's satisfaction.

We need to recognize the nature of conjuncture in our understanding of change in that there are clearly a combination of circumstances and events producing a crisis. Hardy, among others, consistently emphasises this in his writing, underlining the fact that our lives and the meanings we place on them are part of a dialectical process, and often dialogical in their presentation. Marx commented that: "We all take action in the face of life events, these conjunctures, but not necessarily in conditions of our choosing."

My argument would be that our understanding of the landscape in which we live and work is continually, cumulatively, added to by artistic and literary endeavour. Take a cross-section of English cultures at any one time and what will be found is complex network of retained images, sounds and experiences. There is a texture that acts as a 'stage set' to our everyday lives. One example I would venture to suggest is the important link between Hardy and Holst was *via* Egdon Heath, the fictional name the former gave Studland Heath by Poole harbour. At the beginning of Hardy's novel *The Return of the Native* (1878) he describes the characteristics of the heath:

"...a place perfectly accordant with man's nature - neither ghastly, hateful or ugly; neither commonplace, unmeaning, nor tame; but, like man, slighted and enduring; and withal singularly colossal and mysterious in its swarthy monotony...It had a lonely face, suggesting tragical possibilities."

Holst used most of this quote as his dedication to Hardy on the score of 'Egdon Heath', his (Holst's) tone poem, which incidentally he considered to be his best work. Imogen Holst, the composer's daughter, told the lovely story of Holst visiting the aged Hardy in summer, and being taken for a walk across the heath. When the much younger Holst commented on how wonderful he found the heath, Hardy agreed, of course, but said that to really enjoy the place it should be seen in November.

It is sad to reflect that Hardy died three weeks before the premier of 'Egdon Heath' in early 1928.

Thomas Hardy's 'Egdon Heath' as described above sums up for me his understanding of the bonds and tensions between man and nature.

Incidentally, on the question of market towns, one of the features of Thomas More's *Utopia* (1516) was that society should be made up of specifically-created towns twenty-three miles apart. Take a look at any shire county map, and behold: - how far apart are the market towns?

So, despite all these reservations cited above, it should be said that the affection many English people have for the countryside is genuine, and the value of time spent in that diversity of environments remains high. Hubert Parry's 'Jerusalem' may have become a Last Night of the Proms cliché for many, but the potency of William Blake's crusade to build a paradise in England's green and pleasant land still stirs the emotions.

In our own era, the power of musical representations of ideas of an idyllic English village remains potent. Georgina Boyes book *The Imagined Village* (199t) traces the recent folk music revival movement, and lead to the creation in 2004 of a group of musicians and record producers calling themselves by the same name as the book. They sought to explore their musical roots and identity as *English* musicians. This grouping has made links to Cecil Sharp and explored key issues such as a patriotism without jingoism and racism.

What the Garden City movement did was to draw on these sentiments over a century ago, and actively promote these values. The Garden City advocates invariably linked up *these* values with those of the Arts & Crafts movement in all *its* complexity with, for example, a focus on crafts and craftwork that said a good deal about less alienated human labour, and on the many guises of Socialism, including Christian Socialists like Holst.

I would argue that attachment to these values and sentiments is essentially no less true now. But, these values have not prospered in recent years in part due to a lack of discussion and debate, which was much more common among thinking people in the late-nineteenth and early-twentieth centuries. Also, leadership has been lacking in the promotion of debate, for example, from the Labour movement, who really should know better! The 'Bigness' characteristic of 'mass' society was already a key issue for observers in the second half of the nineteenth and early- twentieth centuries. The questioning set in motion by Ruskin and his contemporaries has been continued to this day. The enormous problems; personal, social, and physical; caused by unchecked, indeed actively encouraged 'Bigness', was seen to undermine the core basis of a satisfying everyday life, and has kept most people subservient to the demands of wage labour and increasing, rampant consumerism.

Howard argued that life in the countryside has been systematically undermined by the diminution of the infrastructure. Shops, post offices, pubs, rail and bus transport, and even sports areas, have been affected by anarchic policy and selfishness. The Arts & Crafts and Garden City movements represented a resurgence of both the idea and actuality of 'localism', where like-minded and appropriately idealistic and cynical people who questioned motives linked-up to work cooperatively. Sound familiar? In these respects, I am reminded of Morris' epic tale *A Dream of John Ball* written in 1888 about the Peasants' Revolt of 1381. Courage and solidarity are key themes here, and also the uncertain nature of change. For Morris, there is always "The change beyond the change. How men fight and lose the battle, and the thing they fought for comes about in spite of the defeat, and when it comes turns out not to be what they meant, and other men have to fight for what they meant under another name."

From our perspective in this early-twenty first century, one of the most interesting political aspects of the early-twentieth century was, relatively speaking, just how small a direct role the national State apparatus played in people's everyday lives. It was *local* government that mattered. The creation of the Ministry of Health (and Housing) in 1919 did not delight everyone. Many of those active in local government suspected that the national State apparatus was in the process of 'taking over'. For many people, including leading activists like Raymond Unwin, there were difficult choices to be made between giving a lead and *persuasion*.

So, given the above, why am I looking so favourably on Wheatley's 1924 Housing Act, a piece of *national* legislation, where clearly national government sought a bigger influence? Well, one obvious answer is that Wheatley's Act was part and parcel of his role as Minister of Health. Wheatley, like most keen observers of social change, or lack of change perhaps, continued to draw on their *past* experience to inform their current actions with a certain kind of *future* in mind. Wheatley inherited the stark reality of the era of provision of 'sanitary dwellings for the labouring classes'. The ideas of the 'Garden City' activists, like Howard and Unwin, were directly related to the nineteenth-century debates about the chaotic, de-humanising growth of industrialising cities, and the appalling conditions in which most people lived and worked in 'the slums'. Charles Dickens' description of Coketown, his fictional northern industrial town in *Hard Times* (1854), is worth quoting here:

"It was a town of red brick, or brick that would have been red if the smoke and ashes had allowed it; but as matters stood it was a town of unnatural red and black like the painted face of a savage. It was a town of machinery and tall chimneys out of which interminable serpents of smoke trailed themselves forever and ever and never got uncoiled. It had a black canal in it, and a river that ran purple with ill-smelling dye, and vast piles of building full of windows where there was a rattling and a trembling all day long." (Dickens, p.31.)

Dickens goes on to describe the monotony of the streets and buildings, and the endless routine of the workers; in short, one of his most vivid, and blunt, descriptions of hell on earth for the industrial working classes. We should, of course, beware of seeing early-nineteenth century England as an 'either/or' society. It is a false dichotomy to see industrialising and urbanising England in this simplistic way. Raymond Williams made the point (cited above) about the transformation of communities being complicated, and this view is shared by Edward Thompson in *The Making of the English Working Class* (1963) when discussing 'the rituals of mutuality' that:

"Again and again the 'passing of old England' evades analysis. We may see the lines of change more clearly if we recall that the Industrial Revolution was not a settled social context but a phase of transition between two ways of life. And we must see, not one 'typical' community, but many different communities coexisting with each other." (p.456.)

Throughout the second half of the nineteenth century, the evidence was accumulating around the issue of housing for the working classes. William Booth's *In Darkest England* (1890-1) awakened many a middle class conscience, along with Dickens' tireless reform campaigning supplemented by James Hole's book *The Homes of the Working Classes* (1860s). I have always been interested to consider why, given his obvious abilities as a factual writer, Dickens chose fiction as his vehicle for the enlightenment and entertainment of his readers?

It should also be remembered that the 1890s were an active time for the so-called 'English Realists', a group of writers epitomised by Arthur Morrison. He published several 'fictions', the most well known of which is *A Child of the Jago* set in the East End of London. In these novels, Morrison took up the social realism baton of Dickens, and he was also attuned to the impact of Emile Zola's work, for example, *Germinal* (1885). Morrison's work had a considerable impact on the 'sensitive' middle classes. This combination of fictional 'evidence' and the factual and quantitative enquiries of Booth and his contemporaries contributed to the outpouring of charitable and philanthropic ventures in London and elsewhere. Oscar Wilde was to write a number of plays mocking this philanthropy, and argued that Besant's 'People's Palace' and the like were not the answer to poverty.

There were several acts of Parliament following The Municipal Corporation Act of 1835, which had signalled the beginnings of genuine local government. The 1848 Public Health Act, closely associated with Edwin Chadwick, established a system of local health boards. The 1858 Local Government Act extended the role and responsibilities of local authorities, and The Public Health Act of 1875 moved policy on from the specific sanitation developments of the early-nineteenth century Chadwick era to a wider concern about the environment and aesthetics in relation to housing. However, it is true that one impact of the conventional later nineteenth century policy of the 'bye-law' street was for greater standardisation and less concern with aesthetic matters.

Wheatley knew plenty about the real costs of industrial capitalism, the grinding poverty, and unsanitary and overcrowded housing from his early days in Glasgow (I shall say more about this elsewhere). Wheatley's Housing Act of 1924 clearly reflects his determination to address this crucial issue. His local experience convinced him to put the onus on *local* government to take action. In many instances throughout Britain, local government took up the challenge and the opportunity. This was certainly so in Southampton (the focus of my case study).

Standish Meacham in his 1977 book *A Life Apart: The English Working Class 1890-1914*, touches on several of the issues I have addressed above. Early on in his argument he cites Edward Thompson on the subject of social change over time *and* in relation to class in that a class can best be understood as relationships over time. This values the historical approach to comprehending people's lives in the contemporary world of their own time. The particular nature of relationships between capital and labour, between landlord and tenant, between local authority and resident, between neighbour and neighbour (in the 1920s, say), might be a focus for study. However, an understanding is needed of how those determining relationships were shaped in the preceding decades. So, to assess the everyday life of the working classes (in all their variety) in the post-1918 years, it is necessary to consider social relationships in the years before 1914-18. My focus on the role of the Arts & Crafts and Garden City movements is one aspect of this descriptive and explanatory process.

Meacham argues that the decades before 1890 had been characterised by a good deal of 'liberal'-based cooperation between middle class reformers of varying kinds (including Morris, of course) and an increasingly radicalised working class. This was especially so in the trade union organisation across all sections of the working class, and not just the skilled artisans (the so-called 'aristocracy of labour' as Eric Hobsbawm has described this sectionalisation). The depression of the 1880s and the extension of the franchise in 1884-5 certainly raised the political consciousness of the working class, who in Marx's perception began to see themselves as 'a class in themselves', if not yet perhaps a 'class for themselves' - the leap forward for which the revolutionaries were campaigning. These upheavals eventually led to the formation of the Independent Labour Party (ILP) in 1893 and the Labour Representation Committee, the precursor of the Labour Party in 1920. The emergence of a separate political party to represent the interests of labour in Parliament also eventually led to a decline in working class support for the Liberal Party. It should always be remembered that the Labour Party was essentially a party of labour, where labourism, the promotion of sectional interests, was the dominant ideology and driving force, not socialism or communism.

The discussion about working class culture and the role of ideology that occupied activists and reformers in the late-nineteenth and early-twentieth centuries has continued to this day. These arguments about class formation, and transformation, featured very centrally in the work of Marxist-oriented Sociologists and Historians in the period between the late-1960s and the 1980s. Many of the debates that had occupied designers, architects, trade unionists, social reformers, writers of fact and fiction, and so on, in the late-nineteenth and early-twentieth centuries was invariably 'transferred' to the Academy in the later twentieth century.

The research work and publications of the Centre for Contemporary Cultural Studies at Birmingham University was central to a good deal of this activity. Richard Hoggart was the first director, and established the tone of thinking in the period after his seminal book *The Uses of Literacy* (1957). Hoggart, and later Stuart Hall, Paul Willis, John Clarke, Chas Critcher and Richard Johnson all developed a fundamental concern about the nature and significance of an identifiable range of cultures largely specific to the working classes. One key issue, which has occupied a good deal of my thinking over thirty years, is whether the cultural values of any section of the working class, but especially so the radicalised left in the class, could be seen as an ongoing struggle against the dominant ideology of liberal democracy and consumer culture?

It is the process of development and use of ideology by the capitalist class and their agents has particularly interested researchers. Ideology is seen as a political process. For example, a 'house' is not ideological, although it is self-evidently an object of material culture; but the process of housing policy *is* ideological. For Richard Johnson and his associates, a key issue here is also the value-orientation of the researcher and writer. We know that this was axiomatic for Marx himself in that the research and writing he conducted over many years was first and foremost to further a socialist transformation of society *via* a political and cultural revolution. In fact, this is not so very different from William Morris. "The point is to change society"! (See John Clarke *et. al.* (Eds) 1979.)

Elsewhere in this book, I have discussed the ideas of Harvey Kaye on the development of Marxist historiography. Kaye argues that there is a key distinction to be made between a value orientation to research and writing that espouses a 'bottom up' history of the working class, and working class cultures, and - what is commonplace among liberal historians - a 'history of the bottom' (Kaye, 1995.)

This fundamental concern with the promotion of a self-conscious writing 'from below' returns us to the centrality of what the Chartists argued for 'a *really* useful education'!

In the early-nineteenth century many more working class people were engaging with education in one form or another, often in the do-it-yourself, personal and collective, tradition that grew out of Chartism and the post-Chartist and Freethought movements. I have addressed these issues elsewhere in relation to the trend for a top-down philanthropic movement to educate the working classes, to bring them in to the fold of decent middle class life. But a good deal of this education and experience led to radicalisation beyond the reach of the do-gooders, and this growth in political, literary and philosophical groupings embraced a broad spectrum of concerns with politics, aesthetics and secularism. (See Astley, 1969.)

I would add in summary that the evidence we have of the thinking and action-taking of those in the Arts & Crafts and Garden City movements was very focused on the inter-relation between the past as they experienced and understood it, set against their contemporary life of questioning and struggle, with radical aims in view, their hopes for the future, and a better future for all. This approach has continued in various forms to this day.

I must now turn to a consideration of the role and the importance of Ebenezer Howard (1850-1928).

Ebenezer Howard and the Garden City movement

In Howard's *Garden Cities of Tomorrow* (1898 & 1902), he presented a vision of the utopian city of the future in which humanity lives in a state of balance with nature, and which led to the birth of the Garden City movement. Frederic Osborn in *Green Belt Cities* argues that Howard's starting point was how best to return people to the land. Howard argued that city dwellers continue to desire access to the countryside, and regularly devise ways to 'escape' the metropolis and to be with nature in the countryside. Why not, therefore, give people the opportunity to live and work in the countryside, such as Hertfordshire and elsewhere? (Osborn, 1969.)

Osborn reminds us that in *Garden Cities of Tomorrow* Howard quotes from Ruskin's *Sesame and Lilies* where the latter describes a garden city with a pleasing environment within its boundaries, and the fair countryside beyond (similar in its way to Thomas More's utopian vision). For Howard, this was far from being a unfulfilled pipe dream, and the vision led to the creation of several Garden Cities in Britain. Osborn argues that Howard had a genuine belief in the value and possibility of progress, and that as a 'new town' grew the existing symmetry and functional qualities embodied in the original design would be replicated. Nothing would upset the existing, well-balanced infrastructure based on the needs of all the inhabitants as members of this municipal endeavor. One of Howard's key ideas in this respect is that the 'garden city' should be composed of a number of semi-autonomous neighbourhoods with an average population of five thousand, sufficient to maintain its own school.

7. Ebenezer Howard (1850-1928): his utopian vision *Garden Cities of Tomorrow* (1898; 1902) led to the birth of the Garden City movement.

Each neighbourhood's individuality would be encouraged by its own multi-purpose community centre with all the necessary services, including sufficient shops. Any proposal to increase the number of shops would be put to the popular vote. Howard and his supporters saw these proposals as practical and 'do-able'.

Dugald MacFayden in his 1933 book on Howard and the town planning movement comments on the general appeal of the ideas expressed in Howard's book:

"There was something for every kind of idealist in Howard's plan. There was a chance of self-realisation in a new sphere which pleased the individualist. There was a corporate life, a co-operative endeavor, a communal ideal which pleased the socialist." (MacFyden, 1970 edition p.38)

MacFayden then goes on to sugeest that tenants of private landlords, thoughtful employers, workmen, those seeking a rural re-birth and temperance reformers would all find something to their liking.

However, Howard had his critics, and none more ardent than Thomas Sharp (1901-1978) in his book *Town and Countryside: some aspects of urban and rural development* (1932). Sharp's essential criticism of Howard is that the latter was a social reformer, not an architect or planner, who focused on the social problems created by the degradation of over-populated towns and cities, and the steady dispoliation of the countryside. Sharp argues that nine-tenths of Howard's book was concerned with the socio-economics of social problems. Towns are bad, and the countryside needs regenerating by getting willing people back onto the land. The real, genuine and authentic countryside is to be sacrificed to solve problems created by the town! On this, Sharp says:

"Right up until the industrial revolution...English town-development, though it was backward, was of the normal type, *i.e.,* it was composed of *urban* habitations in close formation. Thereafter began a break-away: hardly discernable at first and showing but a slow progress through several generations, but one which paved the way for the complete and emphatic revolution which was to come later and change altogether the appearance of English towns; and, ultimately, to spread in a lesser degree, to other parts of the world. It obviously arose out of that Romantic Revival which found its chief outlet in literature. Its first indications were apparent outside the town, in the antagonism against formality in the parks and gardens surrounding the large country mansions. It was only gradually that its nature-worshipping tendencies began to break in upon the town itself. Where the wealthy had been content to live in large houses in streets and squares, they now began to favour detached villas surrounded by small 'landscaped' gardens...Here were the first beginnings of 'open-development' and 'garden-cities'' (Sharp, 1932 p.138/9)

With reference to Sharp's point about 'Romantic' gardens, I would cite Rousseau's garden at Nuneham Courtnay on the Thames outside Oxford. On the question of 'garden city' developments, Sharp cites Bournemouth created around 1850 as typical of this new trend, complemented of course by the emergence of the public parks movement in the growing cities of the 1840s and 1850s such as London, Manchester and Birkenhead. In his recent (*c.*2000) book on the spiritual and physical benefits of open spaces, recreation and lidos, Ken Worpole emphasises the embedded cultural value of parks.

Sharp acknowledges that Howard's book was 'epoch-making' and probably more influential than anything similar at the time. He cites the passing of the Housing and Town

Planning Act of 1909 (which mainly banned the building of 'back-to-back' houses and required councils to enage in 'town planning') and argues: "So from Letchworth to the beginning of the War the story of town development is the story of universal adoption of garden-city ideals applied to garden-suburbs, garden-villages, garden-this-that-and-the-other." (p.144)

So, given the considerable impact Howard's ideas had on his contemporaries, how did he actually arrive at that position?

Howard lived for a short time in the rapidly expanding USA in the late-nineteenth century and so witnessed the creation of new towns and burgeoning communities on 'virgin' land. This visit fuelled his inventor-ish character, and on his return he was greatly inspired by Henry George, the well-known land reformer. Howard also knew of the writings of Peter Kropotkin, another advocate of land reform, who shared Howard's growing sense of the need to see the problems of the town and the country as one issue, and take action along those lines. Howard was also moved to social reform by reading the American Edward Bellamy's (1850-98) *Looking Backward 2000-1887* (1888). Bellamy's book was very popular at the time of publication, and certainly engendered much discussion and response.

In his book *The Search for Environment* (1966), Walter Creese suggests that Howard was comfortable with Bellamy's technocratic vision. In his introduction to William Morris' *News from Nowhere*, A.L.Morton describes *Looking Backward* as "...flat, Philistine, but immensely popular." Morris thought it pretentiously vulgar and balked at Bellamy's idea that one monolithic capitalist enterprise linked to 'industrial service' for everyone would solve society's problems. In this respect Morris says: "In short, a machine life is the best which Bellamy can imagine for us on all sides; it is not to be wondered at then that his only idea for making labour tolerable is to decrease the

amount of it by means of fresh developments of machinery."
(Morris' review in *Commonweal* 22 Jan.1889.)

As I have mentioned in my chapter on the Arts & Crafts,
Morris responded to Bellamy's vision more fully the following
year with *News from Nowhere: or an epoch of rest* in 1890.
Bellamy's values are ones of a mass humane capitalism, verging
on the totalitarian, which would of course appeal to many
genuinely concerned social reformers then and now. This was
especially so in the light of the 1867 (and later) Reform Acts
that extended the franchise; but how, then, to manage the
emboldened electorate? Morris and other ardent socialists were
convinced that the values and apparatus of capitalism needed to
be swept away, and that 'the soul of man under socialism'
would be very different. (See Astley, 2006 pages 20-33) In
News from Nowhere Morris set his socialist revolution in the
late 1950s, and looked forward to a time and place of difference
and "a new day of fellowship, rest and happiness."

Morris' utopian romance is clearly influenced by his
involvement in 'Bloody Sunday', the suppression of a
demonstration in London on 13 November 1887. He realised
that the 'failure' of that uprising was a political setback for the
modern socialist movement, and so set about engaging even
more with the cultural struggle against the hegemonic control of
the Establishment with their narrow-ness of vision. Morris re-
doubled his efforts to show what stood in the way of happiness
and the freedom to lead a leisurely life, a life of real choices for
all. Others, like George Bernard Shaw, believed that this
'failure' at last cleared the way forward of these revolutionary
dreamers, and created the necessary space for an evolutionary
socialist transformation to take place using the ideas of the
Fabian movement.

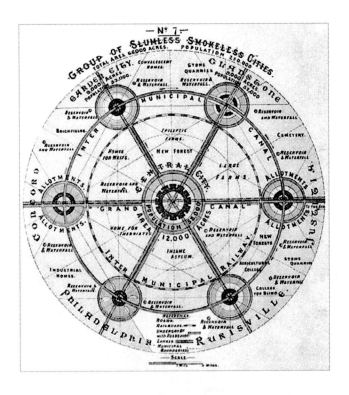

**8. The original Garden City concept (1902) by
Ebenezer Howard.** The masthead title reads:
Group of Slumless and Smokeless Cities.

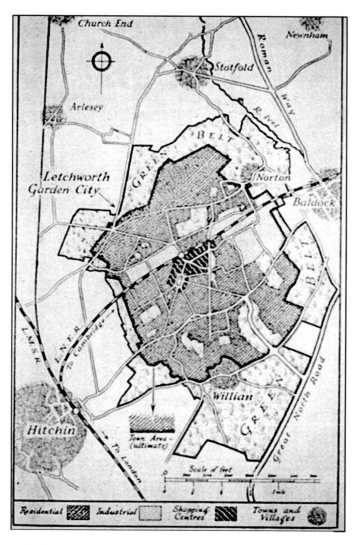

9. Plan for Letchworth: from the book *Garden Cities of Tomorrow* (1898; 1902) by Ebenezer Howard.

Walter Creese remarked that: "Both Howard and Morris based their discussions on an imaginary community that would draw its coherence from the limits of population and the consequent desire for cooperation based on personal acquaintance ...Both had little faith in state initiative or control." (p.150.)

Howard was said to have also been influenced by William Morris' epic poem *A Dream of John Ball* published in 1888 at a time when Morris was formulating his ideas. Howard wanted municipal ownership of land. Morris hoped to restore the primacy of art in determining the environmental quality and texture of the community. And, as Creese emphasises, Morris and his Arts & Crafts contemporaries argued for 'the indispensability of beauty' (p.171). A key issue for Morris and others cited in this thesis was that art had, in the words of Unwin and Parker, withdrawn 'to the gallery', while much of what was developed outside was increasingly ugly and shoddy. In our own era, we seem to have reached the stage where the 'gallery' has become the art, with the *wow* factor, while the content is fairly uninspiring and often ignored, slipping into the background compared with the iconic buildings. Unwin and Parker's words are equally relevant today, perhaps even more so in this age of celebrity and hubris.

I SHOULD add that around this time another utopian thinker had developed ideas on these matters. H.G.Wells in his scientific futurology *Anticipations* of 1902 assesses the likely development of 'urban regions' where 'bespoke' suburbs and/or satellite towns would be built. Changes to communications technologies, from rail to postal services, would create the circumstances to make such developments viable. The bespoke aspect would come from the vernacular, from the particular characteristics of a locale, and therefore avoiding undesirable standardisation. Howard's proposals were also much in line with the popular 'self help' values proposed by Samuel Smiles (1812-1904), and echoed by many others; for example, industrial philanthropists like Joseph Strutt of Belper.

Lewis Mumford said of Howard that:

" . . .[his] ideas have laid the foundation for a new cycle in urban civilization: one in which the means of life will be subservient to the purposes of living, and in which the pattern needed for biological survival and economic efficiency will likewise lead to social and personal fulfilment."

(Mumford, 1945)

Mumford was central to the post-1945 American debates about the contradictions inherent in the development of suburbia: the concept, the reality, and the myth: "To withdraw like a hermit and live like a prince - this was the purpose of the original creators of the suburbs." (Mumford in Charles Haar 1972 p.5)

Much of what the many Americans who wrote about the difficulties associated with suburbs frequently reinforces Howard's fundamental opposition to them. To paraphrase Charles Haar, was it possible for this mini-diaspora to embrace the simple virtues of an agrarian environment while still enjoying the material benefits of industrial capitalism? A syndicalism of the countryside?

Mumford was greatly influenced by the Scot Patrick Geddes (1854-1932), and is briefly discussed in my chapter on Unwin. Geddes in turn was indebted to the ideas of Ruskin (who was not!) and argued like Mumford and Howard that social processes and spatial form are related. By changing the spatial form of an environment, the social structure could be changed, especially so work roles that influenced or determined how people lived. Here we are back with Skinner's issues. It was Geddes in his *Cities in Evolution* of 1915 that coined the term conurbation.

Mumford in turn was a great influence on other's thinking; and, for example, Thomas Reiner dedicated his 1963 book *The Place of the Ideal Community in Urban Planning to Mumford*:

'Dedicated to Lewis Mumford - Utopian in quest of an ideal urban environment in a world of peace.'

Osborn also focuses on the core ideas of Howard and the "the unique combination of proposals": planned dispersal of people and their work, limiting the town size, sufficient space for necessary amenities, the town to be surrounded by market gardens whose produce would meet everyone's everyday needs, the use of planning controls to ensure the desired layout and physical infrastructure with planned neighbourhoods, and land ownership as a matter of cooperative endeavour that looked to the future in a progressive way.

This view of Howard's achievement as someone trying to break the mould is shared by Frank Schaffer in his *The New Town Story*, an account of the various legislation and schemes after 1945. Of Howard, Schaffer says:

"It is a classic story of a pioneer who believed passionately in his principles. Although at times Howard's projects seemed near to failure and even nearer to bankruptcy, he never lost faith in them. Howard can justly be called the father of the new towns. But his preaching and propaganda achieved far more. It marked the beginning of a slow acceptance of the need for planning control." (1970, p.6.)

It is certainly true that Howard was much more interested in social processes than he was in physical forms. Howard did not envisage publicly owned (council) housing for the working classes. He assumed that building societies and other private sources of mortgages, plus schemes like Letchworth, would suffice.

At the opening of the twentieth century, Howard had experienced many examples of public utility societies that had been set in motion by clearly focused, and usually single issue, groups. These would now be called social enterprises. After 1900 there was some growth in co-partnership schemes where a tenant- owned agency could borrow money from the Public Works Loan Commissioners, so long as not more than 5 per cent dividends were paid to investors. (Ward, 2004.) Howard, like Unwin and the younger Patrick Abercrombie, was suspicious of both big business and politicians.

Before saying more about Howard, I should take this opportunity to say a little more about Abercrombie (1879-1957), drawing on his 1933 book *Town and Country Planning*. He starts out by drawing a clear distinction between an attitude of letting growth and change impact on the physical and social environment by 'accident', or, deciding to intervene and plan for growth and change. By the time of the Arts & Crafts and Garden City Movements there were numerous examples of urban/industrial growth that was if not unplanned was certainly un-coordinated, not thought-through, and lacking some sense of coherence. There is in Abercrombie an Unwin-esque holistic design aesthetic, where social and moral goals are privileged. Abercrombie cites Geddes, and argues that when considering town planning he shared with the latter a focus on "place, work and folk".

This commitment fits neatly with Abercrombie's belief that between the 1919 Act and the 1932 Town and Country Planning Act the centrality of the idea of the key relation of planning to building increased to become not only an obligation on local authorities to prepare plans, but a widespread assumption that this should happen.

Howard was of course less interested in the role of local authority building, or in the actual nature and style of building, than he was in the land ownership and site development issues. He also assumed that what was built at Letchworth, and elsewhere, would be funded from private, or sponsored sources, and that his development would deal with the acquisition of the land and its preparation for building. Although Howard saw his plans as being essentially a private development, he argued that to expand on his ideas parliamentary powers would need to be used, as was to happen with regional development and the New Towns agendas of later governments.

Howard's proposal for Letchworth was more like the Housing Association schemes of the 1960-70s where certain interested people would raise sufficient money to gain a freehold to some land for building. The residents then repaid the mortgage collectively, and the residents managed the whole arrangement. I lived in one such scheme in Oxford in the early-1970s.

Howard's 'private equity company' raised the money to build Letchworth, and those that provided the capital were assured a fixed, and modest, return on their investment. All of the rest of the money collected in rents went into the pot to pay for development, services, upkeep, and the like. The State nationally, or locally, was not involved.

While on the subject of land, we should always bear in mind that all the land in the UK is 'owned' by the monarch. Monarchs in the past (Henry VIII comes to mind) had a regular habit of removing land from the current holders, and giving, or selling it, to somebody else usually for services rendered, subsequently deemed 'the freeholders'.

In Howard's day, the King and the State were synonymous,

whereas we now tend to separate the State, especially the Parliament bit, from 'the Crown'. Active ownership of land and buildings in the UK by the Crown is considerable, and mostly in the gift of the prime minister of the day. Not much is ever said about these arcane sets of circumstances, and so the modern citizenry (all of us subjects of the Queen, of course) are allowed to perpetuate the myth that we live in a society where we are all free to exercise our agency. This includes the act of buying land and buildings. Many rebels and reformers over the years have tried to disabuse the populace of their illusions. Tony Benn is very good on this issue.

Howard had very particular ideas about land tenure, as Aneurin Williams in Purdom's book emphasises:

"He (Howard) based his proposals on a scheme of public land ownership formulated by Thomas Spence about the year 1775. This scheme was that the land, subject no doubt to the supreme ownership of the King, should be owned by the local community, or by trustees for them." (Purdom, 1913 p.212/3.)

The issue of land ownership was very big news in the 1880s, not the least of reasons being the visit of Henry George, the American radical, whose book *Progress and Poverty* (1881) caused such a stir. George argued that land is a natural, communal resource returns us to Gerard Winstanley. Howard's contemporaries also regularly referred to Fergus O'Connor and the Chartists arguments for small-scale and collective land ownership.

Howard enthused about municipaltilism. Letchworth has seen the development of the trustees' principle, as has in recent years Port Sunlight, and Bournville among others. Howard and those associated with the development of Letchworth believed that trustees were very different from some 'private' owner of land and the use of the buildings upon it. Howard also regretted the failure of his rate-rent scheme, an all-inclusive payment, and saw a reversion to conventional leases. In particular, he was disappointed that the Co-operative Wholesale Society did not take up the invitation to be involved by developing their shops in Letchworth. He was also concerned that there were not enough 'productive industries' in Letchworth, requiring some residents to travel elsewhere to work.

Right from the outset there had been those, like George Bernard Shaw, who were sceptical about the likelihood of Howard's ideals being realised. After attending the Garden City conference in Bournville in 1901, Shaw wrote to Ralph Neville, the recently appointed chairman of the Garden City Association, arguing that a non-capitalist venture like Letchworth could not be achieved from money market borrowings. (See Hebbert, 1992.)

Howard was always touchy about schemes for 'old English style' suburbs being called 'Garden City'. I have to ask myself whether the Merry Oak estate in Southampton falls into this category. Indeed, critics like Standish Meacham (2001) argue that there is a contradiction in the radical proposals for providing good quality housing for working class families, and the idea of reproducing the physical experience and aesthetic of a somewhat mythologized English country village, which in itself, of course, was characterised by rigid class hierarchy.

As indicated above, a further traditional culture dimension to be acknowledged is that many schemes, like Bournville and Port Sunlight, did reflect social and economic hierarchies and provided 'grander' houses for higher status workers, although Lever the developer of Port Sunlight did acknowledge the special needs of larger families. However, it could be argued that craftsmen had built the houses themselves, and as a consequence their labour had a value that was embodied in the buildings. Plus, as I have already suggested, why not build these aesthetically valued houses to be shared by far more people?

Lever, the creator of Port Sunlight, spoke of the work of Shaftesbury, and that he had read Charles Booth's *Life and Labour of the People of London*, one of several damming indictments of poverty and squalor produced in the 1880s. In fact Booth carried out his study because he was incredulous at the figures on poverty published by Henry Hyndman, leader of the Social Democratic Federation, *via* the *Pall Mall Gazette* in 1885. Booth had to test this information for himself, and what emerged from his comprehensive study was that conditions were even worse than previously thought.

Lever argued that a child that had not known the green and pleasant land would not benefit from education. Not surprising, then, that Lever commissioned what he did. Of course, we need to consider the paternalistic and often controlling tendencies of Lever, the Cadburys and many of their peers.

There is a lovely story about Lever and Port Sunlight, where he kept refusing to allow alcohol to be sold in the 'the Pub'. Eventually, Lever agreed for the issue to go to a democratic vote in the whole village on the assumption that the women would vote against the proposition to sell alcohol. However, the women voted overwhelmingly in favour of change, on the basis, it is said, that they would get their men out from under their feet, *and* know where they were!

The developments at Bournville [designed by the very young Alexander Harvey (1874-1951)] and Port Sunlight chimed with Howard and his ideas for the future of habitation and work.

The evidence is that the creation of Letchworth was another attempt to provide decent housing for people, and is echoed in Unwin's words "We must first see that our citizens are decently housed". There is a 'food comes before philosophy' dimension to this. Hubbard and Shippobottom in their book on Port Sunlight (2005) emphasize this:

"The historical significance of Port Sunlight lies in its unprecedented combination of model industrial housing, (with quite utilitarian interiors) and on a considerable scale at that, with the tradition of the sylvan suburb, in which greenery and picturesque effect form integral elements in spacious planning." (p.6.)

As with other such developments, Port Sunlight brought together the two emerging planning and building cultures of the day: the Arts & Crafts multitude of stylistic influences coupled with the social reformist desire to create much better, and efficient, housing for the labouring classes. These regional developments reproduced local vernacular building, as we would expect, especially if the planners and builders were going to keep to one of Morris and Webb's key dictums: be true to your (local) materials.

Cecil Harmsworth, chairman of the Garden City and Town Planning Association, writing in Purdom's book emphasizes that building Garden City-style suburbs for the 'well-to-do' does not meet Howard's ideal. Private employers-cum-developers like Lever and Cadbury have shown initiative, but "the State itself has been remarkably slack in this regard". (Purdom, p.297.)

Harmsworth points out that the Garden City idea has had much more success in other (often developing) countries. He does say that the (Burns) 1909 Housing and Town Planning Act has been a great help, with Birmingham being the first municipality to develop a scheme for Quinton, Harborne and Edgbaston in 1913. The 1909 Act also provided the means whereby many unsanitary dwellings would be upgraded. In his diary entry for 12 April 1912, Harmsworth reports on a visit to Letchworth by the Departmental Committee on Buildings for Small Holdings accompanied among others by Unwin.

In his book *The Garden City* (1913), to which I have already referred, Charles Purdom makes the point that Garden City ideas did not come 'out of the blue', but reflected debate over many years about ideal towns, utopias, and so on. Substantial knowledge of the worst aspects of the 'industrial revolution' came from very diverse sources, with John Ruskin and the Arts & Crafts movement being just one obvious example. Whether *via* fact or fiction there was a growing sense of the cataclysmic transformation of 'Merry England' into a de-humanising abomination. Early sociological studies like Frederick Engels' 'The Condition of the Working Class in England in 1844' (1892) considered Manchester and other industrialising hot spots, which was widely read, first in Germany and then in Britain and America. Engels' study was followed by several similar exposés of the dire situation in which so many lived (and I will mention some of these a little later on in this study).

These stark realities were a long way from Lethaby's ideal that "every noble city has been a crystallization of the contentment, pride, and order of the community".

This growing knowledge (the scientific and rational fruit of the tree?) accelerated the demand for change, based on a diverse range of theories and proposed solutions. These demands included ideas about a 'Return' to the rural ideal, the garden in the city/the city as garden. We also need to recall that many of our shared stories about returning to the rural idyll draw on the biblical accounts of 'the Fall', of Adam and Eve being cast out from the Garden of Eden. A good deal of our collective thinking about recapturing a 'golden age' of the holistic countryside with all the picturesque trappings of our well-fed imaginations draws on these 'access to Eden' issues.

Purdom argues that 'the old' towns of England had lost their pride, and makes the point that it is only the resources and technologies of the modern age that can cope with the huge growth in population, and deliver sufficient housing of good quality to meet everyone's needs. This theme of the democratic and socialistic management of technology had been a currency for a hundred years prior to the publication of Purdom's book in the early-twentieth century.

Purdom cites William Lever's development of Port Sunlight from 1887 as one form of 'prosperity sharing'. He also refers to Bournville (1889) and the aims of the Cadburys, along with several other enlightened and philanthropic employers across the country, many of them Quakers.

According to Purdom, Howard took these ideas to a different level in his plans for a Garden City, outlined in his book *Tomorrow: a peaceful path to real reform* (1898), re-published in 1902 as I have said above as *Garden Cities of Tomorrow*. Howard envisaged a town of 32,000 inhabitants on 6,000 acres, only one sixth of which would be built up. He saw a 'city' of broad social class where ample employment would be created for all in and around the town, and that existing 'agriculturists' in this part of rural Hertfordshire could be joined by others to make the town as self-sufficient as possible - a concept highlighting the importance of market gardens. The object of all this was to create a healthy, natural, and economic combination of town and country life on land owned by the municipality. Howard shows allotments in his plans, much like those laid out between the houses in Port Sunlight. Howard's town-country criteria were: beauty of nature, social opportunity, fields and parks of easy access, low rents and rates, high wages, plenty to do, low prices, no sweating (cheap labour), scope for enterprise and flow of capital, pure air and water, good drainage, bright homes and gardens, no smoke, no slums, and freedom and co-operation. This is a radical list, which went some way to addressing Howard's two key contexts, the overcrowding of the towns and cities, and the de-populating of the countryside.

In his book on British buildings, Anthony McIntyre underlines this:

"It was (this) breaking up and isolation of men's lives that the socialists tried to combat, with dreams of a community in which work was performed for common well-being rather than for the worker's mere subsistence and another's private gain. This was the object of Ebenezer Howard's proposals of 1898 for a town he called Rurisville. In the sense that it was meant as a place to be in and not a system to move about in...' (1984 p.119)

McIntyre adds to my point above that Howard desired as self-sufficient a town as possible, and certainly was against the idea of commuting via the still expanding railway network. The Cheap Train Act of 1883 was intended to encourage train companies to provide services for the increasing number of London's daily migrants. The new train services being linked to the Bedford Park development in the 1880s was one clear example. Howard wanted people in his ideal town to be able to walk to work, and meet all their other domestic needs in the vicinity. Access to, and constant use of the motorcar, certainly ruined that notion, and throughout the twentieth century most policy and planning accommodated privileged access by car to town centres, and later to the endless sprawl of out-of-town developments. I would add here that many attractive pre-car townscapes have been near-ruined by the pollution of multitudes of parked cars! (It should be remembered that Buchanan's report 'Traffic in Towns' was published in 1963, the same year as the Beeching Report on the future of the railways.)

The Garden City Association was formed eight months after the publication of Howard's book as a way to advance debate and promote the ideas of the book. The Association held a conference in Bournville in 1901 with 300 delegates. It should be noted that Benjamin Seebohm Rowntree (son of Joseph) attended this conference, where he met Unwin, which then led to the commission for Earswick. A second conference followed in 1902, this time in Port Sunlight with 1,000 delegates, and in the same year the Garden City Pioneer Co. Ltd. was set up to pursue Howard's goals. Edward Cadbury was a director, and George Cadbury and William Lever were shareholders. The Pioneer Company was wound up in 1903, and the First Garden City Ltd. was created with authorised capital of £300,000 and a week later the first prospectus was issued. All this activity was carried out by business people and professionals for whom this was commonplace, and led directly to the setting out, and building of, Letchworth.

Mention must also be made of Richard Reiss, a close friend and associate of Howard and Rowntree, and from 1918 the chairman of the Garden Cities and Town Planning Association. A pre-war Liberal, Reiss was a peripatetic Captain in the War, finally being invalided out in 1917. Before the war he had, like his parents, become interested in social welfare and the pressing need to improve the everyday life of the majority of people. In 1917, Seebohm Rowntree persuaded Lloyd George to second Reiss to the recently formed Ministry of Reconstruction. The minister was Addison, and therefore Reiss' concerns with post-War housing matched those of Addison and many of their contemporaries, including Howard. In 1919-20 Reiss was to work with Chamberlain on the Unhealthy Area committee.

Interestingly, after 1918 Reiss decided to join the Labour Party because he saw this as the most logical choice consistent with a radical road to reform. This membership then led him in to association with Henrietta Barnett and the Hampstead Garden Institute. In May 1919, Howard took Reiss to see the large plot of land that was to become Welwyn Garden City, and the whole

Letchworth process was replicated. The Reiss family moved to Welwyn in 1922 (Reiss became a Director of the WGC company), and from the outset it is clear that Reiss and many other key figures in these developments really believed in creating heterogeneous communities.

It was because of his undiminished enthusiasm for the Garden City ideal that Reiss regularly embarked on a series of talks to interested groups of people; for example, on 18 July 1919 in Southampton (a notice for which I discovered in the Ministry of Health journal *Housing*). Reiss was clearly one of many proselytisers in this movement, and - given his concern with helping to create ideal environments for families to prosper - it is not surprising to find his son reflecting later on how wonderful the experience of improved housing environments was for so many children. (I felt much the same way talking recently to the first generation of children who grew up on the Merry Oak estate in the early 1930s).

Purdom acknowledges that the reality of Letchworth was quite different from the ideal Garden City set out by Howard in his book, and in the former's much later book *The Letchworth Achievement* (1963) he talks about 'the struggles' to bring about what they all did. Most commentators of the day thought that admirable though Howard's ideas were that they were hopelessly impractical. Some prominent organisations like The Fabians dismissed Howard's ideas as being akin to preparing the Britain to face H.G. Wells' Martian invaders!

Letchworth was designed by Raymond Unwin and Barry Parker (in 1904) for thirty thousand people on about 1,250 acres, an average of about five houses, or twenty-four persons per acre, a generous standard. Unwin consistently argued against the false economy of overcrowding building sites, such that guidelines were provided for the builders: size of rooms, use of contoured land, approved building materials, and only red tiles! This also echoes Morris and Webb, and reinforces one of the Morris' pet hates - slates! There had been one other important application for the design brief that came from Lethaby.

Cresse makes the link between Unwin and Parker exhibiting at the Manchester Royal Jubilee Exhibition in 1887 (which William Lever attended) and their ideas for Port Sunlight. Creese also argues that Walter Crane was an influential figure in all of this. An associate of Morris, Crane formed the Northern Art Workers' Guild in Manchester in 1896, and had written the catalogue for the 1885 Arts & Crafts Exhibition. Crane's argument was that everyone involved should seek unity regardless of their particular craft; the barriers had to be broken down in order that this new age of artistic collaboration could create the very best for all.

The first residents of Letchworth were professionals and businessmen, and their families, and it is clear that most of them were real enthusiasts for this experiment in living. There was a desire to create 'a new civilisation':

"They hoped to revise all, or nearly all, social institutions, they discussed, as middle class people will discuss, to reform religion, art and social policy, and the application of what they call the best modern knowledge to education and all the affairs of life...Their daring hope of a city that should be something like (Walt) Whitman's city of comrades could not be fulfilled". (Purdom, p.51)

And talk of Whitman reminds me again of Edward Carpenter, who was impressed when he visited Letchworth in the early days of the development.

Despite their best efforts and fine enthusiasms maybe, by the time Purdom had published his book in 1913 Letchworth still lacked a pub! It did eventually have one of course, The Skittles which was originally non-alcoholic. Both dimensions of this particular issue reflect the high profile of temperance values and initiatives at this time.

The second wave of new residents was mainly from 'the artisan classes', probably attracted by the new jobs, but also presumably by the Garden City environment. Purdom says that many of these newer residents did not share the ideals of 'the pioneers'. Worth adding here that the first chair of the new parish council was the Right Hon. Sir John E. Gorst, and the illustrious early leadership may have dissuaded some people from being more involved.

Purdom like so many of his contemporaries asserted that garden city ideas were not faddist, and *must* integrate theory and practice at every stage of development. He goes on to say:

"'If the town (*i.e.,* Letchworth) had no meaning beyond its own borders then its ideals would not matter at all, but so long as it stands for something far greater than itself those ideals cannot be disregarded." (p.196)

There is no doubt that the building of Letchworth did influence town planning, and house design a good deal. Purdom, even in 1913, feels moved enough to take to task those planners who insist on calling their suburbs Garden City style. A compliment to Letchworth certainly, but no more, given the fact that the creation of Letchworth was anti-suburb!

Once again, does this appear to leave my garden city connection with post-1924 suburban development in some ideological difficulty. . .? Yes, it is clear that Garden City ideals certainly did have an influence on the development of garden suburbs. They happened; but, was it desirable, not just aesthetically, but crucially so from a planning aspect? There are questions here whether a town like Southampton needed to build more suburbs. Was the 1924 Act, enhancing the 1919 Act as it did, right to encourage local government to do so?

Gordon Child in his 1996 study of town planning emphasises the key role played by the garden suburbs 'movement':

"...there was the question of land values. London's experience had already shown that redevelopment would be an extremely costly means of re-housing, while land on the outskirts was much cheaper.' (Child, 1996 p.28)

So developing garden suburbs was both cheaper and healthier given the greater space available to meet improved housing standards.

Sidney G. Stanton, the newly appointed Borough Engineer for Southampton, produced a 'where are we now' book on post-1918 housing, reflecting on the influence of the 1919 (Addison), 1923 (Chamberlain), and 1924 (Wheatley) Housing Acts. This book *HOUSING - Housing schemes carried out in the County Borough of Southampton* (1931) was both an assessment of work-in-progress and a celebration:

"The necessity of building houses to let at a small rental was realised in those early days. A large proportion of Southampton's working-class population are dock labourers, whose wages do not allow of a large expenditure in house rents. The principle adopted has been to build a large number of non-parlour houses, and a proportionately smaller number of parlour houses for the people whose position enables them to pay the higher rents demanded for the parlour house." (p.19)

I should explain again that a parlour was a 'best room' in addition to the living room, as it was usually designated on plans. One of my aunts lived in a non-parlour house on the

Merry Oak estate, and I recall the crowded, but cosy nature of that all-in-one room, with the scullery (kitchen) and bathroom at the back of the house. As I have discussed in other parts of this study there were always significant arguments among designers and planners about the necessity, or not, of a parlour.

Purdom in his book anticipates an era of legislation that seeks to create local authorities that are assisted to be progressive, imaginative, and *local.*

This is one of my many links with the 1924 Housing Act, and the key role of subsidies for local government building. It is also worth remembering that the 1924 Act also provided subsidies for private sector development. So although many 'Wheatley' estates, including my case study of Merry Oak in Southampton, were *not* new towns, they most certainly embodied many of the Garden City ideals.

We should also note that the investment that so many people made 'in a better future' is a crucial aspect of utopian thinking and vision. As Geoghegan illustrates with his concept 'imagined communities', there is a dialectical process at work where there is a latent utopia within the existing arrangements of ideas and material culture, including actual houses and estates. For those people in the post-1918 era there was an intoxicating reservoir to draw upon in varying degrees of self-consciousness. (Geoghegan, 1987).

The extension of the franchise, as mentioned earlier, and of which all reformers argued over a good deal, was one dimension of the municipalising of housing. These diverse developments sought to conceive of, and create, a holistic environment, where conviviality and a positive sense of self-determination were evident. There was certainly a sense at this time that everyone could work for the benefit of others, for the community of souls, and not merely for their own comfort and happiness.

There is no doubt that Howard left a huge legacy.

Bernard Shaw, writing Howard's obituary in 1928, summed up his character and achievements with these words: "He was one of those heroic simpletons who do big things while our prominent worldlings are explaining why they are Utopian and impossible."

Reading Shaw's words reminds me of similar thoughts developed in his play *Man and Superman* in praise of the do-ers!

The Road to the 1924 Housing Act

THE HOUSE of Commons, 24 April 1923:

John Wheatley, the Irish-Scottish MP for Glasgow Shettleston, rose to his feet to move a critical amendment to the second reading of Neville Chamberlain's Housing Bill. Chamberlain, the Minister of Health in the Conservative government has, in moving the second reading of the Bill, underlined just how intransigent the problems of housing are: a lack of houses to rent, and chronic overcrowding of poor quality dwellings. He acknowledged that these problems have worsened since 1918, and have deprived people of the "ordinary decencies of life". He is concerned that such conditions present a perpetual danger to the physical and moral health of the community. He is also worried about civil unrest as a consequence of everyday life in such squalid conditions.

He has summed up his moving of the Bill by admitting to the House that this is not a perfect solution to these problems, and is prepared to consider any constructive amendments. However, he does not consider the critique of the Labour Party at all helpful in this respect.

On behalf of the Labour Party front bench, Wheatley - first elected to Parliament in 1922 - thinks otherwise, and proceeds to set out seven points of disagreement with the Bill's provisions, namely that it [the Bill] is:

- inadequate to deal with the present housing shortage
- ignores the difficulty of land purchase and transfer
- fails to provide the means of securing a sufficient supply of building materials at reasonable prices
- throws an excessive financial burden upon Local Authorities

❏ interferes unnecessarily with their administrative powers

❏ fails to reduce the burden of interest imposed on the dwelling house by the present financial system, and

❏ provides only for an unreasonably small type of house.

This last criticism is a key focus of attention for the Labour Party in the 1920s, and in fact is still present as a key issue in Bevan's housing legislation in 1948. This speech of Wheatley's was reproduced in a Scottish Council of the I.L.P. pamphlet *Homes or Hutches?*, and sold for one penny.

Wheatley argues that he feels Chamberlain does not fully understand the extent of the housing problem, which is not one of building but of finance:

"It is part and parcel of that great social problem by which, at every step, we are baffled by poverty at one end and exploitation at the other."

He further suggests that the crisis is felt in every large city where the problem is growing. Glasgow is a prime example, where the medical officer of health for the city has declared 13,195 houses containing 58,000 people not reasonably fit for human habitation. Wheatley emphasises therefore that the lack of houses is not the only problem; the poor quality of the existing stock is a key issue. Wheatley dismisses the Conservative argument that the previous Liberal Party legislation is to blame for the current situation, and points instead to rent increases caused in part by scarcity and the operation of cartels pushing up materials costs by 60 per cent. He pins down the four actions that are needed to provide the necessary housing: land, materials, finance and labour. He argues that the cost of land is not in itself the issue (although he would by choice abolish private ownership of land). It is, he believes, the power by private owners to control access to land, which is the problem. Under the existing legislation Local Authorities could spend two years trying to purchase suitable land, and the proposals before the House fail to address this issue.

Wheatley's performance at the dispatch box was once again met with acclaim. The Labour Party front bench asked Wheatley to lead on this because he had demonstrated a remarkable ability in shaping a cogent argument in the House since his election in 1922. This is important because it made it difficult for Ramsay MacDonald to avoid making Wheatley his Minister of Health in the first Labour Government from the start of 1924; MacDonald would have preferred Arthur Greenwood (who had made his reputation with the TUC/LP joint research and information department), and instead became Wheatley's parliamentary secretary.

It is also quite clear that Wheatley's contributions in the House of Commons after 1922 were shaped by his life experiences in Glasgow, including being a City councillor. In turn his experience in Parliament, and what he said in response to Chamberlain's Bill, led directly to his work as Minister of Health, and therefore the shaping of the 1924 Housing Act. So he knew what was needed in what was really a very straightforward piece of legislation. In view of all the painstaking preliminary work he did with both sides, indeed all sides, of the building industry, Wheatley knew that *his* Bill would be welcomed 'on the ground'. He also had the support of Local Authorities, with the exception of Birmingham - Chamberlain's territory.

JOHN WHEATLEY was very well prepared for his presentation

of the Labour government's Housing (financial provisions) Bill by June of 1924. From the first days of his appointment as Minister of Health in January 1924 (in the minority Labour government), he set about a series of tasks that he knew were essential. In fact even before he officially took office he had begun work on the provisions of the Bill in the period between mid-December 1923, after MacDonald had appointed him, and late January. He identified those he needed to see, and convince, of his seriousness about this legislation. The good impression he made in opposition certainly helped.

Within a few days of taking up his ministerial role he met with leaders of the manufacturers to both discuss his plans and persuade them of the need to join a committee drawn from 'both' sides of the building industry. Wheatley and Greenwood then met, and obtained agreement from the Trades Unions. Tom Shaw the Minister of Labour, sat in on these meetings. This committee, with W.H. Nicholls (a leading manufacturer and employer) as chairman, comprised representatives of nineteen employers and fifteen employees. Their terms of reference from Wheatley were to "assist the Government by advice as to what the industry itself considers can be done in the way of producing working class houses."

The report of this committee was delivered to Wheatley in five weeks, perhaps an indication of just how anxious both sides were to get started on revitalising the industry. (See Middlemas, 1965.)

Wheatley's speech to the House of Commons on 16 April also has some bearing on the final Bill. He began by quoting Chamberlain, who had said when introducing the 1923 Act, that it was not *the* solution to the housing problem, rather a beginning to a solution. (The Act was due to expire in 1925). Wheatley argued that the 1923 Act had not altered the situation of ample houses being built for 'the rich', but beyond the upper fringes of the working class, who might buy, there were those people who needed to rent.

This argument supplemented the work of liberals like E.D. Simon, who were actively campaigning on the overcrowding and slums issues. As with others, Wheatley had often come under attack from the Conservative benches for this 'sob stuff'.

Wheatley went on to make the point that employers needed workers who are fit to do a day's work, and that living in slum conditions did not help. He moved on to say why a subsidy was needed by setting out the costs of a housebuild, which includes the cost of the land, paying the bricklayer, and so on, but argued that the cost of financing the loan to build is considerable even at 5 per cent interest.

Wheatley emphasised that his proposals were not "real Socialism", but "real Capitalism", an attempt to patch up, in the interests of humanity, a capitalist-ordered society. It has to be noted that the inexperience of the Labour government was a factor affecting Wheatley's outlook. There is also the political reality that the labour government was social democratic in its rhetoric, but not in day-to-day practice.

Wheatley made reference to his Report on the industry and what could be done, emphasising that the employers had cited insecurity in the industry, and not trade union hostility, for the chronic shortage of appropriately skilled labour. There were not enough young men taking on apprenticeships as a consequence of this insecurity. The finance aspect of the markets was so volatile that there were these constant fluctuations in building. Wheatley also made reference to the high number of building workers emigrating to the USA.

According to Wheatley, both sides of the industry were looking for a guarantee that houses would be built. His stated target was two-and-a-half million houses over a fifteen-year programme. After three years of building, there would be a stocktaking, which would then usher in the next three-year phase and so on until the full fifteen-year programme was achieved.

In terms of political rhetoric, MacDonald emphasised just how much a priority housing legislation was for the government in an interview he did for the *New Leader* (11 April 1924): "The housing scheme is our most important legislative item. It is really the biggest piece of constructive industrial organization which has probably ever been attempted."

Once again, Wheatley had won over many doubters, and he was offering a pragmatic yet decisive way of breaking the deadlock in the industry that would lead to actually building houses for letting at reasonable rents.

Kenneth Morgan (in 1979) commenting on the situation (in 1919), outlines some of the difficult back story that occupied Wheatley in 1924:

"…building contractors were loath to take part in State housing schemes, and preferred to undertake enterprises that would bring quicker profits than building low-cost, high-density houses. Warehouses, departmental stores, offices, theatres, cinemas, football stadia, and the like occupied the energies of fully thirty percent of the building trade. Another 60 percent (especially small builders) were engaged in the repair of existing property, and only ten percent were engaged in actually building new houses." (p.91)

The Labour cabinet immediately accepted Wheatley's Report, presented on 10 April 1924, and MacDonald stated that this was the government's most important legislative venture. Between early-April and early-June Wheatley entered into detailed discussions with a wide range of interested groups, including the other political parties. By 7 May, the first draft of the Bill was ready, with the key provisions of retaining Chamberlain's subsidy until 1939, with the addition of a £9 per year subsidy for every house built by local authorities to be let at fixed rents. The subsidy for agricultural areas was to be £12. Both these subsidies were for forty years, and the Bill also set building targets:105,000 a year by 1928; 142,000 by 1931; 200,000 by 1934, and 225,000 by 1937.

At this point Wheatley, with his civil servant aides, met the local authority representatives, who were mainly Conservatives. He had to persuade them that his plans would help create a vibrant and functional building industry. Wheatley also had to convince members of the PLP that all this was viable, and most agreed, while Snowden and the Treasury continued to complain about the extra agricultural subsidy. Richard Lyman emphasizes the fact that not all members of the PLP were happy with this housing legislation, and were certainly opposed in principle to the idea of owner-occupiers.

In the main, however, most of these critics, even the majority of The Clydesiders (Kirkwood was usually the exception) kept quiet and relied on Wheatley's judgement. The Tories were in a difficult situation as Chamberlain's Act and all its deficiencies, like continued overcrowding and not dealing with the chronic shortage of cheap rented housing, was still in force and creating the same problems. The Liberals were divided on their response as to whether privately owned and rented housing could solve the problem. But they all agreed that something drastic was needed. (Lyman, 1957.) One aspect of the developing Bill appeared in the third draft, that is, the provision for restricting unreasonable profits in building materials, which became part two to the Bill. Wheatley later turned this provision into a separate Bill because he knew that there would be controversy about such a measure. There was also a part three, which dealt with the payment of standard wages in the industry.

THE SKILL and diligence of Wheatley did not go unnoticed, or uncommented on, by members on all sides of the House. Charles Masterman of the Liberals was particularly fulsome in his praise of the Minister. This, of course, helped smooth the passage of the Bill from first formal reading through the nine clauses and two schedules of the second reading, which was carried by 315 votes to 175. As Ian Wood (1990) points out, only 128 Conservatives voted against the Bill. Wheatley eventually accepted sixty-six amendments, many of which rounded-off necessary provisions that were quite acceptable to the Government. One such amendment was from Chamberlain, namely, that there should be no sale or sub-letting of houses built. Wood adds:

"An odd omission in the bill, that of a fair wage clause in building contracts under its terms, was also repaired by a Chamberlain amendment. On rents to be charged on houses built under its terms, the bill has been accused of vagueness. It sought to return to the principles of Addison's Act by fixing rents in relation to those of pre-war houses controlled by the 1915 scheme. These controlled rents, however, would only be the basis for the average rent each local authority might charge. The average rent was not to exceed the rents of similar controlled houses unless costs incurred by local authorities exceeded their rate contribution of £4 10s per annum per house. Local authorities were, thus, so long as they kept to these conditions, left to their own discretion as to what rent they would charge for individual houses. (Wood, p.137.)

In my Merry Oak case study, I shall discuss the rents set by Southampton council as an example of how local authorities responded to need and costs.

It was evident that by the time of the third reading of the Bill on 25 July 1924, Wheatley was a very tired and not particularly well man. However, the Bill was carried comfortably by 226 votes to 131, with Wheatley commenting in his moving of the Bill that this was not a Socialist measure because the country was not ready for such. It was, however, the very best that he could do at the time. It is worth adding here that Wheatley was almost certainly saying this for the benefit of his divided (as usual) Independent Labour Party (ILP) comrades. As a member of the radical Scottish ILP contingent, Wheatley was well aware of the growing disagreements and disappointments among his compatriots since Labour took office. It was also likely that Wheatley wanted to keep as many Liberals as possible on his side.

The Housing (Financial Provisions) Bill received royal assent on 7 August 1924.

The passage of the bill had taken six months, and was such a success because many people, in many varied organisations, wanted reform, and sought a legislative measure that would address the chronic housing situation in the country at the time. Wheatley was clearly an ideal advocate for this measure, and never claimed it to be a perfect solution. The Act was, for example, only one dimension of the task that lay ahead, the other major concern being legislating on the supply of building materials.

Wheatley wanted to give the government powers of enforcement of supply to avoid manufacturers holding up building. He put a good deal of effort and argument into this measure, but by the time he and the government were out of office in October, the Bill had not been passed. On the success of the Act, Wood comments:

"Under the 1924 Act, house-building went ahead at a pace which even its critics had to acknowledge. Thousands of building workers were brought back into employment under the Act and a record was set in 1927, when 273,000 houses were completed. 'A fine achievement,' Simon later conceded; 'the biggest thing that has been done for housing and employment by any government.'".(Wood, p.142.)

Lyman emphasises that Wheatley's Act was in the form of a 'contract' with the industry (both sides) and the Local Authorities to get on and build houses at subsidised and affordable rents. Everyone was taking responsibility for a measure of planning for the future to replace the chaos of previous years. The Tories did not really have anything else to offer, and only 128 Conservative MPs actually voted against the Bill. During the debate on the Bill, the issue of house-size emerged, and Wheatley opposed the attempt to increase the size because he feared that many would then be occupied by middle class tenants. Lyman summarises that the Bill was well received, and that Wheatley's reputation was greatly enhanced. Even many critics, like E. D. Simon, ended up praising the Act. However, the high rents did remain a key issue, and existed mainly because of the miscalculations on costs.

"Perhaps it was ironic that the Wheatley scheme actually resulted in substantial relief of the housing shortage by the workings of the theory of 'filtering down'...The pressure for accommodations was lessened, even though the people most in need probably had to settle for the houses vacated by the new tenants of Wheatley houses." (Lyman, p.121-2.)

Of the 508,000 houses produced by the 1924 Act, only 15,000 were *not* built by Local Authorities. However, of the two and a half million houses built in England and Wales between 1919 and 1934 only 31 per cent were built by Local Authorities, and only one quarter had had a subsidy. So, more houses, and an improvement in the quality and environment of houses, but still not enough to meet the need:

"The housing problem continued to be unsolved in the twenties because private enterprise built very few houses for letting, because local authorities did not build sufficient houses, and because those that were built were let at rents too high for lower-paid workers, for those for whom employment was insecure, and for the unemployed whose numbers grew to reach 3,000,000 by 1931." (Burnett, 1978 p.234.)

I shall return to some specific aspects of these issues in my chapter on Merry Oak. A key issue at this time was the high number of evictions (the figures were always disputed). Benjamin Gardner, the Labour MP proposed a Bill to replace Chamberlain's Rent Restriction Act, but despite support from Wheatley (although this was not overwhelming) the Bill failed among much confusion. The Labour government did agree to a Prevention of Evictions Bill put up by Simon, which mainly stiffened those terms that applied to landlords seeking repossession for their own re-occupation. One issue here was the uncertainty around whether the Government would have done more on evictions if they had a working majority.

"Thus the great success of the Housing Bill was somewhat offset by the dismal failure over evictions. In housing, with a big, national problem to solve, and the energies of capable men devoted to its solution, there was a bold and ingenious departure, both from the efforts of previous governments and from the clichés of previous Labour Party housing doctrine." (Lyman, p.128/9)

One aspect of this was that while in opposition the Party

could be very anti-landlord, but in office they had to deal with the realities they encountered in terms of actually legislating - not, of course, an unfamiliar problem for social democratic governments.

Wheatley was acutely aware of the limitations of his role in 1924, and essentially did what he believed was possible. Most observers of the 'housing problem' in the late-nineteenth and early-twentieth centuries have seen it as *the* intractable problem. There was growing awareness of the scale of the 'problem', a general agreement in Parliament and among philanthropists and charities, plus some regional working class agitation. Chapman reflects on the situation around 1900:

"Reformers, philanthropists, and local-authority officials struggled to set and maintain adequate standards of sanitation and ventilation, and to provide accommodation at rents which working-class families could regularly afford."
(Chapman, 1971 p.11.)

Chapman sets this list of difficulties against the insecurity caused by the chaotic nature of the ever-changing industrial capitalism. Following Chapman, Morris and Rodger in 1993 argued that regional variety in freehold and leasehold arrangements made a 'national' policy problematic. They identify four reasons why builders (especially private sector ones) had problems in the late-nineteenth century:

❑ Increasing attention being drawn to the quality of housing for the working class, not the least of reasons being the rhetoric of political interventions. As Pevsner among others have pointed out, this in turn is contextualised by the sharp increase in academic theorising on housing need and provision;

❑   The sheer size of the building industry, approximately 10% of the workforce and 30% of gross fixed capital formation. With the ebbs and flows in the industry, demand and supply was volatile;

❑   The existence of a differentiated skilled and unskilled workforce caused tensions in trade union circles. This was to be one of key issue that Wheatley had to deal with as soon as possible;

❑   Builders were invariably seen as the culprits for reproducing slum conditions, which often stood in the way of seeing them as a solution rather part of the problem. (Morris and Rodger, 1993).

There was, therefore, a growing sense of need, a view that a national strategy was needed, with someone in Government to coordinate all this.

I am sure that Wheatley often reflected on the effect of his legislation on the situation in the country, the background to which can be understood to a certain extent by reference to the coverage in the London *Times* between early-1923 and December 1924. The issues raised in the pages of *The Times'* leaders, articles and letters, can be summed up as follows:

❑   The inadequate supply of houses to be rented at a reasonable and affordable level to both middle and working class families;

❑   Control of rents was a key. The Onslow Committee recommended de-control, but even Chamberlain and his colleagues realised the acute shortage of houses in a free market would only ensure rents rising even more;

❑ There was general dissatisfaction that the Conservatives' policy on both issues was unclear; people did not know where they stood on these matters. Chamberlain claimed that his 1923 Act could deliver 100,000 houses, while most other informed people, like E.D. Simon, argued that given the shortage of labour and materials, that 40,000 might be an achievable figure;

❑ The pages of *The Times* also reflect that given the on-going shortage of labour, materials and houses that there would be people seeking to gain profit from the situation. This was considered to be unacceptable given the crisis in housing provision;

❑ There is a consensus in the pages that subsidies from the government are essential, otherwise the increased costs of building and subsidising rents will fall on rate payers in each local authority. This was seen as a major issue for Wheatley;

❑ In this respect, there was a good deal in *The Times* on the need for housing policy to transcend party politics, and clearly there was a measure of agreement on this at Westminster. However, a key sticking point was acknowledged: that the Labour party sought to increase public sector housing, while the Conservatives looked for the main growth in the private sector - building and renting;

❑ There were also ardent voices from the Garden City movement that government should keep out of the process of housing provision, except to give encouragement to mutually-based funding organizations, like building societies, to raise and provide the necessary investment;

❑ There was general agreement that one of Wheatley's tasks was to encourage the growth of apprenticeships. The building workers argued that this could only be done if Wheatley guaranteed his fifteen-year programme to ensure availability of work to absorb the increase in the workforce. Skilled workers, in particular, were concerned lest their status be undermined by an influx of apprentices and unskilled workers. There were six key trades that are regularly discussed: bricklayers, carpenters, slaters, plasterers, masons and plumbers. Note the absence of electricians. There were also comments that the shortage of apprentices was because employers were not prepared to take them on; and, finally:

❑ There was general agreement in the pages of *The Times* that advances were urgently needed in new materials and building techniques. In this respect, it is instructive to consider the keen interest and action by Addison, Wheatley and Chamberlain.

As I have indicated above, the pages of *The Times* reflect the contemporary view that there was a certain pluralism at work, and the general notion of an 'English Pluralism' needs consideration. Peter Lassman in his essay of that title cites Harold Laski, G.D.H.Cole, and later Maitland among those arguing for a view of a group-based political pluralism that reflects the ideas of the German Sociologist Max Weber (writing in the early twentieth century).

Weber argued that a Marxist-style class conflict creating the force for social change was not relevant set alongside the tendency for people to pursue their own interests as individuals by joining in association with other people with similar concerns at a particular time. The notion of 'influential groups' holding sway in politics is a popular one in the 1920s, and many activists and reformers identified the State apparatus as just such a 'group' essentially based on a pluralist approach to change. These trends certainly led many late-twentieth century sociologists to focus on the central issue of 'urban managerialism', *i.e.*, the ways in which access to different forms of housing tenure were managed in a particular locality.

This is an approach influenced by Max Weber as manifested in the 1918-1930 period, and is essentially concerned with the way in which expectations of access to housing were massaged in general, and by the State apparatus and political class at the time. The Whig influence is strong here, and it is possible to see views of the role of the senior civil service in this light. Parliament as the best club in England?

However, and as I have discussed in my chapter on the Arts & Crafts movement, any focus on the management of the 'city' and of housing in the 1920s and 1930s cannot ignore the growing influence of the Soviet Union.

There were significant shifts in the nature of industry and employment in early-twentieth century in Britain. There was increasing reliance on large-scale manufacturing, and patterns of dominant single-location employment. The era of the small-scale, environmentally-integrated, locality-based employment was in decline. The small workshop under the railway arch was disappearing to be replaced by a dependence on large-scale industrial organizations.

In view of the volatile nature of capitalism, once these larger scale sources of employment and income failed, the impact on people and the fabric of the locality was profound. Eventually, and certainly by the end of my period of particular interest (1918-1930), the costs of industrial change were both significant and long lasting. It is not surprising therefore that many people in Britain, and certainly significant sections of the intelligentsia, looked increasingly to the Soviet Union as the alternative, a rational model to replace the chaos of industrial capitalism. This was particularly so in the 1930s.

At the opening of the twentieth century around nine out of ten households lived in private rented accommodation. And as I have said elsewhere this was certainly true even for a small percentage of the upper middle class, who would lease a house for long periods of time. For most middle class people, and almost all of the working class, tenure was dominated by the role of a rentier class. It should be remembered that it had been legally possible to build council houses since 1851, and this does link with the role of charities and the like, invariably working on the basis of enlightened self-interest. In the years after 1918, the situation began to change in significant ways, and we can see that the three key pieces of legislation - the 1919, 1923 and 1924 Acts - that I focus on, played a major role in transforming attitudes, expectations, and the pattern of access to tenure. Far more households were either owner- occupiers or council tenants as a consequence of the legislation. By 1945 26 per cent of households in Britain were in owner-occupation, and 12 per cent in council tenancies. By the time of the 1981 census, owner-occupation was at 54 per cent and council tenancy at 34 per cent, the latter being the high watermark.

The gradual, but significant, increase in the size of the local authority role in housing provision after 1918 inevitably brought with it questions about the management of this resource. The Labour Party became an increasingly influential political group nationally and locally. Labour councillors became the guardians, managers and gatekeepers of an expanding resource, but it is quite clear that with a few exceptions that this was not based on a Socialist programme. Like so much else to do with the role of the Labour Party the ideology was essentially a slightly modified version of the traditional 'top-down' political management of a property-less class of people seeking access to a scarce resource. It should be added that people were increasingly defined by their access to owner-occupation on which was placed an increasingly higher status within an individualistic and consumerist culture.

Sociologists discuss the shift from an ascribed status, the one that class and locality say, gives us, to an achieved status where access to high-value status objects allow change. People in general were classified by their consumption of high-status goods, like housing, rather than desire to develop and foster the utopian Arts & Crafts model of the characteristics of *the person* defining what they owned. The access of the working class to adequate or hopefully good quality housing after 1918 continued to be determined by their position in the economic, political and cultural marketplace.

Once local authorities became major players in housing provision and management, and once changing sources of finance for potential owner-occupiers developed, the focus of attention shifted. The diversity of the privately rented sector, with examples of good and bad provision, was gradually replaced by increasingly centralised means of access to housing. The democratic, and even utopian, aspirations of Howard, Unwin and their contemporaries, were soon replaced by new(er) forms of top-down control over access to housing.

Howard and his Garden City peers mistrusted the State nationally or locally, and we know that many of the enthusiasms for public sector housing and finance for owner-occupation routes to access that grew in popularity after 1918 have increasingly become 'problems'. According to Ward (2004) the concept of public interest was:

"…important legal abstraction resting on a notion of the whole community and supposedly transcending the narrow interests of powerful individuals or social classes." (p.13.)

However, Ward argues that for the town planners of the early twentieth century this was a vague and imprecise criterion for decision-making. One key issue that I have raised before is that there was a 'conservative' view that the high, or even lavish, standards of post-1919 council housing was a problem. The 'high' cost of building (for the A3 house, the standard non-parlour dwelling cost on average £320 in 1934 creating a rent of 11s 8d) got in the way of building more. Lower standards, it was argued, would mean more houses at affordable rents!

SO, HERE we are in the early twenty first century and housing tenure has turned almost full circle. The privately rented sector, alongside a major growth in the voluntary/charitable sector, is a significant provider again. However, culturally this is a 'problem' because the ideal model is for everyone is to be an owner-occupier. Is this still in the public interest?

In Stephen Ward's book *Planning and Urban Change* (2004), there is a 1930s advert for the London-based Planet Building Society, which depicts a long bridge linking a crowded, grey set of back-to-back streets with a bright sunny setting for a bungalow in a wide avenue.

The wording on the poster is "Bridging the gap between tenancy and ownership".

IN DISCUSSING Addison, Chamberlain and Wheatley, and their associates, I have charted the foreground discourse on access to housing, but there were profound changes taking place in society that were much less obvious. One contemporary of this triumvirate was Richard Reiss, chairman of the Garden Cities and Town Planning Association. Following his very successful publication *The Home I Want*, Reiss published *The New Housing Handbook* in 1924, which was indeed a very useful *handbook,* and one that would have been read by a very wide range of people. In his Preface, Reiss writes that Chamberlain has just taken over from Wheatley, and he hopes that the former will attempt to operate the two acts alongside one another (as was Wheatley's stated aim). Reiss certainly hoped that Chamberlain would carry on Wheatley's work with the Building Trade Committee, and look to the recommendations of the Moir Committee on new technologies.

Reiss' book is full of valuable summaries that contemporary readers would have found helpful. For example, he states early on that there are four key issues: the chronic shortage of houses only made worse by the war effort; many houses unfit for human habitation; slum areas to be cleared and the need for planning the future to avoid more chaos. In his chapter on 'The Planning of the House' he suggests the following essentials:

- ❑ Appearance and amenity
- ❑ Health
- ❑ Convenience and comfort and
- ❑ Economy.

In a very Unwin-like way, he argues that there is no value in, or necessity for, skimping on houses or street layout planning. Build to high standards with aesthetic and healthy living criteria to hand and the benefits will be long term. Like Unwin, he suggests that Local Authorities need guidance and advice, not design straightjackets. In other words, locality 'horses for courses'. For instance, on kitchens he says that in Yorkshire housewives bake their own bread, and this should be a design consideration. Finally, for now I would add that Reiss also expresses an interesting view on the rent restriction act of 1915. He is clearly aware of the political turbulence caused by rent increases; for example, in the period that led to 'Red Clydeside' and beyond.

Reiss does not say much about Addison, or the Liberals, but he is clearly aware of the schisms, and as I have said elsewhere the Liberals were the most divided party at Westminster with regard to Housing.

In his book on Lloyd George and Churchill, Richard Toye emphasizes the precarious position of Addison at this time:

"In July 1921 Christopher Addison resigned his position as Minister Without Portfolio, in protest at cutbacks in the housing programme he had inaugurated when Minister of Health. [Lloyd George had moved Addison from the latter position in the spring, in reaction to Conservative 'anti-waste' sentiment, after the cost of the programme had spiralled. This showed how little scruples Lloyd George had about abandoning an ally who had ceased to be useful to him.]...The resignation - although it marked the death of radicalism in the coalition's social policy - proved a nine day wonder." (Toye, 2007 p.225.)

There were, however, other key figures, and one interesting perspective on Wheatley's task and the Labour-Conservative rivalry with regard to housing policy comes from the Liberal (Sir) Ernest D. Simon in his book of 1933 *The Anti-slum Campaign*. Simon was a reformer firmly focused on what he saw as the evil of the slums, and with others like Beveridge, another leading Liberal who spent many years writing about and campaigning inside Parliament and outside for better and adequate housing. Beveridge was to stay very close to this view when in writing his famous 1942 report of national insurance (widely regarded as the blueprint for the post-1945 'Welfare State'), he referred to the five evils that were to be the national challenge after the war had ended. One of these was squalor, a direct reference to the state of housing for the working classes. He also deliberately linked the housing need with the other evils of disease, want, idleness and ignorance.

Simon begins his argument thus:

"Our post-war housing effort has been marked by great achievement and by great failure. The achievement is the building of nearly two million houses, many of them for the working classes, which have set a completely new and very much better standard of housing than has ever been known in this country; a standard we all know, of a decent house standing in a garden, with adequate accommodation and everything that is nowadays considered necessary for civilised life. The great failure is that in spite of this effort the slums are no better today than they were at the end of the war; in fact, they are fifteen years older and have seriously deteriorated. We have a right to be proud of our national achievement. We have a plain duty to be ashamed of our failure, and to leave no stone unturned to put an end to the disgrace of our slums.' (p.3.)

He goes on to say:

"In spite of great national effort in building two million houses in the fourteen post-war years the census (1931) shows us that we are farther away to-day from our aim of one house per family than we were at the end of the war." (p.8.)

By the late 1920s, it was felt that attention needed to shift from the 'general needs' of the increasingly better-off and reasonably well-housed upper working class family to the 'special needs' of those poorest trapped in the slums. The enduring 'problem' of the slums was also refocused on the sanitary dwellings issues of the late-nineteenth century. John Burnett in his book *A Social History of Housing* (1850-1970) argues that the range of problems in 1914 were exacerbated by the war, and that this set of realities were added to by the political commitment to 'Homes for Heroes'.

In April 1919, even the King had his say about the need to take action, citing all the ills that could come from inadequate housing, including unrest, and setting this against the social stability that could be achieved. The Tudor Walters Report was of course to put flesh on all these bones.

Simon adds that, since 1918, there has been increasing pressure, including from the working classes, for more and better housing. He adds that the Coalition government had done a 'revolutionary' thing in requiring local authorities to provide for all working class housing needs that were covered by some other agency. This view is echoed by Kenneth Morgan in his book *Consensus and Disunity* (1979), where he argues: "By the end of the Summer (1918) Addison's ministry had sketched out a totally new social agenda, a socialism for consumers if not yet for producers." (p.24.) This was, of course, while Addison was in charge of the Local Government Board a year before the Ministry of Health was created with the intention (certainly by Addison) of following through on the 1918 agenda embracing among many other issues universal unemployment insurance and the creation of the Whitley Council. The hand of Beveridge was on many of these policy developments. Fisher's 1918 Education Act was closely aligned to these health and housing measures. Morgan also repeats the oft-quoted account of both

Addison's enthusiasm to progress along this social agenda road, and that this did not please all of his parliamentary colleagues, some of whom saw him as a dangerous 'lefty'. Addison was to become increasingly frustrated by the lack of progress.

Barbara Linsley, writing on 'Homes for Heroes', discusses Addison's Act:

"The Act brought about two radical changes. An option to build became an obligation; local authorities were expected to provide for all working-class needs in their district, where they were not met by other means. Secondly, the principle of State subsidy for housing was enshrined in law. The sudden increase in the number and scale of housing schemes by local authorities proved that financial responsibility had been the stumbling block in the past...Additional legislation was needed to make 'homes for heroes' a reality. The Acquisition of Land Act was passed in August 1919 to facilitate and cheapen compulsory land purchase for housing and the Housing (Additional Powers) Act in December 1919 offered grants to private builders prepared to erect houses of the same standard as those by local authorities...The Government's Manual on the Preparation of State-Aided Housing Schemes, published in 1919, stated that new public housing should mark an advance on the building and development which has ordinarily been regarded as sufficient in the past. The 500,000 it pledged to build were modelled on those of the Garden City Movement."

(Linsley in Harwood and Powers, 2008 p.16/17.)

A large part of Simon's book is reflected in these comments by Linsley, and is an indictment of government in general for not doing more, and doing so consistently. He regularly emphasises that all governments, certainly all the ministers of health after 1919, argue that more must be done, that the situation of grossly inadequate housing for many members of the working class, especially the poorest, is unacceptable. However, that is where the unanimity ends. For example, he says that Labour is in favour of State subsidies in general, and to local authorities in particular. This is seen as an absolute point of principle, and a key policy to provide good quality housing in a good environment at affordable rents. The Conservatives are, according to Simon, principally opposed to subsidies except in extreme conditions; for example, by Chamberlain's intervention in 1923.

The Conservatives argue that subsidies increase costs, and also create unfair competition by giving local authorities advantages over the private sector. The Labour party denies this, and points to the unacceptable exploitation by manufactures and suppliers in periods of a growth in building. Simon also argues that 'public opinion' has clearly shown that something should be done, and quickly; it is, therefore, up to the democratically elected government of the day to take action and do something. Simon was well aware of the post-1924 'new conservatism', where reflection on events in Europe since 1917 had convinced many Conservatives that policy should concern itself with explicit opposition to socialism, or - even more of a threat - bolshevism.

Chamberlain certainly played his part in this 'new conservatism' from his position on the centre-left of his Party. Indeed, Morgan also comments on the concerns with unrest and refers to the Commission on Industrial Unrest in 1917, which stressed:

"The effect of inadequate or slum housing and the high rents in generating discontent in mining and other communities. The Housing Advisory Panel under Lord Salisbury the same year had made some surprisingly radical proposals, including a

national campaign for building 300,000 houses, with the State
assisting local authorities with the finance by making up the
difference between the valuation and the actual cost of houses."
(Morgan, p.89.)

Simon also makes reference to the importance of the
development of new, and often cheaper, methods of housing
construction. Addison, Chamberlain, and Wheatley were all
focused on this issue, and in their various ways contributed to
research initiatives. Chamberlain was central to these
developments; for example, his role in the expansion of the
Building Research Station from 1925. It should be noted,
however, that Chamberlain was very keen to hand a key role in
development of new building techniques to his Tory associates;
for instance, Lord Weir, the head of a major Glasgow-based
manufacturer. Weir was notoriously anti-union, and one feature
of Chamberlain's plans was for Weir and others to produce
systems building that would by-pass skilled, and effectively
unionised, building workers. (Swenarton, 2007.)

Simon is generally complimentary about Wheatley, arguing
that the latter's success in bringing together all sides of the
building industry, working *with* the local authorities, addressing
the key issue of building materials, and providing the
'guarantee' of a fifteen-year building programme was a major
step forward.

Simon is also good at identifying glaring anomalies in the
on-going legislation. For example, that charities, the voluntary
sector as he calls them, were able to house larger families of an
average 6.5 children, whereas the local authority average was
4.5. He argues that the charities were able to do this because
their investment was focused in a much more specific and small-
scale manner. He also reflects on the contradiction of 'giving'
rent subsidies *via* local authorities to better-off, working class

families, who could afford the rent, while the worst-off families pay non-subsidised rents in the private sector, and higher rates to pay for the families on subsidies. It was only in 1932 that falling prices *etcetera* made it possible for the provisions of the 'Wheatley Act' to actually reach the lower paid workers. Because the Conservative cutbacks of 1924-7, the 'Wheatley Act' had disappointed many by not reaching more working class families as intended. This brings him to discuss the role of Arthur Greenwood, the Labour minister of health from 1929, and his legislative intervention in 1930. Simon is puzzled by Greenwood's attitude towards housing, citing, yet again, a rhetoric on needs, while being very muted and conservative in his actions. Simon suggests that the 'conservatism' of the ministry might itself be a factor.

"The main object of the Act was to accelerate and cheapen the clearance of slum areas. Under previous Acts, the Local Authority had been forced to purchase the site. Certain amendments were made under the Act which would, it was hoped, make the whole procedure of slum clearance easier and quicker to carry through." (p.36.)

At the time of writing his book (1933), Simon adds that it is difficult to be conclusive about the impact of Greenwood's intervention. Simon was a member of the committee set up by Greenwood to advise on rent restriction, which reported in 1931, with very little impact. Simon emphasises one significant issue, that is, the population increase of England and Wales by two million in the ten years to 1933, with inevitably an increase in working class families needing a house.

Greenwood's Act was not actually implemented until 1933, when it was incorporated into other housing measures. The economic crisis of 1931 had stalled progress, and one of the problems with Greenwood's legislation was its lack of clarity over what exactly was a 'slum'?

There was also a widely held view that as the lower middle and upper working class were housed in improved conditions in the public or private sector, so more accommodation would become available for the lower working class. However, many 'slum' dwellers were very reluctant to give up their tenancies, with controlled rents, to start out on a 'better', but more expensive, path. Plus, would they have the same self-help social bonds that they already experienced? (Burnett, 1978.)

Addressing the clearance of slum housing gave local authorities several difficulties. In Bristol, for example, the city council reflected on this:

"The immediate problem in 1919 was to increase the number of houses. At the same time, building costs were inflated by the high rate of interest and the scarcity of materials and labour; it was impossible to provide houses at prices within the reach of those who required them. The situation was met for the first time by a national grant for housing subsidies made available both to local authorities and to private builders, to enable houses to be let or sold at less than the economic rent or price." (Jevons and Madge, 1946)

The authors of this Bristol report also comment on social problems created by moving 'inner city' slum dwellers, with larger than average families, to out-lying estates. Jevons and Madge acknowledge that in building 15,000 houses, providing vastly improved conditions for tenants, Bristol Corporation had achieved a great deal, but the 'isolation' of families meant that the formation of cohesive communities was difficult to achieve. The authors suggest that given their previous inner city location, and their poverty, made them heavily dependent on social networks for their day-to-day subsistence and survival. This problem was not unique to Bristol, of course, and the many studies of London estate development, along with other metropolitan areas, emphasizes the widespread issues associated with relocation. Jevons and Madge also comment on the tensions that existed between some of the more "respectable tenants and the influx of ex-slum dwellers". (See Young and Willmot.) The new estates in Bristol were certainly garden suburb-style and incorporated all of the contemporary density standards of the 1924 Act, which by definition made large estates even larger.

With regard to the impact of the State over this period, it is also worth mentioning Simon's reaction to the intervention of the national government from 1931. The new Minister of Health was Hilton Young, who introduced a new housing bill at the end of 1932. Simon comments that Hilton Young, like most of his predecessors, was keen to comment on the dire state of housing provision for the working classes, and the need to move people from slum conditions. However, the main impact of the interventions witnessed by Simon between 1931 and 1933 was to slow down the house-building programme even more. The Government had reduced interest rates from 5 to 3.5 per cent, which certainly raised the possibility of the 7/6-rent house. However, Hilton Young played down the role of the public sector and argued that the best option was to encourage the private sector to build more houses for sale and for rent.

"The Hilton Young Act marks a complete change in national policy. Ever since the war, the main energy of Government after Government had been devoted to building new houses to meet the shortage. The Greenwood Act had simply prepared the way for slum clearance to be pushed vigorously when the time came in any district that there was an adequate supply of houses.

Successive Governments had realised that the important thing was a large supply of cheap houses. The National Government had fully appreciated that up to the time of the introduction of the Hilton Young Bill…yet his sole effective action was to repeal the Wheatley Act and so prevent the building of cheap houses to let." (p.56.)

By May of 1933, Hilton Young was actually preventing local authorities from building, even without a subsidy.

Nothing was to happen in house building policy until Bevan's Act in 1948, seen as an essential cornerstone of the 'Welfare State', and part of the response to Beveridge's 'five evils'.

There are two further sources to cite on social context and welfare after 1918 before moving on to discuss John Wheatley in more detail.

First, in his 1921 book *England After War: A Study* Charles Masterman provides a long list of 'issues' in his chapter 'The Aftermath of War'. He cites problems at home and abroad, including in Ireland, all a cause of national concern:

"But the theatres and cinemas are crowded, and the wealthy are occupied in schemes for saving or increasing their riches, and each ex-Service man (the "hero" of three years' ago) is terrified by the advancing cloud of unemployment, or involved in its cold mists, or making frantic efforts to escape from them. Politics have become more bitter and more corrupt. The struggle between Capital and Labour has become more fierce and uncompromising. The efforts of the Churches have become more futile and dim. The elaboration of moral effort outside the Churches has become a voice crying in the wilderness. The newspapers are filled with record of the struggle of one class against another class." (p.13.) This is definitely a 'glass half-empty' view of post-1918 life, and as I say elsewhere, not uncommon among the political classes, and the complete opposite to the optimism and enthusiasm being shown by those pursuing housing and planning reform.

Second, it is necessary to remind myself of the view held by some then and since that in the 1920s and after, that housing provision as welfare was a deliberate strategy by the ruling classes to contain working class frustration and anger. However, if this was entirely the case why did successive governments fail to take appropriate action?

There are also Marxist-influenced ideas that housing policy exists as an attempt by a far from neutral State to stabilise class relations and help the business class by providing a healthier, orderly and accessible labour force. Estates being built close to an emerging industrial plant is an obvious example. The legislative intervention of Wheatley, and even to a certain extent Addison and Chamberlain, was a de-commodification of housing, *i.e.* taking the provision of this essential social service out of the unpredictable marketplace. Of course Chamberlain, like all successive Conservative ministers responsible for housing, sought to shift the balance of provision back towards commodification, the province of the private sector. (See Dickens *et al*, 1985).

10. John Wheatley: his 1924 Housing
Act was the only major achievement of the
Labour Government that year.

John Wheatley

LET ME now turn to providing more detail about the life and times of the man himself: John Wheatley.

He was the first of many children born in 1869 to a family of desperately poor Catholic migrants from Ireland to Glasgow. One family among many. The early part of his life was spent in very overcrowded and insanitary housing, and after leaving school he followed his father down the pit. However, he soon moved on to run a pub, and then work for a Glasgow newspaper, before going into publishing with a friend.

I mention this background briefly because it allows us a window onto Wheatley's direct experience of the hard life endured by the majority of working class people. His experience and growing sense of injustice took him into Irish nationalist politics, and after building a reputation for himself as an effective agitator and organiser, often upsetting the local priests, he moved towards socialism. I should add that an important aspect of life in 'Edwardian' Britain was the very divisive issue of religious education in schools, and in general the responsibility for running schools. The State had ignored calls for a secular schooling and education system, and then had to live with the tiresome consequences. (See Murphy, 1971.)

Wheatley was instrumental in setting up the Catholic Socialist Society. This activity forced him into many debates; for example, with Jesuits, about the tensions between the two ideologies. Possibly these experiences helped to hone Wheatley's political skills? It has to be remembered that until the advent of The Independent Labour Party (ILP) in 1893, the most progressive voice for Home Rule for Ireland of any size and influence was the Liberal Party. The years of Gladstone had kept the Irish question to the fore, but by the time Wheatley began his career in left wing politics the Liberal support had begun to wane. Increasingly, questions were asked in Glasgow as elsewhere, about the continued commitment of Liberal politicians for Home Rule.

By the first decade of the twentieth century, Wheatley had moved closer to Labour politics, and become a council member. His campaigning zeal, and skill, led him in to the £8-cottage movement, and from there to the famous Glasgow rent strike of 1914.

The £8-cottage movement was a direct response to the 1890 Housing Act, and gave Glasgow Corporation power to erect workers' dwellings. Glasgow at the turn of the century had the commonplace very high TB figures, and this public health and housing issue was another key factor in Wheatley's political education. The Corporation was incompetent, and even indifferent, as far as housing provision was concerned, and the £8-cottage movement brought before a Tory-dominated council proposals to provide cheap housing for the working class.

Sean Damer, in his essay on 'State, Class and Housing: Glasgow 1885-1919' (in Melling, 1980) looks at the situation in Glasgow from an on-going class struggle viewpoint. He highlights a constant war of attrition between council officials and tenants, and the regular disregard that the politically powerful had for working class people. For example, one senior academic in Glasgow argued that most tenants were no better than rats! An important point that Damer makes is to see these constant struggles in Glasgow contributing to the demand for, and achievement of, legislative changes over the period he highlights. We all know that social policy comes out of the tensions that exist between the majority of people's needs, and powerful provider's inclination, or not, to meet those needs. The proposals, and passage of legislation required, to deal with provisions like housing and health care are part and parcel of a dialectical relationship where many opposing and competing influences and forces meet. The outcomes can often be a progressive phase where 'on the ground' service providers are enabled to meet needs. Wheatley's Housing Act of 1924 was one such event.

Wheatley was in the thick of debates about many schemes in the offing (as well as his own). After votes and manoeuvrings it was Wheatley's proposals that prevailed. By 1912 the Glasgow Labour Housing Committee had been created, which brought Wheatley even more to the forefront of Labour politics. The war years served to strengthen Wheatley's grasp of local labour politics, and were indicative of his concern to always maintain a strong local power base. Damer makes the point that Glasgow housing struggles are axiomatic with an understanding of legislation nationally. Neither is it an accident that in all these events the Labour leadership in Glasgow was so clear minded in their socialist values, and so able and successful in their organising skills.

Wheatley was clearly among this group of very prominent activists; and, given his increasing importance in the local Labour movement, his candidature for Shettleston in Glasgow for the 1918 general election was to be expected. During the campaign, he argued with the Marxists, yet he was himself accused of being Marxist by other parts of the political spectrum, and the local inevitably right wing press. Wheatley was clearly disappointed that he could not defeat the national coalition candidate. One of the key issues at this time was the consequences following the extension of the franchise to embrace all males over the age of 21, and for women over 30. Nationally, the Labour Party returned fifty-nine members to the new post-war Parliament, and saw Wheatley and his ILP comrades building their local base.

I have already said something of Wheatley's engagement

with the ILP in Glasgow, and it is worth emphasising that the decision to enter government was a difficult step for almost all ILP MPs. Not only was there criticism from the Communist Party for the road Wheatley and some of his associates took, there was also objections raised from within the ILP. Maxton, who was always personally close to Wheatley, was one ILP MP who argued that the compromises that Labour were making while in government weakened their commitment to Socialist policy and practice. As I say elsewhere, there were many MPs, ILP-ers or not, who distrusted MacDonald, despite the role of the Clydesiders in the election of MacDonald as leader in 1922. The ILP was a very strong force within the Labour Party, particularly so in Scotland. Eventually in 1932 Maxton was to lead the ILP out of the Labour Party, leaving the struggle for a Socialist/Marxist perspective extremely thin on the ground. (See Dowse, 1966.)

THE ADDISON Housing Act was passed in June of 1919, and while the legislation broke new ground by offering subsidies to local authorities the building targets were low, and in Wheatley's view totally inadequate to deal with the chronic situation in Glasgow. There was plenty of discussion in the country about the shortage of resources both human and material for construction, and eventually the government decided to direct the subsidies on offer to private builders rather than local authorities, while warning of increases in rents. Leading up to the general election of 1922, reports like that of Salisbury (on rents), and Geddes (on cutting expenditure and selling council houses), only exacerbated political tensions in Glasgow as elsewhere. The election proved a great success for the ILP in Glasgow, taking ten of the eleven seats, including one by Wheatley, the culmination of ten years of hard political work.

In their post-election declaration the victorious candidates concluded by saying that:

"In all things we will abjure vanity and self-aggrandisement, recognising that we are the humble servants of the people and that our only righteous purpose is to promote the welfare of our fellow citizens and the well-being of all mankind."

This stirring commitment is quoted by John Hannan is his excellent and very comprehensive *The Life of John Wheatley* (1988), and I would strongly recommend the interested reader to consult this biography.

According to Hannan, the new MPs were seen off on the train to London with great rallying enthusiasm, and Wheatley was to comment some years later that this election showed that advocating socialist policies did attract voters, rather than frighten them off. This was increasingly a key issue in Labour politics as overtures were made to former Liberal voters, and the like. The Labour leadership argued that these 'floaters' would recoil from full-blooded socialist policies. Does this have a familiar ring?

Despite the reservations of Wheatley, and other members of the Parliamentary Labour Party, Ramsay MacDonald was elected as leader. How prophetic were those reservations to be given MacDonald's later political trajectory. Wheatley's maiden speech in Parliament, on housing need, was well received, and made him much more prominent in the Labour Party generally. However, the patience of Wheatley and his Scottish comrades was sorely stretched by the reality of parliamentary politics, which eventually led to four of them being suspended for a period of time. But, once again, the working class of Glasgow backed their MPs, and it is not too difficult to understand that there were calls for Home Rule for Scotland!

Political upheavals inevitably led to another general election in which the Labour Party increased its number of seats in a hung Parliament. There was talk of coalition, which was vehemently opposed by Wheatley and others, arguing that this would inevitably lead to the watering-down of policies. So, at the very end of 1923, MacDonald was summoned by the King and asked to form a government.

It seems clear that MacDonald, who was already pursuing more links with prominent Liberals, had reservations about bringing the likes of John Wheatley into government, but he did so by asking him to become Minister of Health (MOH). Even *The Times* had to admit that although a bit of a surprise choice Wheatley was very experienced, and well informed.

It is worth considering a contemporary account of the 1924 events, as given by the prominent Liberal, E.D. Simon, in his book *The Anti-slum Campaign* (1933). In his account of those turbulent years, Simon discusses both the 1923 Chamberlain Act and the Wheatley Act. According to Simon there were three key aspects to the Tories 1923 legislation:

- A fixed subsidy of £75 per house of a specified size, and built by private enterprise. (The house my parents bought in Bitterne, Southampton, was probably just such a development.);
- A grant for slum clearance schemes equivalent to half the loss incurred by the local authority; and
- A subsidy to local authorities for building houses to let.

The difference between Addison's Act (1919) and the 1923 Act was that the government paid a fixed sum for each house, and the local authority paid the rest. Simon argues that the only significant effect of the 1923 Act was the subsidy paid to private developers.

The subsidies to local authorities to build were greater in the 1924 Act. Simon makes the same point as does Hannan that one of Wheatley's great achievements was to reach agreement across the industry; for example, to deal with the chronic shortage of skilled labour. Wheatley spent a good deal of time negotiating with trade union representatives, and other supply-side organizations. Hannan does suggest in his biography that Wheatley could be seen as somewhat naïve in his assumption that all trade unionists would swing behind the national house-building goals without reservation, or without using the situation for the direct benefit of their members. He also put considerable effort into bringing his housing legislation proposals before cabinet and Parliament. However, even at the early stages of his brief ministerial career, he could sense the lack of commitment in Ramsay MacDonald, and the suspicion that MacDonald had of those on the left of the Parliamentary Labour Party.

Wheatley also considered the rent of houses under the 1923 Act to be higher than most lower paid workers could afford. This is a point made in the Southampton Borough Engineers' book on their housing programme. Wheatley effectively doubled the subsidy to local authorities, and hoped that this would ensure rents ranging from 9/- to 15/- for lower paid workers. Rents in Southampton in 1929 ranged from 9/- to 11/- for parlour houses, and 7/- to 7/9 for non-parlour houses.

E. D. Simon argues that the 1924 Act put 'great pressure' on local authorities to build, and the hope was that 225,000 houses for rent would be constructed. The cumulative effect of the '23 and '24 Acts was a greater than the expected increase in the supply of labour: 40,000 a year to a total of 775,000 in 1927. The number of houses built in 1927 was 273,000. In all, the two acts gave employment to an extra 200,000 men by 1927. However, this stopped dramatically in late-1927 when the Tories (Chamberlain again) cut the public sector building programme by around 100,000 houses a year. Simon suggests that the boom years, 1923-7 created price increases, with the majority of the increased income going to the building industry. Following the cutbacks, prices fell again to their 1923 levels. On rents, the effect of the Wheatley subsidy in 1929 was 4/2d per week.

Simon argues that the two Acts over-stimulated the market, and so the house-building programme was too great. (Not something that most working class and homeless people would have agreed with!) Simon also reiterates that the Wheatley houses were still too expensive for lower paid workers:

"It was only at the very end of the life of the Act, in 1932 that owing to the fall in building costs, and the rate of interest, it became possible to build the 9/-rent house. And at that very moment in time, the Act was repealed by the Conservative government as being no longer necessary." (Simon p.25-6.)

By the time he was out of office, Wheatley had made a considerable contribution to improving the housing situation for many working class families throughout Britain. Long after he was a minister, the influence and effects of what was most certainly *his* act were evident. His personal reputation was also enhanced:

"Praise for Wheatley's parliamentary performance came from every side. Rayner, a Liberal, who claimed thirty years experience in the building industry as both worker and employer, was wholesome in his praise of Wheatley.
Perhaps the greatest tribute came from a bitter adversary Joynson Hicks: 'No matter whether one agrees with him or not, Wheatley is a great man, a great Parliamentarian'" (Hannan, p.134.)

After nine hectic months in office, the General Election saw the Tories elected, with Labour losing forty seats, and the Liberals being decimated. Wheatley secured his seat, but with a reduced majority of 630.

For the record, it is worth emphasising that Wheatley remained on the Labour backbenches and continued to work with his associates for socialist policies. He made his final intervention in Parliament in April 1930, but his health deteriorated, and he collapsed on his way to the ILP conference at Easter time; he seemed to rally, but collapsed again, and died at home in Glasgow on 12 May 1930.

"The failure of the housing market to provide adequate housing for the poorest households is an enduring feature of housing in Britain. The roots of this failure go back to the end of the nineteenth century when charitable and commercial interests – 'Philanthropy and Five Per Cent' - came together to provide housing for the respectable urban working class. The poorest urban families, and the rural poor, remained at the mercy of market forces." (Ineichen, 1983.)

Many writers on the housing situation in the early-twentieth century have seen the increased State intervention from 1916-17 as a response to the increasing unrest among large sections of the working class.

As I discuss elsewhere in this book, the rapid rise in class-consciousness, coupled with external events like the Russian Revolution in 1917, and in Germany and elsewhere in 1918-19, greatly concerned the ruling classes in Britain. Some systematic and strategic response was considered necessary to avoid greater unrest at home. 'Red Clydeside', major disturbances in London and elsewhere, raised once again the profile of reformers, and reform.

The deep dissatisfaction of ex-servicemen was a further factor for Lloyd George and Bonar Law to contend with.

As Ineichen says this situation hardly lacked exposure to public and political debate. One distinctive contribution to these debates on reform came from Richard Tawney.

Tawney, Beveridge & associates

In 1931, as the first occupants of Merry Oak were settling in, meeting their neighbours and discussing the new homes they were to make theirs, R.H.Tawney was publishing his book *Equality*. It is also worth recalling that this key moral and ethical document was published just eleven years before the Beveridge Report, which certainly reflected the issues about the perilous state of society raised by Tawney.

In his polemic against the iniquities of market-driven industrial capitalism, Tawney offers the reader extensive evidence on the plight of a large proportion of the working classes. He outlines the impact of multiple sources of disadvantage and deprivation, not least the ubiquitous issue of the inter-relationship between grossly inadequate housing and ill health, especially so among children. Discussing the extent of overcrowding, he says:

'...the 9,397 families in Bermondsey over 30 per cent of the total number – living in 1927 at the rate of two or more persons per room, or (those being) brought up in one of the one-apartment houses in the central division of Glasgow, 41 per cent of which contained in 1926 three or more persons per room...' (Tawney, p.126-7)

Tawney reminds his readers that since 1924 (Wheatley's Act) the State had been the main subsidiser of house building, but that even so many of the rents set by local authorities were still out of reach of the poorest, on incomes of less than £3 per week. Many local authorities, like Southampton, were very conscious of this situation (as I discuss below). The State's annual expenditure on housing had increased from £515,000 in

1920-1 to £14 million in 1930-1, a much bigger increase than for any other area of 'social services'.

Tawney and Beveridge knew each other very well from their Balliol and Toynbee Hall days. They both experienced the 'service to society' ethos that dominated life at Balliol College in Oxford at the end of the nineteenth and early-twentieth centuries. Toynbee Hall, founded as a centre for working class education in a wide sense, was opened in the east end of London in the 1880s; and, run by the Barnetts, epitomized the well meaning top-down, liberal, upper middle class do-gooding ethos of the time. This liberal and well educated section of the population believed that intervention aimed at the lives of working people was essential if the members of that class were to be 'saved' from a life of degradation, and thus directed towards 'the best in themselves'.

The service to society ethic had taken hold in part through the headmastership of Thomas Arnold at Rugby School a generation earlier. Thomas Arnold, father of Matthew Arnold, the influential cultural critic, along with the Oxford philosopher T.H. Green, had argued and worked for a set of values that emphasized that the newly wealthy and well-educated products of Victorian society should give something positive to that society. They should in fact seek to create a cohesive society where stability and social order were a paramount goal to avoid chaos and anarchy.

I should also add that Henrietta Barnett, along with Beatrice Webb, were active in the reform 'movement' at this time. They both drew inspiration from Octavia Hill, the housing activist and philanthropist, who epitomized the reformers of the day (and invariably women), and who believed that a 'hands-on' policy was needed: a 'getting close to the needy' set of values that marked a significant change in attitudes towards the poor, especially the 'deserving poor'. Barnett *et. al.* firmly believed that the degradation of the lower orders would continue while they were subjected to slum conditions, where they were in both physical *and* moral danger. (See Susan Pedersen and Peter Mandler *After the Victorians*, 1994). The Housing of the Working Classes Act of 1890 was significant here in enabling local authorities to provide dwellings for the poor. London County Council made conspicuous use of this Act, bringing in Arts & Crafts architectural values to estates: layout, external styling, and improved indoor facilities. The Fabians were keen advocates of this approach to housing need, an aspect of their growing policy formulation for welfare provision, and the gathering momentum for more wide-reaching reform developed at this time as expressed in their published policies. For example, Unwin was recruited to produce a Fabian Tract 'Cottage Plans and Common Sense' in 1902 (Tract no.109). Was his use of 'Common Sense', one wonders, an echo of Tom Paine?

In their editorial introduction to *Cities in Modern Britain* Camilla Lambert and David Weir comment on the rapid growth of cities: "So the early nineteenth century saw a massive and rapid accretion of population towards the centre of large cities, while the displacement of that population commenced almost as soon as the process was completed. By the end of the century, massive areas of working class housing could be found at some considerable distance from the centre of the city. The working class housing estate is not entirely a twentieth century phenomena." (Lambert and Weir, 1975 p.93.) Engels was the first writer to point out these phenomena in his 1840s account of Manchester. He, and then many others, understood the land-values issues behind the clearance of the working class from industrial city centres. This was also a pattern in other European cities; for example, in central Paris.

11. R. H. Tawney
(1880-1962): renowned
economic historian,
social critic and ethical
socialist, he was for
many years a close
associate of William
Beveridge (*below*) since

**12. William
Beveridge** (1879-
1963): economist
and social reformer,
he remains best
known for the
'Beveridge Report'
of 1942.

Courtesy: Imperial
War Museum.

However, we should remind ourselves that clearing working class people from older and smaller city centres was also common place in the twentieth century; for example, in Oxford in the 1950-60s. (John Mogey on Family and Neighbourhood, 1959.) Commercial and retail outlets began to replace people in city centres in the nineteenth century and expanded rapidly in the twentieth. The advent of metropolitan railways systems also made it easier to justify moving large numbers of inner city dwellers, both working and middle class, to 'the suburbs' in one form or another. Dickens was an astute chronicler of this process. 'Slum' in the nineteenth-early twentieth centuries and the 'inner city' later on became pejorative descriptive terms, which made it easier for the state apparatus to justify uprooting people. (Young and Willmott's 1957 research on the dispersal of people from Bethnal Green in the East End of London is a relevant case study.)

All of these degradation and clearance issues were central to Howard's thinking, and shaped his ideas for Letchworth.

Henrietta Barnett had many contacts with Letchworth and Hampstead Garden suburb, and was a keen advocate of garden suburbs. Barnett was also very influential in the emergence of social work, another aspect of the upper middle classes response to the moral malaise and the need to intervene in the lives of the lower working class, with those concerns about social order never far away. (See Mervyn Miller, 2006.)

So, by the late-nineteenth century it was clear to the members of this elite that the increasingly enfranchised and knowledgeable working class were turning to radical solutions to their situation. The last quarter of the century marked a significant rise in trade union organization, especially so among semi-skilled and unskilled workers, and the emergence of modern socialism. The influence of Marx was spreading, and although his particular focus remained on the continental

European scene, his acolytes such as Hyndman and Morris carried the word to a growing number of supporters. It is also important to highlight the role at this juncture of the National Secularist Society, and its attendant 'Freethought' movement. (See Astley, 1969.) The ethical base of the Toynbee Hall reformers was essentially a Christian one. It is certainly true that many of these upper class reformers, like Tawney, were Christian Socialists, and that an important aspect of the 'Balliol' ethos was that each person should come to terms with their own personal God, working out a philosophical 'relationship' that suited them in an era of the rising influence of science and class warfare. The 'service to society' ethos permeated the ranks of the new professional civil service, and their education helped to create a set of values that emphasized a classically informed 'disinterested-ness', a standing above the day-to-day fray of politics and the like. (See Meacham, 1987.)

Tawney became a renowned social and economic historian and reformer in the field of education, especially adult education, with for example his role in the Workers Educational Association, External (or Extra-mural) Studies departments in universities and so on. Tawney believed that teachers were 'bridge builders' (pontifices) and should dedicate their practice to create the conditions that enabled working people to engage with a self- improving education. Green, like his contemporary Arnold Toynbee (after whom the Hall was named) argued that a person's duty was first to educate themselves in the Classical tradition of Plato and Aristotle, and only then to take up a life of service with and for those who were less fortunate. All of these diverse reformers earnestly believed that certain essential basics of everyday life must be in place before anyone can turn their mind to 'higher' things. It was this concern that led them to argue for freedom from economic hardship and for good housing. We can see how Beveridge came to see himself as the bureaucrat *par excellence*, and took him on the road to his 1942 Report that helped shape the post-1945 'Welfare State'. Like so many other liberal reformers, his disappointment with the lack of progress on social reform in general and housing in particular in the inter-war years, only heightened their determination.

In his book on town planning, Gordon Cherry underlines the impact of the housing legislation:

"Between 1919 and 1934 nearly one-third of the dwellings built in England and Wales were by local authorities, and the proportion was higher in Scotland. It was an astonishing take-up, not least because it represented a sharp reversal of attitudes and local authority practices... 'In social welfare terms the subsidized council house was a major development, and was probably as effective as any state welfare initiative in targeting need.' (Child, 1996 p.75.) In fact between 1919 and 1939 four million new houses were built, more than ever before, and by 1939 one third of the housing stock was new. 1,112,000 of builds were by local authorities and 2,886,000 by private enterprise. (Burnett, 1978.)

Mark Swenarton in his 2008 book *Building the New Jerusalem: Architecture, housing and politics 1900-1930* takes a very similar line by arguing that this period marks a fundamental shift in attitudes towards public sector housing. This embraces the way housing estate planning was seen as an acceptable goal for architects. Swenarton argues that the growth of social democracy was a key factor in these developments, an ideological commitment to housing as a key aspect of welfare, the centrality of 'welfarism'. Swenarton also reminds us that there was a view that if cars could be produced *en masse* using new technologies in factories by Ford and Morris, *et. al.*, then why not houses?

There are important links here with the growth in building research after 1917.

Unwin was a key player in all this, and as Swenarton says: "Unwin was, so far as housing was concerned, the expert's expert." (p.4.)

Even so, it has to be concluded that the various interventions of the State from then to now is akin to attempting to empty the ocean with a spoon. Of course, we know all post-Beveridge welfare legislation has been an attempt to compensate the majority of people for the chaos and insecurity caused by market capitalism, but this reality of everyday life still has to be stated, and addressed.

Raymond Unwin and Barry Parker

AT THIS juncture, let me turn to the life and times of Barry Parker and Raymond Unwin, and say a little more about their role in this story. My focus will be mainly on Unwin, the doyen of town planning. Most of what I say from here on *is* in chronological order following the life of Raymond Unwin and, less so, Barry Parker. However, in my desire to address key themes in Unwin's life and times, I do occasionally depart from a strict chronology to explore more fully what I see as key issues that do contribute to a fuller understanding.

First and foremost, they were both involved with the Arts & Crafts movement and its core values. They also considered themselves to be Socialists and democrats. They should both be considered to be utopian socialists, idealistic, and certainly focused on a characteristic of the period, namely that of freedom for the artistic individual spirit. Unlike Marx, say, they considered the conflict arising from class-consciousness to offer a negative prognosis of social change rather than a positive one.

Their influences also embraced Emerson and Whitman, the American poets (Whitman's influential essay 'Democratic Vistas' was published in a cheap edition in England in 1887) and Thoreau, the writer of *Walden: or life in the woods* (1854), which is an account of setting up home in a rustic and frugal environment in order to focus the mind. I would also point to the publication of *Walden Two* published in 1948 and written by B.F. Skinner, the well-known 'behaviourist' psychologist. Skinner wrote a story about an experimental community *Walden Two* that enabled him to tease-out his ideas on operant conditioning; the theory that a system of rewards, more than punishments, can change behaviour.

13. Raymond Unwin and Barry Parker:
pioneers of urban planning.

The members of this largish-scale 'commune' lived as a reward for service in a self-sufficient collective.

This was Skinner's recommended antidote for the rapid decline of American civilization!

Following Unwin's death in 1940 while on a lecture tour in the U.S.A., Barry Parker wrote a memorial notice for the *Town Planning Journal*, where he places Unwin alongside Geddes as the most influential of men. Parker argues that they were both informed by their interest in the practical application of Sociology, an aspect of their open and liberal attitude to education. Parker also echoes the recurrent Modernist theme of planning and building dwellings that were open to sunlight, airy, and of course not overcrowded on a site, a leitmotif of Unwin.

I should also mention that Frank Lloyd Wright (1869-1959), the outstanding American Arts & Crafts architect, was influenced by the same democratic sources mentioned above. Throughout his life, Wright sought unities within nature, including the human habitat, and strived to create the 'usonian', the naturally perfect and inexpensive home suitable for modern life that promoted a democratic ethos.

As I shall elaborate in my chapter on Community, there is a long history of cooperative living, as chronicled by Lynn Pearson's book *The Architectural and Social History of Cooperative Living* (1988). I shall also return to this theme of ideals and experimentation, theory, and practice leading to praxis.

Raymond Unwin, like Morris, wanted the best for everyone and not just a privileged minority. Unwin was to become increasingly focused on housing and town planning, and throughout his career he never lost his commitment to equality of access to a good quality home. Like many socialists of Unwin's day, he had a fear that a greater State role in administering greater opportunity and access to highly valued cultural goods would make town planning, and the like, a controlling and negative influence. Even when he became a civil servant, he sought to avoid this danger. Unwin always argued that if civilization *was* to progress any progress in planning towns and housing would require an enhanced social life that would encourage all of us to engage in decision making within a reasoned context. In my chapter on Merry Oak, I shall return to this key issue in the hope that I can explain my similar commitment to that of Unwin.

Another key influence on Unwin quite akin to Thoreau was Edward Carpenter (1844-1929), socialist poet and activist, who focused on the spiritual degradation brought about by industrial capitalism. Carpenter, like many of his contemporaries, argued for a deeper understanding of, and closer relationship with, nature and the rural life. Unwin was to name his son Edward after Carpenter.

One interesting link to note here is that between Unwin and his associates, and Ebenezer Howard. Like Unwin and Carpenter, Emerson also influenced Howard, and it is not difficult to see why:

"To live content with small means: to seek elegance rather than luxury: and refinement rather than fashion: to be worthy, not respectable: and wealthy not rich: to study hard: think quietly: talk gently: act frankly: to listen to stars and birds, to babes and sages with an open heart: to bear all cheerfully, do all bravely, await occasions, hurry never. In a word: to let the spiritual unbidden and unconscious grow up through the common."

In an article on Carpenter for the Raymond Williams Society journal *Keywords*, Sheila Rowbotham comments that:

"...Carpenter's friend Raymond Unwin created a rural urbanism at Letchworth Garden City, which sported a teetotal pub, a Food Reform Restaurant, a Simple Life Hotel for vegetarians, folk dancing and Jaeger woollen clothing. It also offered spiritual and political heterodoxies of all kinds. Modified versions of Letchworth would be reinvented through other garden cities and the later council estates Unwin designed, all of which sought to bring the countryside into urban life.' (Rowbotham, 2009.)

I should add here that Rowbotham's fascinating book on Edward Carpenter was published by Verso in 2008.

Throughout my study there is a clear assertion that many diverse people have turned their face against large scale urban development.

"Though the philosophy of urban planning has evolved through various stages over the last two centuries, it is not unfair to identify throughout the period an underlying sense of disaffection for urban development together with a conviction that the solutions to urban problems are most easily found by creating new communities in new locations rather than seeking to improve the existing urban framework. This philosophy of "anti-urbanism" is compounded from a number of factors, amongst which are a genuine belief that "urban" life is in some ways less desirable than rural life and, perhaps more importantly, a fear that even if cities are in principle acceptable they have in practice grown far too large." (Murray Stewart, 1972 p.11-12.)

I should also add that many writers on the history of landscape and the environment have commented on the tendency to reject planning, or be accustomed to chaos.

W.G.Hoskins in his *The Making of the English Landscape* says: "...the planned town has always been the exception in England, and derives most of its special interest from that fact.' (Hoskins, 1970 p.278/)

L.E.White also posed the key question "Can communities be planned?" (White, 1950.) He emphasized that the concept of the 'neighbourhood unit' was approaching paradigm status among planners by the 1930s; but, as I discuss later, this often contrasted with the difficulties expressed by the inhabitants of new estates of adjusting to their new life.

Raymond Unwin in his own day was one of the clearest articulators of these issues and problems and sought imaginative solutions to them. Indeed: "He urges students to use intuition as well as the behavioural sciences as tools, and to be ever alert to the psychology of the populations they are dealing with." (Creese, 1967 p.21.) It is also worth reminding ourselves that the early- twentieth century saw an enthusiasm for anthropometrics, the 'science' of measuring human beings, and using those physical attributes to help define and design appropriate spaces for those people to occupy. While this may seem a sensible approach to planning; and ergonomics is derived from this approach; and Galton and the geneticists were to take anthropometrics off into the realms of criminology and racist policy making.

Herbert Gans reminds us that many planners are very bound up in theories about the articulation of physical space in order to achieve certain benefits; people come second. (Gans, 1969.) Housing is generally regarded as a 'social good', a beneficial addition to society. However, this does not necessarily mean that those that subscribe to this view start from the needs of people on an everyday basis, particularly the needs of the poorest members of society. A focus on the needs of extending housing as private property has always been an attractive goal for many planners and designers, and certainly so for many policy makers and politicians. A focus on the needs of every person in a community has had a more troubled history, especially so if that focus acknowledges that what professionals think as desirable does not fit the attitudes and ways of life of many others.

I should also add here a note about a key feature of Modernist architecture, a focus on "light, air and openness", which I suggested was a core issue for Unwin. As I have discussed elsewhere in this study, the 1920s and 1930s witnessed an influx of refugees from a design and architecture background, who went on to have a profound influence on theory and practice at the time. As I have already said in this book, the explicit influence of these émigrés and their colleagues among indigenous designers is not always clear and straightforward. However, if we consider the key issues that Unwin and his contemporaries addressed both before and after the 1914-18 War we can see a clear response to the worst excesses of urbanism as a consequence of industrial capitalism. It should be remembered that at this time a major issue was 'the slums', and what to do about them. The Arts & Crafts and Garden City/Suburb advocates had ample evidence that housing for the majority of people was a public health issue as well as a moral and political one. It could be argued that a good deal of the 'top-down' response to this public health issue was one of enlightened self-interest given the very nature of city life, since the close proximity of unhealthy and diseased people was a danger to almost all. There is also the major theme in the Arts & Crafts Movement of seeking to promote ideas about the value of a symbiotic relationship between nature and a design for living.

Morris was certainly in the forefront of this argument, and the likes of Unwin were socialized into these values, an acculturation process that they willingly embraced. As I have argued, Unwin and his colleagues always promoted the value of orientating houses to the sun, of designing large windows, of providing both 'private' and public open spaces. Their emphasis on the 'greening' of living spaces was central to their design aesthetic, then and later, essential Modernist practice, making life possible. As Unwin, and others were to assert, aesthetics is often a question of the relationships of how things are placed. This is as true in architecture and town planning as it is in music, or poetry and other arts.

"A preoccupation with cleanliness, health, hygiene, sunlight, fresh air and openness characterized modern architecture of the years between the two wars. Representations of the need for "light, air and openness" and a particular concern with health and hygiene feature prominently in the written texts, photographs and films employed to promote the modern movement during the 1920s and early 1930s.' (Overy, 2007 p.9.)

I have addressed the major debate on the professionalisation of architecture in my chapter on Arts & Crafts architects, but I would add here that both Parker and Unwin were uncomfortable with the idea of professional practice on the basis that this status would increasingly separate the architect's values from those of their clients. With some honourable exceptions, the twentieth century confirmed their doubts. Unwin and Parker did see their practice as a symbiotic one, an imaginative process of interaction with the people for whom the building was being done. The imaginative focus was crucial to their ideas on streetscape, and they talked of 'street pictures', a socialization and acculturation process whereby people both saw themselves as integral to the environment, but not passive within it.

For Unwin and Parker, this whole issue was fundamental to

their idea of good architecture and building being educational, a learning experience. They argued that living in a good quality building in a thoughtfully functional environment 'opened the eyes' of the dweller to the prospects of a better life, that is, aspirational architecture that could lead to self-actualisation.

I have a good deal more to say on this issue of the educational role of architecture in my chapter on Merry Oak.

Organising spaces, in which people can live, socially interact and even work, requires a fundamentally different approach and Unwin and Parker applied their 'common sense' focus for planning and design for this purpose. In this regard, Creese has suggested that this "gesture...toward a more positive mental health, and in several senses it was the architectural answer to Unwin's pre-architectural call for a gladder or 'happier' day". (Creese, 1967 p. 17.)

In regard to this issue of working for the 'social good', Stewart adds an additional note on the role of social scientists: "Indeed, from about 1920 the sociological contribution to the development of planning theory virtually disappeared, and the social content of planning was derived until recently almost entirely from the Geddes' heritage of social survey, but as description rather than explanation of social characteristics and problems." (p.19)

As he suggests this was primarily because the positivist methodology of most social scientists was focused on pre-'Welfare State' social pathology among the working class - poverty, unemployment, and so on - rather than developing an interest in the urban environment from a 'bottom-up', more interpretative or even Marxist perspective.

In this respect, Unwin's socialist and Arts & Crafts-oriented contribution looks even more important when viewed from this point in the early twenty first century. I would argue that Unwin was both a theorizer and a practical applicator, and given his professional options, sought the difficult path to progress. In view of this status, he did have power (influence), but that for him was an appropriate use of power in that power + *legitimacy* = authority. So, with the increasing legitimacy that Unwin accrued throughout his many faceted career, he certainly had authority.

In the political sphere, it has also become evident to me that Unwin was much closer to Addison (in political thought and practical deed) than he was to Wheatley. In essence, Unwin could see in Addison a kindred spirit, that of the visionary practical administrator, over and above being a vocal politician. As I have said elsewhere, many of Addison's Conservative colleagues became increasingly irritated by the new Minister's reforming zeal. It was also Addison who increasingly drew Unwin into this reforming role of the new Ministry of Health.

It is clear to me that the guiding principle in Unwin's work is a preference for organic rather than formal development. Whether he was considering the past, or thinking about the future, his aesthetic preference was to ensure that even in new planning developments the outcome, the arrangement of buildings to landscape, the materials to use in building, the roads, paths and so on, should *look* and feel as if this were an organic outcome of the developmental processes. He made this aspect of his core values abundantly clear in his *Town Planning in Practice* (1909). Perhaps there is link back here with Unwin's enthusiasm for Whitman's 'Democratic Vistas'? What is evident in Unwin and Parker's town/neighbourhood-scape designing is an imaginative grasp of parallax, which in this sense means that their curving roads, green spaces, houses, set at expected and unexpected angles to each other drew the eye, and the person, along and through unfolding spaces.

It is important to recall that Unwin wrote this very influential book, with its wide-ranging theoretical and pan-European perspective, while the 1909 Town Planning Act was progressing through Parliament. Of course, this was no accident, and following the Act he organized in 1910 the Royal Institute of British Architecture (RIBA) conference, which put the legislation into a practical context.

At this early stage of his (and Parker's) work, it is clear to see a practical focus. Unwin argues that town planning, and even house design on such a large scale, is a new endeavour for local authorities in their twentieth-century form. He is keen to persuade those in local authorities, borough engineers/surveyors, some architects, and certainly local councillors, to draw on the services of the Local Government Board. Unwin encourages these various stakeholders to use the theoretical and comparative European resource of the Board as a working context for their own strategies. He also advocates the holding of local public inquiries to collect and use needs-based data. This is precisely what did happen, and put Unwin and his colleagues at the heart of all these planning and design developments.

In his essay 'Utopian Thought' Peter Hall makes the point that societies need utopian visions to drive them forward:

"Planning as an activity, by definition, seeks to achieve a goal different from the outcome that would be likely without planning. It assumes that this goal is desirable to the group of people for whom the planning is undertaken. In so far as the achievement of this goal lies in the future, and must therefore involve a degree of uncertainty, one might say that all planning must by definition involve an element of utopianism." (Hall, 1984 p.189.)

I would add that in the twentieth-century discourse on council housing, the many failures in the large-scale developments was consistently referred to as 'failures of utopian ideas', with the working class tenants being invariably blamed ("the wrong sort of people") for disappointing outcomes. So much of this kind of reaction ignores Hall's argument that "Utopia plus social realism, then, seems to be a necessary condition for successful planning." (Hall p.192)

Alice Coleman's *Utopia on Trial* (1985) is almost entirely devoted to castigating the State 'top-down' bureaucrats who imposed a particular form of public sector housing style and regime, which did not allow any significant input from tenants. The twentieth century 'utopian' visions she discusses are essentially paternalistic ones, reinforcing at every turn an environmental determinism, an ideology that rests on the belief that if an environment is changed, usually along some rational and scientific route, human behaviour can also be changed. Singled out for opprobrium are: Howard and Corbusier; Garden City and Radiant City. Coleman is typical of those critics who see such behaviour modification agendas as dystopian, rather than Morris in *News From Nowhere,* or Skinner in *Walden 2,* for instance.

Alice Coleman cites Colin Ward in support of her concerns about cause and effect:

"The important thing about housing is not what it *is*, but what it *does* in people's lives." (Coleman, 1985 p.182.)

Ward's argument here (reflected in Coleman's critique) is to restate the Arts & Crafts mantra that *function* comes before *form.*

Carpenter and Morris, who both had a significant influence on the development of Unwin's ideas, met through the Social Democratic Federation, and although Morris admired the freethinking Carpenter, he did consider him a 'strange cove'. In turn, Carpenter saw in Morris a charismatic dimension to the myriad ideas circulating at the time, and Morris' down-to-earthness, for example, in his workingman's clothing, struck a fraternal chord with him.

Frank Jackson in his biography of Unwin adds:

"To Unwin, the improvement of individual human life came naturally from the social and political beliefs he derived from Morris, and he always believed that the study of man was the foundation of all planning activity." (1985 p.9)

Unwin did, of course, describe Morris as "the great Poet-Craftsman".[1]

Unwin moved from Oxford to Manchester in 1886 for a job as a draughtsman in a cotton mill. Mervyn Miller in his book on Hampstead Garden suburb states that Unwin was unhappy about staying in Oxford to study Divinity because of the elitism he encountered there compared with his experience in the north of England. Unwin consulted Samuel Barnett, who advised him not to stay and study, and so Unwin returned to Chesterfield to serve his engineering apprenticeship before returning to Manchester. He joined the Manchester Socialist Society, and then (that same year) became the first secretary of the Manchester branch of Morris' Socialist League.

In 1887, Unwin left Manchester (and left The Socialist League branch there) for a brief stay (and work) in Staveley (the Coal and Iron Company there), which is close to Sheffield and Chesterfield, where he took on the role of chief draughtsman.

In January 2012, I was able to read, at the John Rylands University library in Manchester, his hand-written diary for the May to September period. This diary was written for his beloved

---

[1] In this sense, it is perhaps worth noting here that Walt Whitman also cast his spell over both Holst and Vaughan Williams, both of whom wrote music based on the poet's work.

Ettie (Ethel Parker, Barry's sister), and certainly comments on how lost he feels not being in Buxton with her. Apart from comments on his daily routine of work on engineering projects, including dealing with workers' housing, and frequent walks, there are references to the many varied people he spent time with including Carpenter. He records in his diary what he is currently reading, which ranges from Auguste Comte (1798-1857), the French philosopher, who is often cited as a founding 'father' of Sociology. Unwin describes his reading Auguste Comte's *Positive Philosophy*, which he admires, as did people from Marx to George Eliot, but he finds Comte too positivist, too focused on a rationalistic and pseudo-scientific explanation of social action.

Unwin's leaning towards a more individual human agency approach to social action is evident in his remarks, and given his utopian socialist ideology and focus on aesthetics issues, this is no surprise. Unwin is also regularly reading, and writing for, *Commonweal* the newspaper of The Socialist League, edited by Morris. In these months at Staveley, he is also reading and discussing Emerson, T.H. Green the influential Oxford philosopher, and James Hinton's *Man and His Dwelling Place*.

What this diary shows is that Unwin is open to a wide range of philosophical and literary influences, which have a bearing on his political *and* aesthetic development. At one point in the diary, there is a quote from George Eliot: "What do we live for, if it is not to make life less difficult to each other?"

By 1903, Parker and Unwin were well established in the Northern Art Workers' Guild, and Unwin's slogan 'Art and Simplicity' reminds us that many of those who commissioned the work of these designers were Quakers. There were even 'Shaker' influences in England at that time, and a good deal of Arts & Crafts design that has survived for us to marvel at today is remarkable for its clarity of style, and what could even be called humble-ness.

However, what is also important here is an issue (and one addressed several times in this study) raised by Ken Worpole, namely whether the growing influence of a Social Democratic political ideology in the late-nineteenth and early-twentieth centuries actually contained a developed aesthetic that embraced architectural design, planning, and the like:

"I believe that it did, and that it was a civic aesthetic focused on collective provision allied to modern design, and strongly predicated on a belief in the benefits of clean water, sunlight and fresh air." (Worpole, 2000 p.10)

Unwin's straightforward and functional approach to planning is exemplified in his Fabian Tract 'Cottage Plans and Common Sense'. (Fabian Tract no. 109, published in 1902.) This project also reflects Unwin's closeness to the evolutionary and practical administering of Socialism into existence ideology of the Fabians. His approach here outlines what are, for him, the basic necessities for a house and a home. We may now regard what he says as common sense, but it is clear that when he wrote this tract most people involved with planning and designing still needed to be convinced. He lists basic requirements: size, light, location, adequate rooms for sensible everyday living, furniture, a garden and so on. The house/cottage must be fit for purpose. The message from Unwin and his associates was clear: whatever the style of house designed and planned, it is essential that it must function, meeting the needs of the users/inhabitants, and not some idealized and abstract notion of how housing should be. There must be flexibility in the environment and design of dwellings that help, not hinder, that is part of the solution and not part of the problem.

The implication here is that society is now (in 2012) is as it was one hundred years ago, at a stage of development when these common sense and essential necessities could and should be provided for *all* families. What is required is the political will to do so.

If we were to look at most critical accounts of post-1950s housing in the UK, we could be forgiven for assuming that none of this discussion went on in the late-nineteenth and early-twentieth century. The architects of High Rise and of the cheapest systems-building schemes seem to have an architectural amnesia, and in league with most local authorities with an anti-democratic disregard for service users. One of the direct results of these years of malaise was the widespread disregard for professional architects, usually attributing the worst set of motives to their practice. It is not surprising, then, that so many observers and users of bleak 1960s and 1970s housing assumed that architects were not capable of imagining anything better.

As Sutherland Lyall points out in his re-assessment of British architecture (published in 1980), one reaction to the previous twenty years of mishaps and mistakes was a return to a 'neo-vernacular'. Lyall does not like it; he sees it as bogus, even though he understands why it happened. He does refer to the fact that architects and planners returned to this stylistic approach because that is what most people wanted. He acknowledges those aesthetic values begrudgingly. (Lyall, 1980.) He cites a 'rustic idyll' aesthetic embedded in English cultural attitudes towards housing, and makes wholly appropriate links to "Rousseauesque ideas' about going back to the land and simple nature". (p.93.) He could also have added that Rousseau was the author of The Social Contract, which seeks to show that "man is born free but everywhere is in chains", freeborn social being longing for a natural justice - the rights of man in fact. And while many critics would dismiss this set of values as Romantic whimsy, this would be a mistake, and certainly most Arts & Crafts practitioners were imbued with this outlook on life, liberty and the pursuit of happiness.

So, to re-focus my attention on the 1880s, I should add that the Fabian influence was considerable at this time: from 1884 to the turn of the century, if often of a contradictory nature.

"There were deep divisions within…society. Unflinching Christians fought desperately against the new Darwinians. Fabian young women tried to burst the suffocating bonds of sexual morality, the Fabians proper attacked capitalism, the workers deeply divided against the employers, the new young novelists challenged the place of literature in life, and even the drama was presently under siege from reckless young Socialists with no conception of the niceties of dramatic subject or construction. More subtle divisions set the Catholics against the non-Catholics, the Socialists against the Marxists, and the scholars against literary historians." (Brome, 2001 p.i)

In an even earlier comment, Brome reflected on the contrary and contradictory life of the nineteenth century given by Graham Hough in 1949:

"In the troubled waters of nineteenth-century thought two main currents can be discerned: the one scientific, positivist and radical; the other antiquarian, traditional, conservative. In England, though opposed, they were not harshly antagonistic. On the whole, they contrived to live pretty comfortably together, and there were many bridges between the two territories.' (Hough, 1961 p. xi.)

Hough also understood a fundamental issue (for me), namely that many of my key players were complex amalgams of characters: "The rival mythologies of the romantic age, the myth of the past and the myth of the future, come to a similar accommodation." (Hough p.xi)

What Hough has to say is also an aspect of the English identity debate: what are the essential characteristics of Englishness? I have addressed this issue in several places in this book, because no matter which particular part of this story is articulated this key debate always returns to tax us.

In 1900, the National Housing Reform Council was established by Henry Aldridge and William Thompson, which began life as a mainly working class organization, but became more middle class with support from Cadbury and Lever. It was essentially a pressure group with good ties to Parliament. Significantly, it was renamed the National Housing and Town Planning Council in 1909 - at the same time as the 1909 Act, and when Unwin and Parker were making their mark.

Incidentally, the term 'town planning' was coined by John Nettlefold in 1905. Nettlefold was the chairman of Birmingham's housing committee and worked closely with John Robertson, the City's medical officer of health. Nettlefold was a radical Tory who published *Practical Housing* in 1908, and became increasingly interested in land reform and garden suburbs. (Ward, 2004.)[1]

---

[1] As for 'practical housing', it might be worth adding here in passing that Morris reflected general Arts & Crafts thinking at the time in terms of houses being fit for purpose. When discussing the interiors of most middle and upper middle class homes, he observed that most were full of very dark and heavy furniture and fittings. Morris once commented that he had not visited such homes without feeling that would be greatly improved by removing 90 per cent of the contents for incineration in the garden! He added that: "If you find anything decent, it is more likely to be in the kitchen than in the drawing room." (Shades of Terence Conran and Habitat here, perhaps).

By 1901, Unwin and Parker had published *The Art of Building a Home* (the emphasis on *the home* as distinct from merely a house is significant, surely). Many of the illustrations in this book are shared with the Fabian Tract of 1902.

Unwin and Parker were: "...treating 'home' as an evolving amalgam of architectural style, domestic technology and cultural values - emphasised over the years with the inter-relation between 'comfort, style and convenience'". (Wright, 1988.)

However, Unwin and Parker were not the only writers in this period that emphasized the importance of 'home'. There were, for example, many pious statements made on the close relationship between Godliness and the home, the link between the altar and the hearth. This approach was echoed by Julia Macnair Wright in 1881 when she said: "Between the Home set up in Eden, and the Home before us in Eternity, stand the Homes of Earth in a long succession...Every home has its influence, for good or evil, upon humanity at large." These dictates were primarily aimed at a young middle class audience, especially so young women approaching marriage or recently married. There were also many guides on how to manage a household, where Godliness and Cleanliness went together. (See Briggs, 1990.) A great deal of this 'Home Sweet Home' ideology was not a very realistic set of options, even for the young middle class, let alone the majority of working class families starting out on adult life, married or not. Unwin and Parker were focused on this concern, with the primary aim of improving everyday lives *via* access to good quality housing.

However, it should be remembered that there was then, as now, a good deal of use of biblical imagery used, especially so in relation to utopian visions. (The title of this book may even be an example?)

Another major contribution to this early-twentieth century housing/home discussion was by Alexander Harvey (1874-1951), the designer of Bournville. In 1906, Harvey published *The Model Village and its Cottages: Bournville* - both a reflection on work done, and a guide to other projects. Harvey was a local man and student at the Municipal School of Art in Birmingham; he was, incredibly, only twenty-one when employed to design and develop Bournville.

Some years' later, in his appendix to Purdom's book on Letchworth, Unwin re-asserts a key issue for him: "That every house should have its garden and should be so placed and planned that all its rooms should be flooded with light and sunshine". (Purdom, p.229.)

Unwin's desire to be involved in the creation of new 'communities' certainly reflects his definition of a community as "a free association of individuals, with harmony between people and their environment." There are certainly echoes here of Morris' *News from Nowhere*, and this would suggest that Unwin's ideas about design drew on the images that Morris' story conjured up, and the values discussed by the protagonists.

I have already said more about this in my chapter on Arts & Crafts and Morris. Unwin and Parker were also greatly influenced by Morris' focus on the ideal of the open living room, with as big as possible fireplace and an inglenook. This was of, course, the oft- copied model of the medieval great hall. This also reflects a major planning value for Parker and Unwin in that whether estate, street, house or living room is the issue, they must provide a sense of comfort and security. Good on the eye and comfortable for the user(s). Unwin and Parker were consistently in opposition to the separate parlour, seeing it as 'sucking up' to a middle class model that actually deprived the family of functional space. I have always found it interesting to note that, in the majority of late-nineteenth and early-twentieth century houses, the dividing wall between the 'front' parlour and the living/dining room has been removed.

In 1902, Unwin and Parker were asked by the Rowntrees to design a model village at New Earswick near York, and the following year they took up the challenge of Letchworth, employed as both the overall planners for the town, and also the architects of several houses and community buildings. They opened an office on site from which they administered the plan layout and construction, a considerable facilitating role. They then moved on from Letchworth to design Hampstead Garden Suburb in 1905, where Unwin then lived in an old farmhouse, the epitome of the vernacular on the edge of the Heath. So, within a very short period of time, these two 'Left-leaning' Arts & Crafts designer/artist/planners had accomplished a good deal. It is also worth mentioning that Unwin continued to make a clear link between Garden City principles and their application to suburbs; for example, in an Article he wrote in 1920 for the MOH journal *Housing*. I will say more about this journal shortly.

In his 1967 book *The Legacy of Raymond Unwin*, Walter Creese enumerates the defining philosophy of Unwin and Parker, with the:

- ❑ village as an animate symbol
- ❑ necessity for understanding the past
- ❑ Middle Ages as the historic standard.

The indispensability of beauty, and their 'twelve houses to an acre' criterion for building, while not always achieved, this remained benchmark to chime with their slogan "nothing gained by overcrowding!"

As I have suggested above, one crucial dimension of this ethos was to be found in their enthusiasm for the *cul-de-sac,* which creates a sense of security and intimate-ness. They always argued that there are important psychological dimensions to this aspect of planning. In an extension of their focus on the role of nature in people's lives, they were also fond of naming streets after trees and plants, and this is to be found on the Merry Oak estate.

They shared the conventional Arts & Crafts belief that "what has been joylessly made cannot be joyfully used". This also aligns with the general Arts & Crafts reaction to the growing standardization found in mass production that moves ever further from the individuality worked into the product by the craftsman. There are echoes of this in our day with increasing numbers of people turning to handmade goods of all kinds, and also for organic produce and Fair Trade.

In his book on Unwin and Garden Cities, Mervyn Miller quotes from Unwin and Parker's *The Art of Building a Home* (1902):

"The village was the expression of a small corporate life in which all the different units were personally in touch with each other, conscious of and frankly accepting their relations...it is this crystallisation of the elements in a village in accordance with a definitely organized life of mutual relations...which gives the appearance of being an organic whole, the home of the community, to what would otherwise be a mere conglomeration of buildings.' (Miller, 1992 p.36.)

I should add here that Unwin's visits to New York in the 1920s only reinforced his opposition to high-rise solutions to urban planning.

As already cited, Unwin's *Town Planning in Practice*

published in 1909 soon became the 'bible' for those many forward-thinking Edwardians, whether they were conscientious professionals or adventurous local politicians. As John Betjeman points out in his chapter on Architecture in Nowell-Smith's *Edwardian England* (1964), there was a growth in good quality design and building. Many of the designer/architects that are discussed in this book were in their prime in the first two decades of the twentieth century, and even if many of these better known people designed for the wealthy, or the newly aspiring middle classes, the influence of good design was considerable; this was the 'spirit of the age' that was inspiring localised ideas about private and public sector housing for a much broader section of the population. Unwin was central to this, which is a key reason why he was sought by politicians like Addison, and with this later work became *the* central figure in planning. For John Betjeman, the period 1901-1914 was a golden age of ideas and action, and praxis through design and building.

One of the distinctive features of Unwin's *Town Planning in Practice* was the conspicuous reference to his Continental European contemporary Camillo Sitte. George Collins in his 1965 book on Sitte says that he, Sitte, and Unwin both used the technique of comparing photographic examples of good and bad town planning. Collins argues that by the 1880s "students of municipal reform visited the Continent...and made reports that emphasized the technical and administrative excellence of German cities". (Collins p.86.) Collins argues that Unwin and Sitte were very much alike in their translation of Garden City ideas into a vision of the garden suburb. Sitte was clearly influential in Britain, despite the fact that his writings were not translated into English until the 1940s. Enthusiasts had to read the original German, or French translations, or rely on the many summaries and interpretations of Sitte's work that were circulating in Britain. Collins also emphasizes how both Garden City and Arts & Crafts ideas had enraptured many in Germany, with Sitte and Muthesius being two prominent examples.

Unwin and Parker continued to take commissions together, and apart when their business partnership ended in 1914. Contemporaries saw a clear difference in the nature of these two men, Parker the aesthete and utopian, and Unwin increasingly the practical applicator, prepared to be a committee man, who was clearly in for the long haul of information-gathering and education.

Unwin was a 'front and back office' man. Although it should be said that by the mid-1920s many of his peers regretted the fact that Unwin was 'buried' deep in the Ministry of Health apparatus, hidden away. It is quite clear that Unwin was still exerting a great deal of influence, but it is true that to a certain extent his work for the Ministry and so on kept him away from developing his own architectural practice. Addison certainly needed Unwin, and the former did comment on the reality of 'starting from scratch' when the Ministry of Health was created in 1919.

As Swenarton points out, establishing a radical, public sector and 'homes fit for heroes to live in' housing policy from within the new Ministry of Health was fraught with difficulties; not the least of reasons for this was the desire by Addison & Co. to take a national lead, being much more directional in their dealings with local government. The power of municipalism in the land was still considerable, and Addison's new centralised and centralising approach was not universally welcomed (especially so in Birmingham), and perhaps over the years a cynicism developed in both men, that is, in a distrust of certain people's motives. (Swenarton, 1981; Olechnowicz, 1997.)

One of the innovations of the new Ministry of Health's housing department was the fortnightly journal *Housing*, and I thought the reader would be interested in a brief selection of contents over the journal's life between 1919 and 1921.

The first issue of *Housing* (sixteen pages in all) was published on July 19, 1919 at a cost of 3d - although two free copies were sent to councils across the country. The journal was aimed at Ministry staff throughout the country (the MoH was regionalised), local government staff (as I have said a body of people to be 'won over'), and interestingly, the press. The editorial for the first issue was written by Addison, who said of the journal:

"Its aim is to assist all who are concerned with housing by giving them in a regular form information and advice based on the mass of cases and problems which came before the ministry. We desire to make available to all the best that is being devised in house plans or lay-outs, and any features of exceptional interest in the schemes that come before us." (no.1 vol 1. p.1.)

Each issue of the journal was a very mixed bag, with a diverse range of issues raised; for example, the use of concrete, case studies of housing developments in particular places, with plans and photographs, a parliamentary report, an article on housing in Germany, a list of meetings and conferences, a summary of recent publications and useful journals (*The Architects Journal* is cited), and a survey of active housing schemes, both urban and rural, and with regional data.

One of regular features of the *Journal* was a 'contributed' article, and this first edition carried an anonymous piece from the Garden Cities and Town Planning Association. A major issue in the article is the promotion of public utility societies, and how these are engaged in a scheme of educational propaganda in order to inform the public about the possibilities that exist to get on and build houses! In view of the enhanced role of government, and past examples to show the way, the

Association's writer stresses the opportunity to "set a permanently higher standard of working-class houses throughout the country." (p.11.)

From Issue 2 (2.8.1919) onwards there are frequent references to Public Utility Societies (PUS), and an article here carries a definition of a PUS:

" . . .is a co-operative society formed for the erection of working-class houses…incorporated under the Industrial and Provident Societies Acts, with limited liability and must limit its rate of interest and dividends to 6%. It can get financial assistance from the Government by the Ministry of Health and must give security of tenure to tenants and a share in the management of the society."

The assistance from the Ministry included a loan of 75 per cent of the original capital cost of the approved scheme and an annual subsidy of 30 per cent of the loan charges on the whole of the capital borrowed. A PUS only required seven people to set one up at an initial cost of £4. This was the Government's version of the Letchworth model, and then and since caused debate about whether this is a better model for raising capital to build and manage rather than a more direct State role; that is, council housing. In the early-twentieth century, this mixed provision model was commonplace.

In issue 5 (3 Sept 1919) is a 'contributed' article on The Labour Housing Association (set up in 1898 as The Workmen's National Housing Council) and supported by the Parliamentary Committee of the TUC.: "Its main purpose has always been to encourage local authorities to provide good houses for the people, with all the conveniences demanded by health, comfort and taste, and to exercise to the full their powers under various Housing Acts" (p.67.)

The author of the article adds that their work is supported by architects committed to the provision of good quality housing for the working classes, and all are taking a share in the task of "educating public opinion".

Throughout the pages of the journal there are articles from and about women and their needs. There are also regular articles on technical matters; for example, innovations in building methods, including factory-made components to be assembled by less skilled workers. These technical matters are also supplemented by pieces on 'architectural education', and the need for all schools of architecture to teach about taste, design, building techniques, and the value of these processes to improving social life. The vernacular style is regularly seen as a preferred model. These 'professional' concerns are also linked to articles on Town Planning, and how this rational approach to providing for needs in the community is the way forward.

Another regular source of articles in the journal are exhortations by Addison and others to speed up the process of submitting schemes and getting on with building. It is clear to see that throughout the 1919-1921 period Addison is increasingly frustrated by local politicians and bureaucracy.

By March 1921 *Housing* has changed to a monthly, and in May 1921 Addison's voice is replaced by Mond, who starts out by discussing the problems of building caused by rising costs and the burden on taxes. These are the first signs of shifts in commitment to the post-1918 agenda on housing.

Also at this time (1919), Unwin edited a collection of articles, with pictures and plans for the Local Government Board entitled *The Nation's New Homes*, with a forward by Addison, the then president of the Board. (This monograph was published by The *Daily News* in London and Manchester, and at 6d. was aimed, and reached, a fairly wide audience. The anonymous (I have my suspicions that it is Unwin) opening essay is 'The New England': "…the new England of which all housing reformers dream is to be a fair land. The homes we build, therefore, must be beautiful as well as healthy and convenient. In design they should vary with local architecture and custom, and local materials should be used as far as possible. Thus, they will strike no discordant note, but harmonise with their surroundings."

These values were to be typical of the message that Unwin and his colleagues sent out from their base in the Ministry.

TO RETURN specifically to Unwin, and his diverse influences and role, Standish Meacham in his book on the Garden City movement argues that Unwin along with many of his contemporaries had real difficulty in reconciling their utopian socialism with the realities of the modern and modernizing capitalist world. Unwin identified the growth of capitalism with individualism (nothing novel there) and how this acted against community. As Meacham says, Unwin was a part of the growing interest in 'Community', its creation, maintenance and destruction. I see the hand of much later twentieth century reformist sociology in this as well. This focus on (re)building community *via* a benign welfarism was seen as an antidote to class antagonism; the "End of Ideology' to quote Daniel Bell, the American sociologist, who was so often in tune with his British contemporaries. If the working class could be helped to find a better place in which to *know their place* then this might create social stability and promote social order, and so achieving a key goal for many of Bell's peers: society as a self-adjusting system. With the advent of new estates, the visual differentiation seen in housing environments could perhaps be narrowed and thus demonstrating the veracity of claims about social mobility and a growing classlessness?

Unwin, clearly influenced by Ruskin, Morris and Carpenter

et al, drew on a mythologized past to argue for a better, more just future. In supporting this view Meacham quotes from Unwin and Parker's *The Art of Building a Home* (discussed earlier):

"The essence and life of design lies in finding that form for anything which will, with the maximum of convenience and beauty, fit it for the particular function it has to perform, and adapt it to the special circumstances in which it must be placed." (p. 84 of Pedersen and Mandler.)

Meacham adds a further thought on the specific issue of design style:

"They acknowledged the paradox implicit in their search for designs suitable for a democracy with the patterns of England's feudal past. Yet where else to look? Too often the new 'strikes a note of defiance with surrounding nature' and the harmony of the individual with nature remained central to their definition of democracy. Hence the appeal of an old building, which seems 'almost to grow out of the ground on which it stands'." (p.85-86.)

In all of this there is an old-style Englishness that is very reminiscent of G.K. Chesterton and his associates. Although Unwin, like Orwell, came from the 'lower upper middle class' he could not be bracketed with the Toynbee Hall types, although there are areas of common concern, such as their wish to counteract the ill effects of a rapid industrialization, urbanization and secularization by an appeal to 'community'. This was articulated as a necessary cultural homogeneity of interests and of 'better selves' who would draw on the past in order to re-create the best of this. Meacham, in his piece on Unwin in

Pedersen and Mandler's book, says of Unwin that "He saw it as his mission to design houses suitable for a democracy of individual selves." (p.80.) There is an Unwin family anecdote that the younger man spoke to Samuel Barnett when the latter was trying to set up Toynbee Hall. Apparently. Barnett said to Unwin: "Are you more interested in making people good or making them happy?" Unwin's reply is lost to us. What many of these 'Englishness' enthusiasts left out of their ideas was an acknowledgement of the enormous struggles 'in the past' that had brought English society to where it was. Morris and some others saw the dangers in this unrealistic view of English class history, but many other advocates of the 'Englishness' ideal did not. (Meacham, 1999.) There are still identity issues still unresolved to this day.

At the end of 1914, Unwin joined the Local Government Board as chief town planning inspector, then the Ministry of Munitions to design workers' villages at Gretna and Eastriggs. This purpose of the wartime work, mainly carried out between 1915 and 1918, was to house munitions workers. Both Lloyd George and Addison were central to the Ministry of Munitions. One other person working at this time was Frank Baines, an Office of Works architect who was responsible for the Well Hall estate in greater London. Baines 1,000 houses and 200 flats were built in what was called at the time 'picturesque traditional' and was very Arts & Crafts in style. Baines' work, and other similar ventures were criticized for being too elaborate and therefore costly. Good designs for the one-off house of a wealthy client, but not very practical for mass housing schemes. The more popular, cheaper to produce, style was the neo-Georgian, or 'Queen Anne' as seen in Bedford Park, in west London, and later to become a factor in Unwin's favoured hybrid style.

One of the promotional aspects in selling Bedford Park

houses to a diverse, but quite 'arty' and bohemian middle class, was how healthy it was to live there. The man behind Bedford Park was Jonathan Carr, a young and ambitious businessman who wanted *his* garden suburb to reflect the aims of Ruskin and the Aesthetic Movement. He initially employed Godwin, but replaced him with Norman Shaw before long.

Unwin was very familiar with all these eclectic developments that added to his source material to be drawn upon in the future.

Of the wartime legacy, Swenarton says:

"By the early part of 1918 it was certain that the promised post-war public housing would be developed on garden suburb lines at the low densities favoured by housing reformers - twelve houses to the acre . . .in urban districts and eight to the acre...in rural areas. It was by no means clear, however, which direction the architecture of public housing would take. The evidence available to *The Builder*...suggested that the picturesque style school was in the ascendant, an impression confirmed by the prominence of picturesque designs in the prize list of the competition organized in 1917 by the LGB and the RIBA." (p.24)

Unwin, like his contemporaries, was seeking practical solutions, and as Swenarton says: "There were also more positive grounds for espousing simplicity of design. To Arts and Crafts designers of a certain persuasion it was to be preferred on aesthetic grounds as well. Faced with the harsh realities of low-cost housing, the picturesque and ornamental could be seen as a 'sham', a pretence reminiscent of the speculative builder. To architects like Unwin, 'rightness of form' could be obtained only by a simple type of house without any false pretensions." (p.27.)

This approach by Unwin and his associates does of course bring them much closer to the continental Modernists whose mantra was that all unnecessary and un-(even dys-)functional detail or ornament should be avoided: "As is well known, the design of standardized housing for the working classes was a central issue for the theoreticians of the European modern movement." (p.29.)

Swenarton also refers to the Housing Congress held in 1916, and dominated by the Liverpool School, the academics in the University there; for example, the well-known Patrick Abercrombie. A key outcome of this event was a focus on simplified styles of housing that would be cost effective. However, with hindsight it is clear that the advocacy of simple styling was more to do with saving money than with aesthetic considerations.

As an aside, I would add that the arrival of Lloyd George as Prime Minister in 1916 signalled a considerable growth in political advisers in Whitehall. Indeed, LG employed so many special advisors that they had to be accommodated in temporary huts erected in the garden of 10 Downing Street, and were dubbed Lloyd George's 'garden suburb'!

From 1917, Unwin had a major role to play in the Tudor Walters Committee (named after the chairman, a prominent Liberal MP and a director of the Hampstead Garden Suburb Trust) which was set up to consider the issues around building construction for housing for the working classes, and usually referred to at the time as 'the experts committee'. The report produced by the Tudor Walters committee became *the* guide for planners. Sidney Stanton, the Borough Engineer in Southampton responsible for Merry Oak (my case study estate and much else) would, like his fellow professionals throughout the UK, very likely have read and used the Tudor Walters report. There was at this time a widespread view that the development of housing plans was best left to borough engineers and the like, within a context of the growing acceptance for 'town planning', a pragmatic and 'professionalising' approach to problem solving. The report was, as Swenarton says: "...a thorough going treatise on the theory and practice of low-cost housing design, encompassing matters as diverse as town and site planning, internal layout and servicing of houses, availability of building materials and new systems of construction." (p.25.)

Not surprisingly, Unwin brought his socialist sympathies to this project, not the least area of his concern being the size, and amenities of the housing. Cottage designs and improved standards were much in evidence. Plans were included in the final report indicative of the quality that Unwin and his associates advocated, while always keeping a close eye on costs. In 1917 Unwin was appointed as the chairman of the Buildings Materials Research Committee. The research profile of the Ministry steadily increased, and Unwin became Ministry representative on the board of the Building Research Station (BRS), which was set up in 1921 as a late response to the Tudor Walters Report (and pressure from Unwin). This was, of course, to become Chamberlain's pet project and he appointed R.E. Stradling as the new director of the Station in 1924. Stradling and Unwin were to remain good friends for many years and continued to work together. The work of BRS expanded considerably over the coming years, with Chamberlain seeking funding over and above what had been previously allocated. I wish to return later to discuss some of the practical outcomes of the work of the BRS as it affected actual house design and building.

THE PROVISIONS of the Tudor Walters Report, eventually published in October 1918, with an established target of 500,000 houses, set the tone for what was to follow with the Addison,

Chamberlain and Wheatley Acts - all within six years - 'Homes fit for Heroes'. In the various reports and recommendations that appeared in these years, Unwin in particular maintained his insistence that any indicative plans were only for guidance, and should not be seen as the only style of housing. However, these Ministry pattern books were created, and clearly did have an influence on local architects and planners. Indeed, as I have suggested above, the anti-architect feeling that emerged in the 1960s and 1970s created a wish for a return to a 'pattern book' approach for local practitioners to follow thus circumventing the form over function designs produced by many architects for buildings and schemes that they would probably not have considered suitable for their own use.

In his book *Raymond Unwin: Garden Cities and Town Planning* (1992), Mervyn Miller reflects on the utilitarian approach that soon came to dominate the post-1918 period of building. This was especially so in the provision of public sector housing (no surprises there), and is echoed in the many years to follow when attempts to agree generously-sized dwellings for working families would be whittled away by the mean-spirited conservatives of all political parties.

As indicated earlier in 1919, Unwin was appointed Chief Architect in the newly created Ministry of Health with Addison as the first minister, and with a clear link made between housing and health. It is clear that Unwin and Addison were close in their values, and equally frustrated by the impediments to the work they both saw needed doing. Jackson, and others, have suggested that Unwin's decision to give up a successful private practice to become a civil servant reflected his desire to bring a practical, hands-on approach to his ideas, perhaps one aspect of his Fabian sympathies.

Several of those writing of Unwin in admiring ways have emphasized these practical aspects to his life.

One such commentator on these matters was Patrick Nuttgens. In his 1972 book *The Landscape of Ideas,* Nuttgens says:

"He was a practical planner, not an academic theorist; but he recognised from the start the fundamental importance of the idea of the community and the practice of corporate life in moulding the form of the environment." (Nuttgens, 1972 p.91.)

Unwin was also very active in building construction research during and after the War. A good deal of what comprised the Tudor Walters report was on the technicalities of securing the resources needed to build large numbers of houses as economically as possible. In this respect, he is close to Wheatley's work as Minister in 1924 while trying to bring together the various stakeholders in the building industry in order to do more.

Unwin was to remain influential in this role as well as chief technical officer for building and town planning until 1928 when he retired from government service, and then turned increasingly to academia. During his time at the Ministry, two housing manuals for site and house plans were issued (as discussed earlier). Unwin also edited a small manual on design. So along with contributions for the Ministry periodical *Housing* in all this 'back office' work Unwin was true to his conviction of striving to bring the centralised resources of the State to the on-going concerns with house design and town planning.

However, I should not allow my enthusiasm for the garden suburb ideal to cloud the fact that many of the suburbs that were created between the 1880s and the 1930s were not a success, and did not live up to the ideals of Unwin and his associates. This was often so because the realisation of these developments was in the hands of inexperienced local authority politicians, borough engineers, and other officials. This is especially so in the apparent failure of many estates to create a cohesive community of like-minded and cooperative citizens. Then, and since, developers of all kinds have assumed that the provision of certain houses built in a particular environment will in itself be sufficient to meet the social role of cohesiveness. This is clearly not the case, and I have addressed this issue more fully elsewhere in this book.

What is less clear was the nature of his relationship with John Wheatley in 1924, other than as a key advisor within the Ministry. Wheatley and Unwin came from very different socialist cultures, and the special nature of Glasgow politics should never be underestimated. For example, Hannan in his comprehensive biography of Wheatley does not mention Unwin. Clearly, Unwin was there, behind the scenes so to speak, and was still active in his advocacy of decent housing, and planning, for working class people. It may well be that his influence within local government circles was what really mattered?

Sidney Stanton, who as I have already mentioned, was the Borough Engineer in Southampton from 1928, and the person directly responsible for Merry Oak and the other 'Garden City/Arts & Crafts' style suburbs, had moved from South Shields council. This area of the northeast of England had major housing (or lack of it) issues, and Stanton must have brought these concerns with him to Southampton. Stanton was born in Dudley in 1890, and married there. From local records in the Southampton archives, it is evident that Stanton took early retirement in 1944-5, moved away to Barnet, where he died in 1948 aged 57. I have been unable to trace any surviving family members with whom to discuss his life, role, and values.

The 1931 *Housing* booklet that I have already referred to is very Arts & Crafts in its design, and clearly indicates some strong cultural influences. Miller confirms that most local authorities did not employ architects, and therefore relied on their Borough Surveyor, and not always to good effect. So, once again, was Southampton fortunate to have Stanton in post? We know that the Council did employ a local private architect to draw up plans, but all those records in the possession of Southampton City archives just give Stanton's name. This architect was almost certainly W.J. Green, who was appointed on a professional-fees basis for work done in the mid-1920s. He drew up eight designs, which are then regularly referred to in council minutes before and after Stanton's appointment. As suggested above, my suspicion is that Green, along with many others around the country, would have drawn on the sample plans and layouts created by Unwin; for example. In his *Town Planning in Practice: An introduction to the Art of Designing Cities and Suburbs* (1909).

In his book on Unwin, Frank Jackson emphasises the centrality of Unwin's influence:

"Though Unwin painstakingly tried not to tread on stylistic toes in discussing site layout and architectural character, his belief in the kinship between community and form led him towards a mediaeval and picturesque mode of design as the most unified in historical terms." (Jackson, 1985 p103.)

I am reminded just how close many of the ideas on planning expressed by Unwin and Parker have found their way into twenty-first century thinking. In my Introduction, I mentioned the Principles of Intelligent Urbanism (PIU) movement. PIU as a doctrine evolved from the city planning guidelines formulated by the International Congress of Modern Architecture, primarily an American late-twentieth century phenomenon.

In brief, the ten principles are:

- ❏ a balance with nature
- ❏ a balance with tradition
- ❏ appropriate technology
- ❏ conviviality (all very Ivan Illich), which itself has six aspects based on 'a place for...' the individual, for friendship, for householders, for the neighbours, for communities, and for the city domain
- ❏ efficiency
- ❏ human scale.
- ❏ opportunity matrix, *e.g.*, a range of sources of development help
- ❏ regional integration
- ❏ balanced movement, *e.g.* integrated transport systems.
- ❏ institutional integrity, *e.g.,* a local government that is accountable.

Most of the above will not come as a great surprise to any thinking person, and some, or all of these principles would be on a list of the basics required to plan the development of viable places for people to live and work. The fact that it seems these ideas have to be regularly 're-invented' by successive generations might suggest to us the lack of attention paid by the State (national and local) to these principles?

I should add that Geddes and Sitte are among the writers who have addressed the idea of *Sharawaggi*, a Chinese term meaning irregular gardening. This in turn is partly derived from the Picturesque landscaping movement, where aesthetics over-ruled symmetry. One of the ideals of the garden suburb has been to excite the eye and the imagination.

However, this is much easier to achieve in the small-scale, and more expensive developments; for example, in the clear differences between Letchworth and Hampstead Garden Suburb.

Other writers on the essential ingredients for everyday life have made similar lists as the PIU one. William Michelson is an example; he suggests:

"The analysis of social life reduces the variations in response to urban form to five dimensions: life style, stage in the life cycle, social status, value orientation, and personality." (Michelson, 1970 p.v/vi)

Did Merry Oak come near to meeting these criteria?

Before moving on, I should add some comment about the lasting effects of Unwin's planning era. As I have already said, the increasingly complicated, and increasingly conservative politics of the 1930s led planning and housing into a *cul-de-sac* that Unwin did *not* design. During the Second World War, there were many discussions about the future of Britain after the war. The debates of this period tend to be dominated by accounts of the 1942 Beveridge Report, but the Labour Party was also busy discussing planning and housing as exemplified in the Party's 1944 pamphlet 'Your Home'. In addition to an obvious discussion about the need to develop a coherent strategy and a practical approach to planning, there was attention also given to the role of the citizen in planning the physical environment. However, what is evident from all this post-1945 activity and enthusiasms is that many of the lessons of the 1920s were not learnt. There is much talk about 'educating' the citizen in order that participation as a desire can be realised, but little seems to have been done. Coupled with a lack of fundamental 'grassroots' engagement with people of all classes, was a failure by local Labour councils (with some honourable exceptions) to impose themselves on this social and cultural process.

Many people whinged about inherently conservative officials and bureaucrats, but did not do anything about it, allowing the former to hold sway over change, or the lack of it. The appalling management of post-1945 council housing stocks was a further example of this problem, and my feeling is that many Labour councillors simply did not trust their working class constituents enough to engage with them in a meaningfully democratic way. What seems very characteristic of the immediate post-1945 period is a reactive, rather than a genuinely pro-active, response to the needs of planning and housing. As has often been the case, local and national administrations, and often Labour Party ones, are easily persuaded to adopt a penny-pinching attitude towards reform. 'This seems like a good idea, but how much will it cost?' I certainly encountered this approach in the 1960s, often arguing with Labour (and other) local politicians that working class families did have an equal right to access good quality services, including housing. These negative attitudes to providing a good quality service were not confined to housing; schooling suffered a similar u-turn on policy and practice after 1945.

As has often been argued (see Tiratsoo, 1998), the sociological and mass observation-type evidence post-1945 emphasised the overwhelming desire of most families of all classes to have a privatised home life, their own front door, a garden, privacy, and access to a functional set of services.

However, to end on a more optimistic note, it should be added that in 1944 the Labour Party did endorse and adopt The Reilly Plan, named after the professor of civic design, whose approach to planning neighbourhood layout, street orientation and housing, was genuine Unwin!

Unwin was transformed by his involvement in the Garden City movement. It set the foundations for his future work on the garden city suburb, his lasting legacy. This is certainly Standish Meacham's argument in his conclusion on the lasting value of the Garden City movement, with the focus on a "physically beneficial and aesthetically pleasing" environment.

"Above all, it had generated a set of principles and ideals that gained acceptance not only in Britain but throughout much of the western world. The years before 1914 witnessed...the spread of the garden city gospel in Europe and America - indeed, throughout much of the world. Howard's book was translated into French, German and Russian before 1914. By that time Garden City Associations had been established in eleven countries, and an International Garden Cities Association founded."

(Meacham, 1999 p.178-9)

It is also clear that these early-twentieth century initiatives led to the proposals for improvement to housing contained in the 1961 Parker-Morris Report.

The centrality of Unwin's role in all of this is clear, and there is substantial physical evidence on the ground.

Community

BEFORE TURNING my attention to the Merry Oak estate, my Southampton case study, I need to provide the reader with some context and say a little about 'Community', and how this connects with what I have already argued in this book.

Wheatley's intervention, building as it did on Addison's pioneering work, came close to the aspirations of many Arts & Crafts enthusiasts by combining a measure that would both address the chronic need for good quality, functional and aesthetically pleasing houses, and would also provide for affordable rents. This provision also coincided with a phase of influence by those who sought to create what was considered to be the most pleasing and valued form of housing, planning and community infrastructure development.

Many other inter-linked developments reflect the ideals of The Diggers, the seventeenth century land reform movement, such as allotments, the right to roam, and sufficient time and resources to engage in solo and group cultural practices of high value: making things, engaging with the arts, especially perhaps music, sport, and so on. (I will return to the Diggers shortly.) The value of all this to a community of like-minded people is what Raymond Williams referred to as "a structure of feeling", the summed-up and recognisable sense that a people have of themselves, for good or for ill, which is also evident to observers.

For over a century, sociologists have been studying 'Community' social relations, and those social relations that can be seen to constitute a community; this is largely because in the industrial societies the forces causing migrations between rural and urban areas (in both directions) have been such a potent issue. For example, a good deal was written in the early-twentieth century on the social and cultural disequilibria caused by these migrations, especially so the dramatic population growth of industrialising towns in the nineteenth-century, most of which did not have any parliamentary representation until after The Reform Act of 1832. Most writing on community has emphasized the importance of shared values linked with local cultures, encompassing shared work and everyday life experiences. The social bonds that make up a community involve looking at fraternal, sharing, and caring aspects of people living in the same place. German sociologists call this *gemeinschaft*, a holistic sense of belonging, attributable in large part to a primarily homogeneous culture. The trouble with most studies carried out by Sociologists, or Social Anthropologists (those working in industrial societies and deciding to 'come down off their colonial veranda') tend to attribute certain kinds of behaviour, both individual and collective, to such social bonds. In reality, there is often very little in common with what social theorists and researchers have said about communities and what the real people 'on the ground' say.

It is clear now that most communities are indeed made up of people who may share a good deal in common culturally, including a history of place, which may be relevant in terms of their sense of identity, and also in the often harsh realties of social change in access to work, and so on. But, many people who live in a particular locality and do in fact invest psychologically and practically into a 'community' may have very little in common, other than a post code, with most other people. What is more commonplace are in fact "communities-in-the-mind". (Pahl, 2005,) Insiders and outsiders, observers near and far, may like to believe that such and such is true of certain people in certain circumstances. Behaviours will certainly be attributed to aspects of 'community' life, possibly social cohesiveness. Perhaps the big question is always going to be whether being a member of a physical and social community (a particular group of people in a certain locality at a specific time) will have a (raised) political consciousness that engenders a social solidarity that will impel them to take action collectively?

A key issue that has been regularly discussed is that of the social stratification in any particular place. This might be strata based on social class, or status, or ethnicity or gender and so on, or a combination of these. Whatever the mix, there will be evidence of hierarchies in *that* 'community', and this will almost certainly affect most aspects of everyday life.

Schooling and education is one clear example, and Gary Easthope is typical of sociologists who have addressed this issue. In his 1975 study, 'Community, hierarchy, and open education' Easthope suggests that the idea of community can be looked at fundamentally in terms of the relationship and conflict between individual freedom and collective organisation and centralisation in people's lives. Easthope argues that schools are inherently hierarchical, and are but one key aspect of hierarchical societies. Basil Bernstein in his pioneering work in the 1960s (see 1970) of the link between social class and language acquisition and use, demonstrated that this is also a core aspect of how, and why, a society, or community is stratified. These factors affect life-chances, and the 'snakes and ladders' of everyday life.

"Working-class community rests on the division of labour in society. The working-class family has few, if any, financial assets. The man has nothing to live from except his labour and his skill. His job is unlikely ever to give him enough money to build up capital, let alone employ others. This...economic division, whatever else it does, pulls the working class together as a group; and as a self-conscious group." (Jackson, 1972 p.164-5)

Since Jackson wrote this, a number of working class families have joined the 'property owning democracy' that was a cornerstone of Thatcherite policy. However, forms of stratification as discussed above have not disappeared.

One recurring motif in middle class writing about working class life and working class 'communities' has been a desire to return to a 'golden age' of community. As I have argued elsewhere in these pages it is true that many working class individuals and families did struggle to adjust to their re-location to new and aspirational estates. These estates were almost entirely designed and built without any consultation with the users, old and new, and tended to concentrate on housing people as soon as possible while focusing less, if any, attention on the infrastructure needed for people to function successfully in their everyday lives. Nicholas Taylor in his 1973 book *The Village in the City* raises this issue and cites the famous 1950s Young and Willmott study of the migration of Bethnal Green residents to the new LCC estate 'Greenleigh' (actually Debden in Essex). Taylor emphasises the tendency for middle class observers to succumb to nostalgia (even to memories that are not theirs!) in over-stressing the value of the old and squalid compared to the new.

It has often been argued that the old life in the homogeneous community was better. Young and Willmott did at least avoid the worst excesses of this patronising tendency, arguing that new housing in itself does not make for a 'community', and did actually emphasise the way in which the resettling of families did encourage a 'turning in' on a more private family life. The advent of commercial TV in the mid-fifties (with access *via* a rented set) was certainly a contributory and reinforcing factor here. Taylor also echoes my own belief that a good quality dwelling in a well-planned environment will always be a cornerstone in providing for a good quality of life. However, this is not enough in isolation from other essentials like a sufficient and secure income, good and accessible social welfare services, cheap transport, and so on.

The social anthropologist Anthony Cohen has been one writer confirming that most 'Sociology of community' sought to confirm that the social and physical structure of a community determined its meanings for those who were members of that social group culture.

The 'old' were carriers, daily reproducers and reinforcers (for example, through social controls) of that culture as valued heritage and tradition, while the young were expected to be socialised into the dominant norms and values - a process of acculturation often resisted by the young.

This structural determinism did dominate most thinking on sociology and ethnography. Emile Durkheim's 'social facts' of everyday life (this is how it is) was a significant influence on both approaches. Cohen argues that even when symbols are used in this approach (as we would expect of Durkheim) they are taken as read, unambiguous guides to the cultural meanings in question. However, this is all too simple because we have to take hermeneutics in to account, and even the double hermeneutic of interpretations being made of other people's interpretation of social reality. (This problematic draws on the concept of *emic,* the insider's view of a culture, and *etic,* the outsider's view, for example, the researcher). Just because someone lives in a particular place, within certain boundaries and apparently a member of some culture group does not mean that they put the same meanings on place and social life. We have to accept that 'community' is a mental as well as a material-based construct. (Cohen, 1985.)

The title of Cohen's book is *The Symbolic Construction of Community*, and it is the 'symbolic' that is so volatile here when coming to discuss suburbs and 'suburbia', in Unwin's day and ever since. *Urb* is the Latin for city, and *sub* is usually translated as 'under' or 'before'; for example, a case is before the court, which means that it is 'under' the jurisdiction of the court. So, a suburb is under the sway of the city; it is a related compartment, or as the dictionaries have it, 'an outlying part' of a city. As I have argued elsewhere in this book, the 'suburb' has often been vilified, cast in the role of a rest home for middle class escapees from the turmoil of central city life. However, as Paul Oliver argues in his edited book *Dunroamin: The suburban semi and its enemies* (1981), the growth of suburbs (private and public sector) in the 1920s and 1930s did not signal escape, but arrival. Le Corbusier, among other 'modernists', railed against the suburb, but unfortunately the accommodation built in his name has not survived as well as the suburbs he despised. His approach brought about, more often than not, the triumph of form over function to the extent that so many such buildings, while looking heroic on the distant skyline are, for one design, construction or management reason or another, dysfunctional. I am just looking at Osbert Lancaster's famous 1938 cartoon of a small part of a suburban road with very Arts & Crafts style houses!

Ray Pahl, one of the most prolific sociological commentators on community in the twentieth century wrote in 1964 about 'urbs in the rure', one of many studies of the migration of people from city to garden suburb or garden city. The aesthetic debates for and against suburban life have often focused on the familiar symbols; 'sunburst' windows, roses in front gardens, tree-lined avenues, and small, integrated parks, regular references to Arts & Crafts motifs, and so on.

Ebenezer Howard argued against the even further spread of the suburb, and yet he was writing and planning at a time when the Arts & Crafts dominated suburbs of the late-nineteenth century were at their zenith, never more popular. It has often been the alleged conservative politics and 'lifestyle' of the suburb that has upset critics; but that measure is a very weak one as Merry Oak, like many suburbs, has not corresponded to that description in any simple way.

These issues take us to Williams' conceptualisation of a 'structure of feeling' in the sense that values that *are* shared do have meaning and give coherence to people's understanding of who they are: their *identity*.

Williams was influenced by (but critical of) F.R. Leavis, who in the introduction to his 1933 book *Culture and Environment* argues that:

"...literary education, we must not forget, is to a great extent a substitute. What we have lost is the organic community with the living culture it embodied. Folk-songs, folk-dances, Cotswold cottages and handicraft products are signs and expressions of something more: an art of life, a way of living, ordered and patterned, involving social arts, codes of intercourse and a responsive adjustment, growing out of immemorial experience, to the natural environment and the rhythm of the seasons in the annual cycle. That is why it is difficult to take revivals seriously. It is not merely that life, from having been predominantly rural and agricultural, has become urban and industrial. When life was rooted in the soil, town life was not what it is now. Instead of the community urban or rural, we have, almost universally, suburbanism." (Leavis, p.1-2.)

The 'organicism' of Leavis seems attractive, but is in fact a set of values built on the shifting sands of very elitist attitudes about the need to respond to the coming of mass society undermining a homogeneous culture. What Leavis and his supporters claimed as *the* high culture that was, or should be, universal was always a very partial view, that is, the wishful thinking of a bourgeois who turned his back on demands for a more democratic and open multi-culturalism. People 'knowing', and being in their place, was more satisfactory for all.

As always, language plays a crucial part in any consideration of these issues. I am reminded here of Richard Hoggart's seminal book *The Uses of Literacy* (1957), where among other issues he describes the way American popular culture has drawn (younger) people away from their shared and common-place language. This in turn rendered people susceptible to a new consumer culture *via* the language of advertising, and so on.

Communal support exists on the basis of shared and understood inter-relationships between personal troubles and social problems, or issues. A homegrown resilience develops to deal with adversity, and altruism is effectively built into the fabric of everyday life. Sociologists use the concept social capital to emphasise the deep reservoir of local know-how that people come to rely upon. However, I would add that it has been argued in the 1920s and 1930s that there were ideologically driven political moves to weaken and nullify the continuing influence of local co-operative ventures, and even the Co-operative movement itself, in favour of the spread of liberal individualism and a consumerist approach to everyday life. (see Neil Killingback, 1988)

These concerns are discussed in some detail by Lynn Pearson in her 1988 book *The Architectural and Social History of Cooperative Living*. Her approach to these developments emphasises the growing independence of women in both thought and deed. One of the main aims of cooperative and communal living was to release women from the everyday burden of domestic chores. The early-twentieth century was already a period of labour-saving technological innovations, and these coupled with a collective approach to essential domestic work offered an opportunity for more women to seek satisfying employment outside of the home. Walter Crane in a 1905 article was not unique among Arts & Crafts practitioners in advocating the design and building of dwellings that facilitated such cooperative approaches, and which could incorporate resources for education and leisure. Many Fabians were enthusiastic advocates of cooperative living, and Unwin and Parker certainly addressed such ideas in their early books; for example *The Art of Building a Home*.

There are clearly echoes of these ideas in much of the utopian fiction of the time: Bellamy's *Looking Backward;* Morris' *News from Nowhere*; and, later, Skinner's *Walden Two*. Men and women were involved in these late-nineteenth and early-twentieth century discussions, and these issues drew attention to the increasing number of women practising as architects. Women had been excluded from the RIBA until 1898, but there were at least twelve practising female architects in London by 1891.

However, despite all the promising pre-1914 developments, and the greater role of women in work outside of the home during the war, progress was limited or even thwarted by male vested interests. During the war there were several committees of active women focused on planning and housing, and these carried on afterward; for example, submitting evidence to the Local Government Board/Ministry of Health up to and including the Tudor Walters Committee, where most of this evidence was ignored.

An example of the concept of social capital in practice would be cooperative housing schemes, and Colin Ward, one of our leading contemporary writers on housing, identified difficulties for any group of local people engaging in their own development in his 1986 review:

"Progressive councils everywhere built their new estates on the fringe of the city or made wholesale clearance of the old streets to provide new blocks of flats. As the years went by, the professionals of the housing industry produced larger and larger schemes of more and more idiosyncratic appearance, which met every single standard that authorities had decreed for housing provision, but which were less and less liked by the tenants who were obliged to move there…There has been very good and very bad public housing, but none in which tenants have had a hand in the design or the management. The price paid for not involving tenants has been very high indeed." (Ward, 1986)

I have said more about this issue in my chapter on Raymond Unwin.

In the mid-1980s, Ward was merely emphasising that the accumulated local social capital was being ignored by planning experts and authorities who, yet again, thought they new best; with a focus on form before function; and certainly did not feel it was appropriate to involve tenants in the provision of their own housing even though this was paid for from taxes, and done in the name of local citizens. It is hardly surprising, then, that many working class families chose the owner occupation route as soon as they could, and certainly took the 'right to buy option' in large numbers.

Again, to paraphrase Williams, the overlooked reservoir of local experience and know-how, makes for a 'knowable community', not just of the present, but importantly in shared memories, good and bad, of the past.

The contemporary realities of these issues are well summed-up by Anna Minton in her absorbing new book *Ground Control: Fear and Happiness in the twenty-first-century city*; for instance, in her discussion of (quite literally so), 'the building blocks' of conviviality. She reminds us that a great deal was made of the prospects for progress, harmony and happiness by New Labour, "Things can only get better" they sang!

Well, clearly things have got worse for many people since 1997, and if civil society is to survive the current chaos of casino capitalism and an authoritarian state apparatus, which actively supports a banal and vulgar media directed by celebrity-fixated consumerism, this is surely not the way forward.

"We cannot shop our way out of this malaise. Something radical needs to happen, and soon." (Minton, 2009.)[1]

This viewpoint also reflects the work of several radical, even Marxist, theorists in the 1980s and 1990s. Manuel Castells was one such thinker and writer, who adopted a structuralist Marxist perspective (much in common with Louis Althusser, another French thinker) to discuss the urban question. Castells started out by taking an uncompromising view of urban movements by suggesting that they were always second-best to specific class-based politics in a capitalist, industrial and urban society. However, by the 1980s he had modified his view to argue that non-party political-issues based social movements did in fact have an important role to play. He acknowledged that most of these movements *were* urban-issues based; for example, around tenants' rights, or fending-off unwanted development, road building, and the like. These movements, which drew on existing social capital did engage people with a localised politics that emphasised for people the lack of genuine democracy in a society that prided itself on being open and democratic in its forms.

Many local and regional urban movements soon realised that they shared many issues in common with other groups across the country; and indeed beyond the UK, and as a consequence sought out many alliances. Manuel Castells was one theorist who emphasised that these experiences did in fact raise political

---

[1] In 2012, Minton added a sequel to her book addressing the lack of community benefit to be derived from the Olympics developments

consciousness along with an awareness of the real limits to liberal democratic political structures. At the same time the German sociologist Jurgen Habermas, a Marxist, and the last member of the Frankfurt School, developed his ideas on 'communicative action', arguing that rather than being open and with freedom of speech, the rulers of capitalist liberal democratic societies sought to close down discussion about the adequacy of contemporary political institutions to actually represent the views of the majority of citizens. At the moment, we are very much back to these critiques once more.

Ray Pahl (who I have already cited) argued that a key underlying feature of any community, or locality, was the politics of resource allocation. In his 1970 book *Whose City* Pahl argued for the following criteria related to resource allocation:

❑ There are fundamental *spatial* constraints on access to scarce urban resources and facilities. Such constraints are generally expressed in time/cost distance.

❑ There are fundamental *social* constraints on access to scarce urban facilities. These reflect the distribution of power in society and are illustrated by: bureaucratic rules and procedures; (and) social gatekeepers who help to distribute and control urban resources.

❑ Populations in different localities differ in their access and opportunities to gain scarce resources and facilities, holding their economic position or their position in the occupational structure constant. (Pahl, 1970 p.215)

These factors can, according to Pahl, lead to conflicts over the allocation of valued resources; conflicts that both local and national politics is required to deal with in one way or another, in one groups interests or another…And, in 2012, in the era of 'Localism' we should quite literally, 'watch this space'.

There is a further key issue that flows from the above, namely the concept of an 'Ideal Community'. Thomas Reiner argues that 'Ideal Community' is a legitimate place to start a planning design discussion. The protagonist can set out the key criteria; what makes up 'the ideal'; against which any actual developments in thought and deed can be measured or assessed.

'The Ideal Community is deduced from basic assumptions about the good life' (Reiner, 1963 p.15)

So, in this sense the Ideal Community is a utopian vision, what should be. Part of Reiner's aim is to discuss the way or extent to which ideas like utopia are programmatic, and actually lead to changes in social life. Do the goals set out translate in to the Ideal Community that is sought? This is one example of the widespread and lasting influence of the Arts & Crafts and Garden City movements.

This line of argument raises the key question for 'planners' of whether some proposals stand more chance of success than others? Do proposals need to draw on existing high value ideas (and crucially, images) embedded, in the existing culture that can be 'awakened', drawn upon and moved from the residual perhaps to the emergent, as part of an argument for change. I would argue that it is clear to see this happening in the proposals for planning and building design in the 1920s and 1930s that drew upon the ideas and images from the Arts & Crafts vernacular. While considering the complexity of such cultural contexts, I should add at this point that there are also myriad methodological issues here, and I can only briefly allude to them. Williams' work is often seen as the most well known example of 'culturalism', an approach to understanding social relationships, and human actions that emphasise the agency (role and scope) of ordinary people to transform everyday life. Our lives may well be conditioned to a great extent by powerful external forces; but, and it is a big but, we are the ones who take the action in the face of everyday life events. We mediate the world through our vision of it, for good or for ill. And this is not just a personal response; it is also collective, in our shared interpretation and understanding of life's ups and downs. We develop values, and theories about what, who, and why, and take action accordingly. In Social Science, these methodological influences are referred to as 'the cultural turn', and marked a point in the 1970s especially when many sociologists in particular realised that fathoming the mysteries of human society had to go beyond statistics or studying the lives of great men.

One of the reasons why sociology experienced the 'cultural turn' was because of the deep dissatisfaction mentioned above. There was a tendency in the hegemonic 'structural-functionalist' grand theorising that represented the person as a 'social clone', a 'sleepwalker', and generally someone who because of the power, or dominance, of social institution led socialization and social control, had little agency, or choice-making capacity or cultural creativity. Societal influences, the dominance of sets of values and social norms were seen as both inevitable and necessary if, against all the rapidly changing modern world odds, social order was to be maintained.

There was implicit in most Sociology the idea that creativity was essentially a leisure activity of the middle and upper classes, and where it did exist at the margins in working class life, was exotic, deviant and probably dangerous. Most 'normal' people were to be encouraged to bend their selves to the obvious needs of mass society; work, family, deference to one's betters, legality, be unquestioning, grateful and certainly not oppositional to the *status quo* of class, gender and race orthodoxies. Sociologists of the 1950-60s became increasingly influenced by the work of the Frankfurt School on the one hand, and the (once again) growing atavistic and liberational ideas of the working class-focused adult education. It is no accident that those such as Leavis, Williams, Hoggart, Thompson, Hall, and Willis, *et. al.* developed their ideas about 'common culture' in this growing democratic milieu. As Williams would have it, a 'structure of feeling' that was most definitely oppositional. No surprise, then, that their values reflected the growth and influence of a post-1945 literature, drama, cinema and so on, that embraced Sillitoe, Storey, Barstow, Livings, Mercer, Loach, Garnett, Potter, and the rest.

One link with this alternative and oppositional cultural creativity with the Frankfurt School was the belief that this 'home grown' working class focused account of real life would challenge the elite/high art cultural hegemony of the British establishment. It is also the struggle between the politics of everyday experience, recognising shared needs and addressing them, compared and contrasted with the political abstractions; derived from studying Politics, Philosophy and Economics (PPE) at Oxbridge; of generations of middle class do-gooders 'leading' the Labour movement.

However, a note of warning is required here about the blanket use of the word 'culture', and especially the role of Williams. There has been a tendency since 'the cultural turn' to argue that everything is an outcome of culture, and if that is the case there is not much point in talking about it because clearly it is just like the 'Blackpool' running through a stick of rock! Williams certainly argued, as I do here, that there are many aspects of our everyday lives that are essentially materialist, not the least being our own unique biology. Of course, many aspects of our 'ways of life' are influenced if not determined by the language we speak, the rituals we attend to, the stuff we believe and has meaning for us, and the shared understandings we have.

It is because these *cultural* dimensions of our lives can and do make a difference that it is worth discussing them. In this sense, culture is ordinary, but in selectively relevant ways.

Otherwise, my advice is not to bother with it!

Historians have also struggled with such issues, particularly in regard to popular memory. Many historians would now agree that "memory is larger, or something more, than history." (O'Keeffe, in Moore and Whelan, 2007 p.5.) O'Keeffe suggests that what constitutes 'our' memory is certainly shaped, or influenced, by historical narratives. We, ordinary persons, social beings, living our everyday lives, certainly remember 'the past', but how accurate is this? What is the veracity of the anecdotes we share? Of course, Social Historians and Sociologists, among other researchers, seek out, and record, the stories that people tell.

Stefan Collini in his 1999 book *English Pasts* addresses these concerns: "Historians who also venture to write as social critics exemplify in a distinctive way the tension at the heart of the intellectual's, especially the academic intellectual's, cultural authority." (p.85, Collini, 1999.)

Collini discusses Gertrude Himmelfarb's *The Demoralization of Society* (1995), which focused on the issue of the shift from Victorian virtues to modern values, and charts the way in which the collective authority that dominated everyday life then has been supplanted by the values of possessive individualism.

This view is a conservative one, but also one that cannot be completely dismissed from a wider discussion about the prevailing sentiments required to maintain civil *society.*

Collini also draws on the mid-1990s writing of Raphael Samuel, a very different contributor to these debates, about what constitutes 'history'. Samuel's 1994 book *Theatres of Memory*, a collection of disparate essays, seeks to offer up a democratised view of history; for example, in the need to place a high(er) value on the 'popular memory'. There is nothing new here as the bread and butter of the social historian. Indeed, a good deal of what I say in this essay emphasizes the way in which so many people associated with Arts & Crafts constantly drew on folk traditions and idioms; or indeed assumed ones, in the pursuit of their own style and the justification for that style.

Samuels' approach was a contradictory one in that he claimed this democratic methodology, seeing *everyone* as 'the historian', but he also valued the role of those, like himself and his acolytes, who spent their working lives *as* Historians. However, the reader will have noted by now that I prefaced this essay with reference to 'a memory', and therefore I, too, am placing some value on this aspect of human consciousness. As I discuss elsewhere in this book, Samuels was also debating with Patrick Wright on what constituted an appropriate sense of the English past.

Also on this key question of memory, I should mention the perspective of the writer Siri Hustvedt, who commented that: "Narrative is a necessary organising force in our lives, a way of making sense of disparate and fragmentary sensory and cognitive material that bombards us all the time from outside."

As I have already suggested, that perspective may be an individual or collective one, and indeed many 'communities' have enthusiastically embraced the idea that oral and written histories of persons, places and culture groups should be elicited from 'the people' and developed as a matter of record, and so place a certain, higher, value on that record. One of the key issues that we all have to address is why do some memories exist, while much else of our lives has gone? Why is it there appears to be a process of value judgements placed on what we do remember? It might well be the case that some memories are coaxed, or even coached, from us. Memories are certainly a reservoir that both our conscious and unconscious mind draws on, often linked to some potent emotional agenda. I am reminded here of Dennis Potter's writing, particularly so his later TV plays like *Blue Remembered Hills* (even if he did relocate 'the hills' from Wenlock Edge to the Forest of Dean), *The Singing Detective*, and the last two plays *Kereoke* and *Cold Lazarus*. This last play poses some interesting questions about the use of memory for commercial and political purposes.

What I have suggested here about 'community' could well contribute to our use of collective memory; for example, of 'our' community. My later chapter on Merry Oak reflects this. Our identity, our sense of self, of who we (all) are, is most definitely linked with these cultural processes. It is also true to say that many of these narratives take the form of music and song, and these are collected, and deployed, in a creative cultural process of enlightenment.

GERARD WINSTANLEY is the most well known person associated with The Diggers, the mid-seventeenth century land reform movement that was in turn a part of The Levellers movement within the Parliamentary forces at the time of the Civil War in the seventeenth century. Winstanley and The Diggers sought to gain access for all people to land, the very essence of creating the conditions for life. The Diggers argued that private ownership of land and its use for the creation and harbouring of wealth leads to economic and political power and oppression. Indeed, when a group of the Diggers were brought before Cromwell to be examined about their activities they refused to remove their hats on the basis that this man was just their equal. The Levellers, led by Lilburne and Overton, had set the tone by insisting on the sovereignty of the people and casting Parliament and Government as the servant of the people, not their master. Through good government the people would be able to appreciate agency within the collective response to satisfying their needs. People could expect government to act in the interests of all by, for example, securing the means of a decent, honourable way of life that guaranteed fair and reasonable access to the core necessities of life: peace, freedom of association, food, shelter and the expression of their creativity.

There are threads of continuity from The Diggers to the schemes (usually utopian socialist ones) from the eighteenth century onwards to establish communes. Indeed, one of the regular responses to the harsh realities of urban life within industrial capitalism has been a return to 'the land'. Whose land has also always been a key issue, and we should not forget the work of Fergus O'Connor and other Chartists in their bid to establish communities that were democratically owned and run.

In my chapter on Raymond Unwin, there is a brief discussion on the ideas of Edward Carpenter, a well-known late-nineteenth century champion of all that the Diggers and their descendants argued for.

Diverse forms of commutarian dissent have run in our collective consciousness, as have its practical applications. One such example of this is in Stanley Buder's book *Visionaries and Planners* (1990) where he cites Paul and Percival Goodman's book *Communitas: Means of Livelihood and Ways of Work* published in 1947:

"…they emphasised a fraternal associationism in both design and values to break with the values of consumer capitalism and its tendency to force life and its various roles into tightly sealed-off compartments" (Buder, p.202.)

Just because many of these responses are less visible today does not mean they cease to exist, or be potent influences. Indeed, the evidence here in England is that there is a queue of pioneers wishing to join the growing number of purpose-built 'communal' co-housing schemes. (See 'Love they neighbour' *The Guardian* 24 October 2009.)

I feel that it is inevitable that such discussion as this will bring us to an assessment of 'Utopia', and an assessment of just how important this concept was during my period of interest.

In his essay 'The Necessity of Utopia', Mark Holloway says that the nineteenth century had seen great hope placed in the advance towards 'Utopia'. This was certainly there in Marx and Engels, of course, who in many ways argued that the enormous potential of the industrial revolution could and should be harnessed for the liberation of all humankind. Many of the Arts & Crafts pioneers shared this goal; and their engagement with a variety of 'socialisms' demonstrated this. Morris certainly wrote about, and then spoke, at length on this, and I return to this particular theme elsewhere in this book. Holloway emphasises that by the mid-twentieth century the utopian vision had increasingly soured, and a turn to dystopia was clearly evident: "Utopia had not entirely disappeared, however. It had slipped out of the atlas onto the drawing-board or into the government white paper." (Holloway, 1984 p.180)

My particular interest in Arts & Crafts and Garden City influences on planning and building fits well with Holloway's reference to 'the drawing board'. It should also be acknowledged that after 1942 with the Beveridge Report, and then after 1945 with the implementation of 'the Welfare State' many working class families believed that they had indeed arrived at the shores of utopia, and that life could only get better for them, their contemporaries and their children. This was certainly true with the still-linked concerns with health and housing that Bevan addressed in the late-1940s.

If Wheatley had had the opportunity to do so in the mid-1920s he might well have achieved as much or more. However, we also need to acknowledge that when the 'utopian' goals that are set come closer to fruition, aspirations move on, and shifts in dominant ideologies do have a significant impact on social policy.

I also need to offer a word of caution on the extent of interest most ordinary people have in either the politics of progress or themselves as 'big picture' agents of change.

"It is true that the English are kindly folk. But a good deal of what is praised as tolerance is merely indifference, based on a dwindling interest in politics and also a false feeling of security. It is not so much that these people are monuments of patience and kindness as that they do not really care about what is happening in public affairs." ~ *J.B. Priestley.*

This statement of matter-of-factness from the English author in 1935 could have been written yesterday in 2012 as a not altogether unreasonable or surprising response to prime minister David Cameron and his 'Big Society' rhetoric.

The Priestley quote comes from *England Arise: the Labour Party and popular politics* in 1940s Britain by Steven Fielding, Peter Thompson and Nick Tiratsoo (1995), and reflects their central argument concerning the limited view of politics that most people hold, then and now. These authors argue that in general terms politics means voting, and not much else most of the time. As I have said elsewhere in this study, and raise again in my chapter on Merry Oak, the evidence suggests that most people, most of the time focus first and foremost on the home, the family, friends, and the immediacy of work, and so on. Not the bigger picture. In my experience, people in Britain are motivated to take action, become involved on the basis of a particular issue, and often not 'connecting-up-the-dots' of context. The history of the labour movement in Britain since the end of the nineteenth century, with its tribal focus, is testimony to this narrow, even blinkered, view of everyday life.

One reason for this 'indifference' that Priestley suggests is that working class people in particular have been consistently told that they do not really have anything worth saying, and developing and encouraging political education has always been a very low priority for the ruling elites.

The Labour Party has occasionally ventured into policy initiatives on forms of political education; especially leading up to elections; but have always been cautious about raising political or class consciousness. Over successive generations, the leadership of the labour movement has offered a top-down vision of politics, (as with my comment about PPE above) invariably demonstrating their fear and distrust of working class independence and militancy. It is not surprising to note the manner in which working class families have been offered a 'bread and circuses' approach to everyday life, kept enthralled by a frivolous and self-referential popular culture.

Predating the quote from Priestley above, Godfrey Elton in his 1931 version of *England Arise* raised very similar concerns, emphasizing the difficulty then of *moving* people, and stirring them into action. This is after all what 'movements' are supposed to be about! Elton drew very specifically on the galvanizing rhetoric of Edward Carpenter's Socialist song 'England Arise', and the importance of this form of rallying cry in 1883-4. (Elton, 1931)

As I have discussed elsewhere in this study (for example, in what I have to say about the key role of Raymond Unwin), questions do need to be asked about the aim of planning communities. Can communities be planned? Who should and does do the planning? There is no doubt that Unwin and his associates poured considerable amounts of goodwill and optimism into the task of housing people, particularly so working class families. This is evidently true in the politics of John Wheatley, and generally of most of the planning and housing legislation of the period from 1919 to 1939. There were then, as later, high hopes of genuine reform and progress, the outcomes were mixed, short-term success gone sour. . .an anti-climax.

Gustav Holst and Ralph Vaughan Williams, who have already been mentioned in this book, are good examples of this artistic response. Like Delius and Finzi, they have often been categorized as 'English Pastoralists'.

Holst talked to his students and musical colleagues about the recovery of the early English music tradition, lost for two hundred years prior to the early-twentieth century. Both he and his friend Vaughan Williams sought to incorporate the best of that tradition into their music, often drawing on folk idioms that had vanished, or under- valued, for decades. They did not believe that a 'return' to a recovered English folk was *the* answer to the development of music, but they were open-minded and inquisitive.

Holst, Vaughan Williams, and Elgar, of course, were all the inheritors of the dominant influence of Teutonic music (Holst's family were German), and were well socialized in to the German musical hegemony of the time. Elgar met his first real success in Germany and spent very enjoyable times there, and was deeply upset by the jingoism of the 1914-18 war. Holst and VW were determined to (re)create an English music, and drew directly on their discovery of English folk songs (as I have already indicated). Both these musicians wrote and talked vigorously about the need to create this English music and were well versed on all the developments around them; for example, with the publication of *English Country Songs* (1893) by Lucy Broadwood and Fuller-Maitland.

Vaughan Williams wrote a good deal about a national music,

and about folk music; this piece, for example, is from his 1955 essay on 'The Folk-Song Movement':

"Music, like language, derives ultimately from its basic beginnings...About fifty years ago, Cecil Sharp made his epoch-making discovery of English folk-song. We young musicians were intoxicated by these tunes. We said to ourselves, 'Here are beautiful melodies of which, until lately, we knew nothing. We must emulate Grieg and Smetana, and build up, on the basis of these tunes, a corpus of compositions arising out of our country and character.' And we proceeded to pour out Overtures and Rhapsodies and Ballad Operas to show the world that we were no longer a land without music." (Vaughan Williams, 1996 p.235)

I would add Bela Bartok and Zoltan Kodaly (among many others) to Vaughan Williams' list, since their musical composition was enhanced and developed along with their nationalistic Hungarianess, by their 'discovery' of, and uses of, folk forms.

There is also something important here about 'style'. What I mean by style is a negotiated, or re-negotiated, cultural space for role performance, of whatever form, such as music, design, architecture, clothing fashions, and so on. We all seek to express our sense of self, our identity, through the creative actions we take; however, there will be social control forms of circumscription of our attempts to do so. Struggles will ensue, which will take many forms dependent on the people and situation; but out of these struggles, and in a dialectical way, a new 'space' or style will come about. This is a further aspect of the relationship between residual and emergent cultures that I discussed above.

No one who has listened to the music of Holst and Vaughan

Williams could accuse them of being stuck in nostalgia or in the least 'chocolate-boxy', since there is plenty of Hardy-esque darkness among the light!

One obvious Hardy connection to traditional English singing traditions is in his novel *Under the Greenwood Tree,* where the Mellstock locals have a run-in with the new and aesthete vicar about unaccompanied singing in church, and the singing of carols at Christmastime.

Both Holst and Vaughan Williams wrote many carols and hymns, 'In the Bleak Midwinter' being one of Holst's best known based on Christina Rossetti's poem. These tunes were often written with non-professional choirs and musicians in mind. Vaughan Williams, the agnostic of the two, delighted in the verve and jollity of Christmas, another triumph of Dionysus over the Puritans! It is always worth recalling that Cromwell actually banned Christmas Day-singing in church as an unnecessary intrusion. Fortunately, many of the singing traditions were continued in the countryside out of sight and sound of religious fanatics.

On the advice of Cecil Sharp (the folk song collector mentioned above) Percy Dearmer, the idiosyncratic churchman, persuaded Vaughan Williams to produce 'The English Hymnal' published in 1906. This was a monumental task, especially, as Vaughan Williams noted, since he had wade through Victorian treacle to get to the music.

In his 1989 book *Vaughan Williams: and the Vision of Albion,* Wilfred Mellers says:

"Vaughan Williams demonstrated that the human spirit, however abused by industrial materialism and bureaucratic institutionalism, lay dormant, awaiting resuscitation. His life's work was to be, in Blake's sense, a rebirth of the Human Imagination, in a new vision of Albion." (p.2.)

Those who know the music of Holst and Vaughan Williams, these two great *Englishmen*, will understand the strong evocation of 'pastoral' alongside the evidently modern dimension to their music. Those who have not experienced the joy of Holst and Vaughan Williams are advised to start now, where they will also find a darker side to *their* pastoral evocation of England's 'green and pleasant land'. I should add that Vaughan Williams began the sketches for his Pastoral Symphony (his third symphony) in 1916 while 'in the trenches'. The symphony had its first performance in January 1922, and when listened to today still creates a vivid mixture of light and shade, hope and despair, or at least dismay, reflecting the complexity of cultural meanings we have about the pastoral.

One key cultural value in any musical or narrative form would be a shared pride in a local community, often so in the struggles to cope with the 'snakes and ladders' of everyday life. There is invariably a real sense of 'to everyone according to their needs, and from everyone according to their means' in the cooperative and collective approach to life. Reciprocity is evident alongside empathy. As I suggested earlier, a necessary and realistic altruism is often incorporated into the very fabric of working class life. The size, and even spatial layout of a community, for example, in a visually manageable location, can be crucial to a sense of security encouraging a together-ness rather than isolation and indifference.

However, it is clear from research done over many years that the provision of housing is not, in itself, enough to meet the criteria for what constitutes an effective and efficient community in these respects. There have to be other key social institutions: shops, schools, a pub, a 'church', a library, sport and other leisure facilities, and social care and health service providers to help with certain problems. Whether these are all provided by the local or national State is another matter. There also has to be a stability of incomes at a level to sustain people of all ages. Food comes before philosophy, and these several materialist realities represent a key set of factors for everyone.

Elsewhere in this book, I have engaged with the debates around the virtues and vices of suburbs, and it is worth reminding ourselves that the North Americans of the 1940s and 50s had very mixed emotions on the subject. Lewis Mumford, Charles Haar and the Goodman brothers are mentioned, and I would wish to draw the sociologist David Riesman into this brief discussion. Riesman was one of several thinkers of the 1950s who asked the almost heretical question: "Affluence for what?" He made an extensive study of the mores of suburbia, and concluded:

". . .what is missing in suburbia, even where the quality of life has not overtly deteriorated, is not the result of claustrophobic conformity to others' sanctions. Rather, there would seem to be an aimlessness, a pervasive low-keyed unpleasure."

(Riesman quoted in Haar, 1972 p.35)

Anyone who has read Richard Yates' novel *Revolutionary Road* (1961), or seen the recent film version, could not fail to note Riesman's verdict on the fate of the 'organization man'.

One aim of enlightened planners, like Howard and Unwin, has been to incorporate all of the elements of the self-sufficient community within the social matrix that gives structure to everyday life. Democratic controls over these institutions may only come through a further series of struggles, or enlightened 'wardenship' of localities. What form that wardenship takes, and who organises it, would say a good deal about the members of any community. I shall return to these issues when discussing Merry Oak, my case study in the next chapter.

"Now and then Utopians (realists in the long run, that is, rather than of the moment) actually undertake to plan their physical surroundings. Instead of setting loose controls over broad categories of land use, they specify in detail the character and location of this structure, such and such a space.' (p.iii Tilley in Michelson, 1970.)

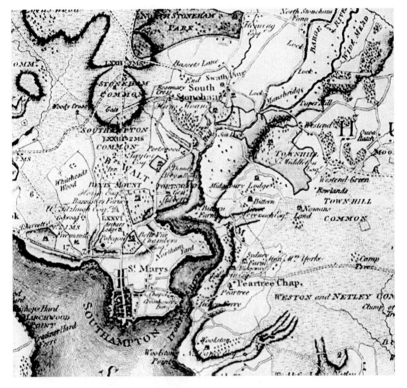

14. Southampton antique chart: the Bitterne area
of the city is the location for the *Access to Eden*
case study of the Merry Oak housing development.
Courtesy: Bitterne History Society.

Merry Oak

NOW IT is time for me to turn my focus on the Merry Oak estate in Southampton, and Joan Rolfe's anecdotal memoir is a good place to start:

"The new estate, regarded as probably the most attractive of all council-housing, consisted of varied styles of well designed houses; those in Merry Oak Lane (later renamed Merry Oak Road) were semi-detached with two reception rooms and usually allocated to larger families. Other houses were smaller, but all had indoor bathrooms. Those applying for tenancies had to produce marriage certificates, evidence of low income, and must have children." (Joan Rolfe in *The Book of Bitterne*, 2007 p.137)

Merry Oak was the name of an early-nineteenth century house built in parkland next to the expanding parish of Bitterne, where I was to grow up. The estate was an extensive wooded area, but by the 1920s the Errington family had abandoned the house, which fell into disrepair. The Council bought the land, and set about developing a housing plan that would go some way to meeting the chronic shortage of affordable rented accommodation for working class families. Houses were also made available for elderly people, so my sense of the development was that a 'community' was planned from the outset. The planners thoughtfully used the existing park-like environment, and many pastoral characteristics were incorporated into the scheme.

It is interesting that the word 'estate' seems to have slipped effortlessly from meaning a large area of land and buildings owned by a member of the gentry to a planned area of housing for people of lower classes. The eighteenth century estate builders engineered, often quite literally, a return to the 'natural' look, or at least their idealised version of it.

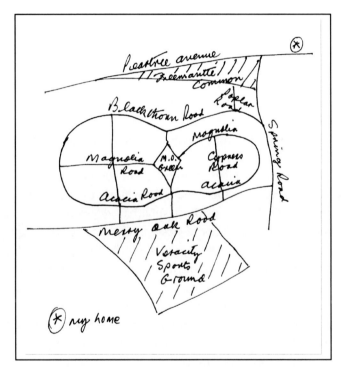

15. Merry Oak estate located in the the Bitterne suburb of Southamption. (*Author sketch.*)

There had to be vistas, groves, grottos, follies of 'instant' ancient buildings, especially those in thrall to the Gothic, and the ha-has, which every estate had to have to keep the beasts out of the garden. This was picturesque, evoking nature, or even mocking it, pastoral and romantic, and expressing a certain mastery over nature commonplace in an era so devoted to 'progress'. Of course, there are links here with the public parks movement often complementary to the housing estates of the late- nineteenth and early-twentieth centuries.

Arts & Crafts styles and motifs are very evident in what was done at Merry Oak, with the curvature of the roads, the houses, and infrastructure artefacts like well covers, and seating areas. So, in fact the *new* estate was made to look older, as if it had 'always' been there. This is a commonplace feature of the vernacular architectural design which Morris, Webb, *et al* inherited from their teachers. The roads were named after trees, or other flora. The provision of a school was included in the overall planning, the first phase of which was opened in April 1935.

The famous twentieth century architect Louis Kahn once said: "Architecture is the thoughtful making of space." One of the great difficulties with most suburban developments is that the buildings are the focus of design, and not the whole space. This invariably creates the impression of buildings dropped into a space without consideration for 'positive' or planned spaces between buildings, as distinct from unplanned, and usually 'negative' spaces. Merry Oak was planned holistically, with the spaces between the roads and buildings contributing to the overall feeling of inclusion. It is classical design in the sense of being created for a specific set of social functions, not just to provide dwellings for people. The planning of buildings and spaces is quite like music, since it is often the spaces between the notes that are crucial to the overall effect; this is a question of relationships that I have discussed elsewhere in this study.

Arts & Crafts values stressed precisely this; there is a desire to create aesthetic interest, adventure; excite the eye, and take it on a journey. The meanings people place on a particular environment are to some extent influenced by form and response to function: does it work and do a job well? This is almost certainly one dimension of what constitutes a 'neighbourhood'. We know that a neighbourhood is more than a physical and geographical entity. The likes of Unwin knew this intuitively, and set about designing accordingly.

There are also issues of creative imagination at work; is this a thing of beauty? The design work of Raymond Unwin is central to these concerns, and for Unwin and his associates it was crucial that at last there should be a vigorous response to the environmental and housing chaos that an anarchic industrial capitalism had brought about.

The call for a reasoned, aesthetic and socially just response to *planning* the environment was loud and clear - for those that wanted to listen. There were plenty of people in Southampton who *did* listen, and were prepared to act.

So, when considering the planning and design work of the 1920s that created Merry Oak, the recent past of building chaos, slums and overcrowding should also be recalled. Standish Meacham reminds us of the poor standards of housing and environment even for the better-off members of the working class, who could afford a higher rent. The combination of shoddily built, patched-up, dirty and insanitary housing added up to the slums that were the constant focus of Edward Simon and his associates in the nineteenth century. Meacham adds that in most working class districts any variety was provided by the type of factory, or railways or canals that tended to dominate the landscape.

"Wherever the neighbourhood, and whoever its inhabitants, visual monotony was almost certain to be its most distinguishing characteristic. Whether houses were two-up, two-down or larger, back-to-back or open to a court, they stretched the same across the landscape, aligned together at the streets edge, built of a common stone or brick..." (Meacham, 1977 p.32)

As I have suggested elsewhere in this book, there is a lasting issue to address over the identification and policy development around public health. The very specific early- to mid-nineteenth century focus on necessary sanitary dwellings for the labouring classes derived from a complex mixture of the urban spread of disease, the displacement of vast numbers of migrants as a consequence of agricultural and industrial capitalism, fear of revolution, and humanitarianism. Housing, or the lack of it in an adequate, appropriate and safe form, was a problem the State at national and local level could not ignore. However, the 'problem' label stuck to many or most policy rhetoric, and became deeply embedded in national cultural values about the provision of public sector housing.

The 'problem' label has continued to have a profound effect on general attitudes to living in a home provided by the State as distinct from choosing the decent and liberal freedom option of being an owner-occupier.

Jeremy Seabrook raised some relevant questions about the nature of superficial change to housing circumstances in an article for *New Society* in 1985. He considered where Beveridge's 'Five Evils' were forty years' after the creation of the 'Welfare State' in 1945. On the 'evil' most closely associated in Beveridge's mind with housing and environment, he said:

"And what of Squalor'? The dismantling of 'classic' industrial area - the 19th century slums and tenements, mills and factories - was to have done away with all these cruel sites of suffering...But this has been the mere landscaping of capitalism. The squalors of contemporary life aren't to be found in the infested interiors, with their orange-box furniture...Nor even are they to be found in the stinking breath of open drains and offal-strewn canals." (Seabrook in *New Society* 28 Feb.1985)

Seabrook goes on to suggest that superficial changes have been provided by the outpourings of a banal and vulgar 'Americanised' popular culture, the media and consumer led gloss. This is all part of what Seabrook has referred to as 'the great consumer swindle'. He argues that post 1945 'welfarism' has transformed, changed, the appearance of life, but beneath the shiny if shoddy surface life bears a great resemblance to the 1880s or 1920s.

In spite of all the positive aspects of the Merry Oak development, Joan Rolfe points out that the provision of the new estate did not please all local private sector dwellers, and that as a child she often experienced snide comments about those who lived in Merry Oak. (Rolfe, 2001.)

Lynsey Hanley comments on this form of negative response in her memoir *Estates* (2007). Though mainly discussing the post-1945 estates, she does argue that many 'outside' observers found many of the mid-war estates plain and monotonous. The architects of Merry Oak could certainly not be accused of that design and planning failing. Hanley does in fact acknowledge that many of "The cottage estates were handsome, self-contained and meticulously planned." (Hanley, p.66.) The advantage for the residents of the new estates in Southampton was that although built on the outer periphery of the town they were small-scale and well integrated with existing and future housing development.

The importance of green places and spaces is seen as important now as it was then:

"One of the defining characteristics of suburbs is the amount of green space, in particular the mixture of public and private green space. Indeed, one of the greatest assets of the suburbs is that they have more space generally. But the challenge is to make the best use of this space." (Sarah Gaventa in 'Keep alive our lost Elysium', 2009.)

As I have mentioned elsewhere, gardens and gardening were increasingly important to all classes, among these the new occupants of council housing who actually found themselves with gardens to tend!

Morris and his Arts & Crafts associates devoted a good deal of their time to discussing the role of gardens, and put this into practice. These discussions and practices still echo today, and over the years has come to be seen as the 'cottage garden' style.

In addition to Morris, there were three key protagonists in this 'movement' away from the formal gardens and bedding schemes of the eighteenth and early-nineteenth centuries: William Robinson (1838-1935), Gertrude Jekyll (1843-1932) and her close collaborator the architect Edwin Lutyens (1869-1944). Robinson and Jekyll were passionate anglophiles and argued that what might be appropriate for 'the continent' was not so for England.

Their gardening styling reflected directly the vernacular approach in design and especially architecture that became increasingly influential in the nineteenth century.

Robinson's most well known book *The English Flower Garden* (1883) was a huge success, and still resonates today. (The 2011 Chelsea Flower Show was dominated by Arts & Crafts gardens.). He had set the dramatic changes in motion through founding the magazine *The Garden* in 1871.

(For a very thorough introduction to the history of Cottage Gardens, I would recommend Geoff Hamilton's 1995 BBC TV series book of that name.)

As an interlude, here are some photographs (over, 16-20) of various aspects of the Merry Oak housing estate.

16~20: Aspects of Merry Oak *(Author photos)*

MAGNOLIA RD

The landscaping of Merry Oak was an important aspect of the overall planning process. In a 1930 talk, 'Southampton: Past, Present and Future' (published as an article in the *Journal of the Institute of Municipal and County Engineers* in 1939) Sidney Stanton makes reference to the 1924 Housing Act:

"The erection of houses under this Act was commenced in September 1925 on the Woolston Estate between this date and March 31, 1928. After the latter date, the erection of houses were pushed forward.."

He goes on to enumerate the Merry Oak building between March 1928 and 1930: 26 non-parlour houses at an average cost of £341 per house, and 14 parlour houses at a cost of £406. In addition to this, the existing contract allowed for a further 248 non-parlour, and 46 parlour houses to be built, and eventually they were built on the second 'half' of the estate site.

The houses themselves, with a combination of a limited number of designs as was usual, were very cottage-like in their appearance and layout. My photographs show some of these characteristics (see montage images included here.) There was some interior panelling and decorative tiling, especially as a part of fireplaces. The similarity in design and layout merely mimicked urban middle class housing, which had since the eighteenth century been built by speculative developers for sale, or more likely for rent. It was commonplace for middle and upper middle class families to obtain a long lease on a house that remained in the freehold of the developer, who in turn was often a major local landowner responding to the increased demand for houses that matched the increased prosperity of the already reasonably well-off.

The actual design of the houses in Merry Oak was the work of a local architect, W.J. Green who in 1925 was asked to draw up a set of eight designs for the proposed housing developments in Southampton, including Merry Oak. Those designs were submitted to the Southampton Council Housing Committee in May 1925. These plans remained in the control of the Council, and were 'inherited' by Sidney Stanton when he arrived from the northeast of England.

IN HIS 1924 *The New Housing Handbook*, which I cited earlier, Richard Reiss discusses the pros and cons of a Local Authority employing a full-time architect. However, as in the case of Southampton, if this is not considered to be appropriate, Reiss sets out a scale of professional costs:

"Where a Local Authority decides to employ an outside architect, the fees payable to him represent 5 per cent of the building costs on the first twelve houses and 2 ½ per cent on the next sixty, and reduced amounts for any more over sixty."
(Reiss, 1924 p. 82.)

It is worth adding here that in 1920 Southampton's mayor, Sidney Kimber, was invited to a housing conference called by Lloyd George and held at Downing Street on 15 February. Lloyd George spoke first, followed by the Chancellor of the Exchequer, and then Addison. Addison was then to chair a committee that was set up by the conference to discuss planning and building issues. Kimber was a member of that group along with representatives from London, Cardiff, Hull, Bristol, Manchester and Liverpool, and claims to have learnt a great deal from meeting with council leaders from these metropolitan areas. I note, yet again, the absence of a representative from Birmingham. Wheatley was to experience a similar situation in 1924. (Kimber, 1949)

Compared with working class families' experience of

housing, the Merry Oak houses were of generous proportions; and as already said had such luxuries as an indoor bathroom, most of which were on the ground floor next to the kitchen or scullery.

On the issue of sculleries, it is worth noting that the 1923 Report by the Women's Committee of the Garden City and Town Planning Association observed the trend to push all cooking out of the living room with its range and into the scullery, 'the modern workshop' and they therefore stressed the need for larger and better equipped sculleries or kitchens. I would also add that the limited influence of Continental Modernism on the styling of most 1920s and 1930s housing was invariably restricted to kitchens and bathrooms.

One of the effects of this trend was that, by the end of the 1930s, most interior design pundits had declared that the old style farmhouse living room/kitchen with its range was finished, out of date, obsolete. One wonders what they would make of the ruralised urban middle class enthusiasm for the Aga?

These concerns also embrace changes in the nature of fireplaces, and the mid- to late-nineteenth century changes to heating and cooking technologies. This is yet another example of the importance of seeing change to everyday life *via* a cultural materialist perspective.

Muthesius, that valuable German observer of English house and home mores, argued that 'the fireplace' was deeply embedded in the English cultural consciousness. The improvements in gas and then electric technologies gradually pushed the open fire to the margins, and as can be readily observed over the past few years the majority of new housing comes without fireplaces, and /or open fires at all - or at best new-ish gas technology versions of the 'living fire'. Close to where I live, new houses have been built in an eclectic late-nineteenth century style with chimneystacks, but with no *actual* fireplaces, of course. In this period of change, there was also an increase in household management publications, cookery books and various aimed at a 'mass market'. Cassell's Book of the Household published in 1897 is one such well-known example.

The functional and aesthetic influence of the Arts & Crafts movement is clearly to be seen both externally and internally. Of course, the decoration and furnishing of the interiors would have varied according to the taste and disposable income of the residents. However, the council not only maintained the external collective spaces; they also made random inspections of house interiors to make sure that the tenants were maintaining standards.

There is no doubt that there was a high demand for affordable housing at this time, and Joan Rolfe alludes to this when she says:

"In 1930, there were hundreds of families on the waiting list in Southampton and hopes rose when building started at Merry Oak. Few people could afford to buy a house and often private rents were high." (Rolfe, 2001 p.7.)

Joan Rolfe also refers to the very tight margins in income and expenditure for families when her parents were allocated a 'parlour' house with a slightly higher rent. She says that for many years the front parlour was devoid of furniture, while her parents saved enough money to buy a three-piece suite! In the meantime, the living room continued to be the everyday focus of family life, with the parlour saved 'for best'.

Joan Rolfe in commenting on these tight margins emphasizes the effects of low incomes: about 40/- (£2) for unskilled workers, and a little more for the skilled. We know from the Council literature that the Merry Oak estate was aimed at the majority of unskilled dockworkers. The onset of 'the

Depression', with short-time and unemployment, meant real hardship for many families coping on benefit of around 28/6 per week, with rents around 14/-. (Rolfe, p.45.)

There are also reminders here of the enterprise and self-help of residents utilizing their back gardens to grow 'fruit and veg' to meet everyday needs. This echoes allotment schemes and so on in so many garden city/suburb style developments over many years.

Joan Rolfe's memoir is abundant in its reference to neighbourliness and general conviviality. This aspect of social bonding is important in terms of the everyday support that neighbours can bestow on each other, adding a social and psychological security that relying on "the kindness of strangers" might not.

One factor here is that most people's lives were very similar in most everyday aspects of living standards *and* expectations. It was not necessarily that people 'knew their place', more perhaps that they knew they *had a place*, a collective space, to share, and have pride in?

Most evidence on the social interaction of people in a particular neighbourhood has suggested that working class people spent more time with their kinship network, while the middle classes tended to spend their leisure time with friends. However, this view depends heavily on the geographical location of contacts with family and/or friends that vary between classes, especially where working class families move to new estates some distance from members of their kinship group.

Working class men were more likely to separate their daily contact with co-workers from home and family-oriented time, with the possible exception of going to the pub. As I have suggested already, households (especially so women members) are more likely to seek contacts with, and support from, those that are nearby regardless of whether they are family or not. But, yet again, these trends need to be seen in the context that for a long period of time now men have had more leisure time than women. (Willmott, 1987.)

IT IS clear that Merry Oak was primarily built for, and occupied by, 'the respectable working class'. Skilled manual workers and their families joined in the 1920s and 1930s by the growing number of clerical and other white-collar workers. The growth of what came to be seen as the new segment of the lower middle class meant in reality that many of these families were no better off than skilled and semi-skilled working class families. There was certainly an increased demand for fictitious capital, mortgages and the like, to assist these new socio-economic strata to become owner-occupiers. Also, from a middle class perspective in general, the style and size of housing changed because after 1918 many such families could not afford, or did not seek, servants.

It was also the case that after 1918 there were less men and women seeking employment in service. As a consequence, the growing number of middle class women, whether housed in Southampton or Metro-land, became full-time housewives, and Britain increasingly became a land of 'Janet and John' families.

One of the reasons why early-twentieth century council housing was invariably seen as patronising by outside observers stems from the rules and regulations that tenants were expected to sign up to, and adhere to, or lose their tenancy. As I have suggested here, the residents of Merry Oak, like estates across Britain, tended to be from the upper working class because of the level of rents charged. It is clear that throughout the twentieth century until at least the mid- to late-1970s, the 'respectable', more skilled white men could access council housing, and certainly felt a pride in their home and locality, and more likely to accept elements of social control. (Collins, 2004.)

It is no surprise to find Joan Rolfe and her contemporaries commenting on the sharp contrasts from those early years to now, these reflections emphasising the virtual destruction of public sector orientations, and collective, if selective, class values. Throughout England, estates like Merry Oak have increasingly been dominated by the values of possessive individualism, lives blighted by enslavement to a rampant consumer culture. A.H. Halsey has been one prominent sociologist focusing on changes to the nature of status in the last two hundred years. He has argued that the fake egalitarian status that has been deliberately promoted *via* a media and politics-led consumer culture has sought to hide the continuing class-based inequalities of modern Britain that are reflected in access to good quality housing. (Halsey, 1978.)

I HAVE been working my craft as a sociologist for several decades now, and have for some time concluded that the most significant dimension of social life is our values. As a population in general, we have been directed away from a set of values based on conviviality, mutual support, shared problems and solutions, and a focus on equality and fairness. We have been encouraged to see our lives and choices as acquisitive individuals, and where "There is no such thing as Society."

Set against this is the value of social capital; the accumulated awareness, experience and knowledge of people in their own localities. This social capital, a powerful cultural reservoir, needs to be accentuated, promoted (even recovered), and drawn on. Local people need to take responsibility and make decisions, and have a say in how their 'public' money is spent in a fair and equitable way.

One consistent theme that appears in assessments of the success or failure of the late-1920s and 1930s estates is concern with the lack of adequate infrastructure. Many of the estates built at the time (for example, Becontree in London) were little more than very big concentrations of housing for working class families recruited into nearby industry like Fords in Dagenham. (See, for example, Darrin Bayliss' 2003 article 'Building Better Communities: social life on London's cottage council estates, 1919-1939'.) The lack of infrastructure issue appears regularly, and was commented on by Ronald Frankenberg in a chapter on urban housing estates, in his well-known study 'Communities in Britain' (1966). In that study, Frankenberg argued that the London County Council combined a lack of interest in the fate of the new estates with a tendency to expect other agencies to plug the gaps in service provision, which invariably did not happen. A further key issue for the new estate dwellers was around the strengths and weaknesses of a 'go it alone' policy by the residents. In his article, Bayliss comments on the suspicion that surrounding private estate dwellers had about 'little Moscows' being created on the one hand or the 'invasion' of middle class do-gooders like the various forms of the Community Association movement.

This range of problems did not emerge in my conversations with those who were children in Merry Oak in the 1930s. They consistently talked in positive terms of the social networking and cohesion they remembered as characteristic of life then.

One of the reminiscences included by Joan Rolfe in her book is by Moira Mortimer, who as a child in Merry Oak in 1930 witnessed a visit by 'the then Housing Minister'. This was almost certainly Arthur Greenwood, who was the Minister of Health in the second Labour government (1929-31), and as a consequence, just like John Wheatley, also minister of housing. Apparently, Merry Oak was a 'blueprint' estate!

Moira Mortimer also recalls an estate gardener who cared for the public spaces, and again as elsewhere, there were clear guidelines on the use and protection of the estate. There were certainly many more fenced areas than would be found now. The inclusion of the wooden summerhouse on The Green central to the estate layout is a further indication of a desire to create a garden village aesthetic. All that was missing were some animals. The planners of Milton Keynes solved that problem!

Of course, the estate looked very different when it was first set out. There were, for example, very few cars (most working class families could not afford such luxuries). The growth of car ownership over recent decades has, of course, changed the dynamic of these spaces, affecting the appearance of house fronts, use of gardens, and roads and shared spaces.

ONE OF the aims of this book is to consider the educative value for adults, and particularly for children, of living on the Merry Oak estate. I intend to consider this 'added value' in relation to their 'everyday lives'. In this respect, therefore, I will consider some of the theoretical work done in this area of study. I have made the argument that this added value of an aesthetic and social experience goes beyond the expected value of being well housed at an affordable rent.

"True education is concerned not only with practical goals but also with values. Our aims assure us of our material life; our values make possible our spiritual life. In its simplest form, architecture is rooted in entirely functional considerations, but it can reach up through all degrees of value to the highest sphere of spiritual existence, into the realm of pure art." (Quoted in Blake, 1960.)

These are the words from 1938 of Mies van der Rohe, a world famous architect of Modernism. He knew well, was praised by and indebted to Frank Lloyd Wright, who in turn was the USA's leading Arts & Crafts-inspired architect/designer.

Van der Rohe advocated that 'building education' came before the development of design education. His view of the value of good building has a clear parallel with what happened in Merry Oak and elsewhere in the same era.

Those who were children on the estate in the early 1930s have told me that they had enjoyable lives, with ample space to play. This was true of the estate itself, with its village green layout and the access children had to the adjacent varsity recreation ground with its sports role.

Those children, now in their 70s and 80s, recall the supportive nature of adults, their parents, for example, towards other people living on the estate. There appears to have been a fund of social capital at work here, and I cannot rule out the likelihood that the general feeling of well-being created by the estate 'atmosphere' did make a difference. Of course, I am in to double hermeneutic territory here, but given the overt social cohesion aims of the planners and builders it is a likely outcome.

What I have elicited from the children of the 'early 30s' is a sense of them and their parents of just standing inside the door of their changing lives. I have also been told that schooling on the estate was enjoyable for most, most of the time. It was routine, and teachers as agents of socialization and social control, as is usually the case with working class children, played a conventional role. Most commentary on the schooling of the working class children in the 1920s and 1930s emphasises the unchanged nature of attitudes towards such children's abilities and expectations. They were consistently seen as limited and limiting. In the vast majority of cases, schooling was provided at the lowest common denominator level, sufficient in fact to prepare children for their ascribed roles in life. (Rubinstein, 1970.)

So, in part my argument here is to what extent did the children's experience of life on the Merry Oak estate both serve as an *educational* experience, and raise their expectations? An education of the senses, perhaps? I shall explore these specific issues later.

There is also an issue here about the 'suburban child'.

"Suburbia is, or was, a state. I say "was" because the state of Suburbia is passing away. Its great days are already over. In time I hope it will be given the history it deserves, complete with footnotes and maps and an acknowledgement of the civilising influence it has had upon the larger world...a definition of Suburbia. What, and where is it? Simply, as the Suburban child sees it, it is between the shops and the fields." (Kenward, 1955 p. 1-2.)

Kenward's nostalgic Edwardian 'high summer' homage is a further 'golden age' example to add to several others discussed in this book.

It is relevant to note here that English Heritage have published two working papers 'The Heritage of Historic Suburbs' and 'Suburbs and the Historic Environment' on the value and conservation of the suburb.

Colin Ward in his 1977 book *The Child in the City* also addresses the children's perspective. In his early chapter 'Paradise Lost' he suggests that self and industry/advertising-created ideas and images promote myths about happy, idyllic childhoods, *our* childhood, the lost personal landscape. This is also invariably a rural landscape and one reason why the likes of Kate Greenaway and Laurie Lee have remained popular. Ward links this talk of usually reactive nostalgia to the more pro-active goal of creating an environment the goal of which is happiness, especially so for the child.

I do not have time here to explore the current literature on the happiness of children, now back on the political agenda.

However, I would strongly recommend Paul Martin's 2005 book *Making Happy People. The Nature of Happiness and its Origins in Childhood* published by Harper.

In general, I am supported in my observations of family life by Ross McKibbin (1998) in his drawing on a considerable amount of primary community-based studies emphasising the central role of women in social networking, and the value of this sociability in general to the social cohesion in everyday social life. (p.182.) McKibbin makes reference to the value to families of these survival networks, which as the primary research suggests, were essential to people coping with the vagaries of industrial capitalism.

A link I wish to make here is with the concept of 'everyday life'. I would argue that to understand the value of Merry Oak, and similar estates, recognition must be given to the quotidian. By this, I mean the importance of a reflected-on everyday-ness that promoted well-being and social cohesion. I am also arguing that people in this setting were reflexive beings, and could see the value of what they had.

As I have already argued in discussing 'Community', a good deal has been said about social bonds, and how the shared experience of living, working, playing, raising families, and so on, the essence of the quotidian, promotes cooperation. These everyday processes of living, the cumulative character of social interactions, lead to the formation of social capital that can then in turn be drawn on in times of need. For example, in periods of individually or mutually experienced hardship not uncommon for working class families, there is a fund of goodwill and know-how to be drawn on: psychological, emotional and practical support, that exists independently of whatever the State apparatus might provide.

In this respect, the outline of Zimmerman and Pollner is relevant here:

"The world is *experienced* as an intersubjective world, known or knowable in common with others." (Zimmerman and Pollner, 1974 p.84.)

Of course, I would have to acknowledge that the cohesiveness and continued well-being of particular families, or of a neighbourhood in general, will ultimately be determined by there being sufficient incomes to sustain those people. Many idealistic post-1950s public sector housing developments in particular foundered largely because of this. Subsistence is not enough, regardless of the intrinsic value of housing and environment; there has to be a reasonable, socially acknowledged standard of living that can embrace a quality of life. Where people live and who they share that neighbourhood with makes a major contribution to their quality of life, but 'food comes before philosophy' to paraphrase Marx, and therefore aesthetic value *etc. etc.,* ethos will soon diminish and seem irrelevant if people's income is not sufficient to provide a decent and secure everyday life. This should also remind us that a good deal of the recent research on, and discussion about happiness, emphasizes that money is not the only or even most important measure beyond a certain mean.

This brings me to saying more about the concept of 'everyday life' in particular relation to Merry Oak, and how my observations here are relevant to our understanding of the value of such public sector housing in general.

Henri Lefebvre in *Everyday Life in the Modern World* (1968) makes the point that the role of everyday life in literature should not be underestimated, and he cites James Joyce and *Ulysses*, as a celebration of the quotidian. For me, this is an example of the role and importance of cultural creativity, which both individually and collectively has both an intrinsic and extrinsic value. Individual creative action demonstrates a purposive response to everyday life experience, which can then be shared by and with others, near and far, whose reflexivity leads them into similar social actions, a shared and enhanced consciousness.

Lefebvre makes the point that philosophy is essentially not a 'noun' form, but a 'verb'. I have always argued that the same is true of Sociology, and History, where practice, the essential role of method and praxis are at its heart. However, the value of the accumulated knowledge that is the Humanities in all its diversity, invariably seen as the 'noun' stuff, is important.

On knowledge and everyday life Lefebvre, argues that Socrates' advocacy of the maieutic method is key, *i.e.*, the 'midwife' that brings forth what is already there. However, Keith Jenkins (1991), for example, among 'post-modernists', have serious reservations about this straightforward relationship of substance, enquiry and understanding. Jenkins draws a distinction between the 'past' and History. He cites David Lowenthal's assertion that 'the past is a foreign country' in that whatever we write about the past is selective.

In spite of the empathy we may feel for those subjects of our enquiry, we are essentially creating a view of those lives and events that has more to do with literature than anything more positivistic. Jenkins argues that theorizing came late to academic history; this is, perhaps, because it was imbued with a positivist methodology, while the 'literary turn' came much earlier to other academic disciplines within the Humanities and Social Sciences, Sociology being a clear example.

I would argue that the cultural materialism of Raymond Williams is a good example here, in that he produced a series of studies *Culture & Society 1780-1950* (1958), *The Long Revolution* (1961), and *The Country and the City* (1973), which are in their form literary, sociological and historical. Whether all other members of those academic disciplines would recognise these studies as such is another matter, of course. But Williams, along with other writers of the same period, were offering historical accounts and reconstructions of everyday life, which included a good deal of both biography and autobiography. For instance, Richard Hoggart in 1957 with his U*ses* of *Literacy*: sub-titled *Aspects of Working Class Life*. This is especially true of Williams, who alongside these non-fictional accounts of everyday life, wrote novels like *Border Country* (1960), very much an autobiographical work. As for Richard Hoggart, he was to become the director of the Centre for Contemporary Cultural Studies at Birmingham University, located within the English Literature Faculty, a new development that really started the Cultural Studies phenomenon in the Britain.

My own writing, in the past, and now in *Access to Eden*, is similar in approach. I do acknowledge the historiography, and collect and analyse examples of the discourses of the period under examination, which are drawn from a diverse range of sources that illuminate everyday life, and also consider the interpretations of these debates and discussions by 'historians' up to and including the present day.

My analysis and reflections on this 'past' can then be refined by the work of members of other disciplines with an interest in my period and subject of study. This can provide a quite different view of the place, time, events and people. My own methodology leads to a multi-perspective consideration of the subject matter. This critical exercise is clearly a modernist approach in not accepting a single and fixed perspective on the 'past' in question. This method embraces a conventional triangulation of evidence, with a broad disciplinary approach.

I am aware, of course, that for many people this is a damning indictment of my woeful eclecticism that marks me out as a 'Jack of all Trades, but Master of None'! I have grown to live with that reality. In thinking about 'everyday life', it is also important to emphasize the material-culture dimension to the quotidian, and the shared experience of inter-subjectivity. As Lefebvre argues: "Everyday Life is sustenance, clothing, furnishing, homes, neighbourhoods, environments...call it material culture if you like." (p. 21.)

In his speculation on the nature of industrial capitalism, Lefebvre suggests that changes to 'society' are incorporated into the rhythm of everyday life, and reflected on, and responded to, *via* forms of creativity, which are in themselves a rise in the consciousness factor (as I have suggested above). He also considers the possibility that a loss of substance in life is identified, not unlike Weber or Freud's *disenchantment.*

Lefebvre draws on David Riesman, the American sociologist writing in the 1950s (and mentioned elsewhere in this book) and Herbert Marcuse, an exile from the Frankfurt School, both of whom were writing in America in the 1950s and 60s, and both tended to concentrate on 'outer directed' man, to the neglect of the 'inner directed'. Both Riesman and Marcuse are notable for posing key questions associated with the post-1945 'American Dream'; instance, "Affluence for what?" This in turn returns us to the issues around what constitutes happiness. Marcuse's *One Dimensional Man* from 1964, an account of how consumerist industrial capitalism has 'domesticated' and enslaved people, is typical of this approach. I would also cite Philip Slater's 1970 essay 'The Pursuit of Loneliness: American Culture at Breaking Point', which has as its front cover a detail of Edward Hopper's painting *Nighthawks* - one of the most stunning visual accounts of alienation I know.

Lefebvre was also influenced by Georg Simmel (1858-1918), the German social scientist, often seen as one of the 'founding fathers' of Sociology. Simmel was particularly interested in the inter-relationship between the 'forms' or social structures in which people's lives are lived, and the cultures, of everyday ways of life that constituted the content of those lives. He was also exploring the way in which the agency of people (their scope for choices) was influenced and shaped by contextual circumstances at a particular historical moment.

One of Simmel's most influential essays is 'The Metropolis and Mental Life' from 1903, where his studies on the impact of rapid urbanization took him into Psychology as well as a radical form of Social Anthropology many years ahead of its time.

"The deepest problems of modern life flow from the attempt of the individual to maintain the independence and individuality of his existence against the sovereign powers of society, against the weight of historical heritage and the external culture and technique of life."

He added that the city is not a spatial entity with sociological consequences, but a sociological entity that is formed spatially. Or in other words the very spaces that we occupy, alone or with others, both reflects the existing social order with forms of class segregation and so on, and sets the tone for what might come about in the future. For me, this is an interesting perspective on the 'new' life taken up by tenants, by adults and children, moving in to a housing space like Merry Oak.

Throughout his account of concerns about everyday life, Lefebvre touches on the key Base & Structure argument at the heart of Marxist debate with regard to a cultural-materialism understanding of everyday life. In the sphere of Marxist historiography in the last sixty years or so, there has been considerable debate about whether material conditions (and economic relationships) determine consciousness is the complete explanation as to why people act in the way they do. Bruce Brown in his *Marx, Freud and the critique of Everyday Life - toward a permanent cultural revolution* (1973) highlights the cyclical rise in re-thinking Marx's critique of capitalism and the nature of society that stems from this; for example, the way capitalism has changed its nature, thus raising key questions about hegemony, and what the response of the revolutionary left could be or should be. He emphasizes that in the 1960s there was a re-focus on the role of the manipulated inner self, as well as the public self, hence the rise of interest in Freud, Reich, *et. al.*.

Brown cites Lefebvre's reflecting on the re-discovery in the 1960s of Marx's use of alienation to explain levels of consciousness and action taking whether the people concerned were in paid employment or not. This chimes with the rise of the Feminist movement, and the key issue of emancipation through access to paid employment and a degree of economic independence. Of course the reality for many middle class women was then, and still is, that having a demanding job is not all that it is said to be and not necessarily liberating given all the other familial demands on them. Many professional women have also experienced the 'glass ceiling' where they can see the potential trajectory their career might take, but are invariably left frustrated.   Even an era of 'sexual liberation' has not been that rewarding for many women.

As Harvey Kaye suggests in his book on British Marxist historians in the twentieth century (1995), a growing number of these thinkers, most members of the British Communist Party at least until 1956, were increasingly questioning the orthodoxy of 'base and superstructure' thinking.

This 'economistic' Marxism was increasingly seen as another form of repression, and methodologically not embracing a comprehension of the culturally creative agency of the person as an aspect of their social being. This also leads Kaye to argue that the then dominant positivistic methodologies overlooked the issue of historical specificity of social life at any one time.

This in turn raises questions about a 'total person' view, and the need to unite the personal with the political. (echoes of feminism again). Brown argues that this is one reason why the

1960s saw a new interest in Marx's Economic & Philosophical Manuscripts of the 1840s, where there is much discussion on alienation and the 'inner person'. This certainly had a big influence on the Frankfurt School, and Marcuse in particular. But, the British Marxist Historians were also taken up with this viewpoint, which led them in turn to argue for an explicit 'bottom-up' approach to understanding the historical specificity of a particular time, or event, or individual and collective social action. As Kaye says:

"Not only do the British Marxist historians stress the importance to historical studies of the experiences of the lower classes, they also insist that the lower classes themselves have been active participants in the making of history, rather than merely its passive victims' (p.229)

However, Kaye also makes the important point that while looking at the experiences of those 'at the bottom' we should not underestimate the degree of accommodation by the working classes with their situation.

The work on the 'Aristocracy of Labour' by Eric Hobsbawm, or the commonplace view by Historians and Sociologists on the left that the 'welfare state' is a mechanism for buying the silence of the working class (while they pay for it themselves), should remind us of hegemonic issues, and ideas of false consciousness.

"The Surrealists sought a method of cultural revolution based on a new conception of human possibilities and aimed at unlocking all the barriers, both physical and psychological between the conscious and the unconscious, the inner world and the outer world, so as to create a *sur-realite* in which the real and the imaginary, thought and feeling, would fuse and dominate all of life." (p.24.)

Brown argues that the Surrealists and particularly Reich suggested that purely material suppression of the working class was passing, but was being replaced by a class struggle around sexual repression.

A free libido was seen as the great liberating force - Reich *et al* could not anticipate the extent to which the ruling class would manipulate capitalism to commodify sex, and sell it back to the working class as just another cheap, vulgar and banal consumer object. Feminists attempted to deal with this, but got lost (especially middle class women) in their desire for personal freedom in their sexual relations - *Cosmopolitan* and the road to orgasm!

Reich's attack was also aimed at the patriarchal family, which has now been replaced by a largely unstable miss-mash of arrangements that do not really meet people's needs.

Brown argues that in the 1920-40s the leadership of the Left - whether Social Democrat or Communist Party opposed this revolutionary cultural movement - and moved to isolate, and often expel, those who proposed theories challenging the traditional patriarchal approach to everyday life.

And even though Reich and the ideas of others resurfaced within the 1960s New Left, the overwhelming repressive nature of commodity capitalism had taken such a stranglehold by then that such culturally revolutionary ideas were swimming against the tide. The Gay movement has been more successful, and the work of some Feminists and the likes of Jeffrey Weekes have raised these issues again. But this has not really challenged the 'puritanical' hegemony. Brown emphasises the difficulties in changing the *status quo* because of 'bread and circuses' on the one hand, and the dead hand of the growing institutionalisation and standardization of life on the other. The hegemonic grip of the ruling class and their agents is very profound and the role of education has gradually been replaced by an overt work-oriented curriculum, where most of the arts and social studies have been squeezed out. Of course, the traditional individualistic and Humanities-oriented education in the private sector has continued virtually unchanged.

So given these issues, I do have to ask if an awareness of 'everyday life' issues on the 'estate' act as a bridge between the private world of the person and the family, and the more open spaces of the social domain that the vast majority of us are required to make our way in for a wide variety of reasons, some voluntary, some not. Once again, this raises the key question: how much agency do we have?

Lefebvre is keen to distinguish between 'social' space, with use-value and collective intent, and the spaces given over to profit generation and/or commercial entertainment. (The writing of Anna Minton is also relevant here.) These latter spaces are manipulated from the outside and have no democratic element to them. These situations provided tensions for residents of estates, public and private, in the 1920s and 30s as they do now. How residents respond to these attempts at 'external' forms of social control has and will vary, but in general what does happen is that even in neighbourhoods where people could be regarded as 'hidden behind their front door', threats to their agency will unite people in opposition to these external threats.

Doreen Massey in her essay 'Space-time and the Politics of Location' in 'Architecturally Speaking: art, architecture and the everyday' (2000) edited by Alan Reed, says this:

"The spaces through which we live do not only consist of physical things: of bricks and mortar, streets and bridges, mountains and sea-shore, and of what we make of these things. They consist also of those less tangible spaces we construct out of social interaction, such as the intimate social relations of the kitchen and the interactions from there to the backyard and the living room. The relations of neighbours: talking across the back wall, the more formal hello in the street, the annoyance when they come home noisily and very late, yet again, on a Saturday night. These lost spaces are set within, and actively link into the wider networks of social relations that make up the neighbourhood... Social space is not an empty arena within which we conduct our lives; rather, it is something we construct and which others construct about us. It is this incredible complexity of social interactions and meanings which we constantly build, tear down and negotiate." (p. 49)

Massey goes on to suggest that the loss of that valued familiar can lead to a nostalgia, which then has cultural resonance.

In 1884, Unwin had his own thoughts on these everyday contradictions in life:

"Either all genuine liberty of life and action will be lost to the individual through enslavement to the impulses of mass control; *or* planning on cooperative lines must be adapted to secure that a free space and sphere may be allotted and preserved for the individual within which he may be free to exercise his liberty and initiative for the *good of all.*' (Quoted in Creese, 1967 p.9.)

So, social change will happen, and we have abundant examples of the negative and positive impacts of such phenomena. The point is: can a generation of designers and planners work together to replace chaos with reason and *shape* a much better future for all?

As Owen Hatherley suggests in *Militant Modernism* (2008), given the enormity of the tasks that face us, and the disappointments that designers and planners (even of the stature of Unwin) face, our responses to social change *can* be seen as

"...the common contemporary phenomenon of nostalgia for the future, a longing for the fragments of the half-hearted post-war (1945) attempt at building a new society." (p.8) Or, as I have said elsewhere, it is not the *loss* of democracy that upsets us so much, because we have never really enjoyed it, but the loss of *hope* that we will achieve that aim.

The many years that Unwin spent in his official roles made him very aware of the endless compromises that face our attempts to make significant changes. This is echoed by Richard Hornsey in 'The Spiv and the Architect' when he touches on linked issues around the 1940s; for example, on policies to transform the metropolitan space and 'engineer' the everyday culture of people's lives to accept a trade-off, and acceptance of a control of space in return for social order, and even freedom from the impact of the deviant elements in everyday life. This was a top-down 'educational' process. In this regard, Hornsey links planning and design with the wider welfare model that *via* the social democratic ideology, delivered care, services and benefits to 'the people' in a *rational* way. But, in the case of public sector housing and its planning, this is not a very democratic way.

As an instance of the contradictory nature of planning interventions, which I have discussed elsewhere in this book, is that despite the obvious benefits of the mid-nineteenth century public parks movement, there were many vested interests to be noted.

The parks were seen by their promoters as a 'green lung' for the burgeoning city, a space that had a civilising and calming influence. It is quite clear that this was invariably the case, but these parks, these 'democratic' open spaces were 'policed' *via* the use of local bye-laws that controlled what could and could not be done, and what would not be tolerated. Even in the realm of joining planning with access to green spaces, the top-down values of the Victorian middle class were very evident, and lasting.

MY ASSESSMENT of Merry Oak is that for the generations of people who lived there, or indeed as with my small sample of residents who grew up there, the creation and running of the estate brought many benefits. As a place to live, as a personal and collective social space, this estate offered a good start in life, raising expectations and demonstrating that there was actually the potential for a better life. I am also sure that the experience of Merry Oak residents was shared by thousands of other estate dwellers throughout the land, that is, people who had been 'given' reasons to be hopeful, and perhaps even 'Access to Eden'.

I have sought to demonstrate that the contribution of good design and planning to this potential and actual well-being is there to see, and an established model for us to follow in the twenty-first century.

Conclusion

IN THIS brief conclusion, it is my intention to pull together the threads of my argument and make an assessment of the degree to which my aims set out in the Introduction have been achieved.

I hope that the reader has been able to follow my argument, and feels now that what I have discussed has made sense, while being enlightening and interesting. I also hope that reading this book will encourage some further exploration of these ideas and issues.

The main aim of this book was to explain why and how the 'Wheatley' council housing estates came in to existence, and with what effect, including the key issue of how they actually *looked* on the ground.

I have argued that those people who were instrumental in creating these late-1920s and early-1930s estates drew significantly on Arts & Crafts values and Garden City ideals in developing a response to the chronic housing shortage after 1918.

There was, of course, a very diverse range of people, from politicians to civil servants to local authority engineers and architects, who were all focused on the need to provide public sector housing for large numbers of families as quickly as possible. This was particularly true with the over-riding necessity to house working class families, that is, those in greatest need as a direct consequence of rapid urbanisation, population growth, a lack of planning and building control, and the inadequate supply of both sanitary and reasonable quality housing. The plight of the 'slum' dweller was both a cause for those offering humanitarian and philanthropic responses, and for other more radical socialist based agitation for social justice.

The ideals of the Garden City movement, with Howard and all his associates, became a fundamental focus for many such people.

What is also characteristic of this period is the legacy of aesthetic considerations for the actual physical form that the new housing should take, questions around what design features of both the house and the local environment should follow.

As I have argued in this book, the late-nineteenth and early-twentieth centuries were a period of modern history when increasingly shared aesthetic values in regard of housing and landscape became embedded in design culture, and indeed a paradigm for practice, both in theory and in everyday use. This is where the values of the Arts & Crafts are seen at their most significant.

Of course, there were interminable debates over styles and the details of development, but in general there was in place by 1918 a clear understanding about what had to be done, and how this might be achieved. As I have argued in this book, the inter-play between Arts & Crafts and Garden City helped to create a consciousness of both the problem and some viable solutions. What developed was a 'can-do' attitude among a growing range of articulate and energized activists. These complex inter-plays also created the conditions for the experiments with the 'garden suburb', which is of especial interest to me.

My case study estate, Merry Oak, exemplifies these cultural developments in the way that the very conception of this housing estate, and the form it took, is representative of experience, expertise, enthusiasm and energy of the era. As I have argued in my Merry Oak chapter, there was also the opportunity to develop an educational form to these developments on the ground. The users of these housing services stood to have their consciousness raised in several ways; for example, in a growing awareness of an entitlement to an improved quality of life as a consequence of access to new and improved standards of welfare provision in everyday life.

As I have argued in my study, my understanding of welfare here is of well-being, a creative sense of a more satisfying and fulfilling life, and a recognition of both raised expectations for the future, days of hope, and actual access to housing. Home life is central to well-being, and the scope for a developmental, incremental, raising of standards, and increasingly the security that comes *via* surveying an horizon of opportunities. There was scope here for intrinsic and extrinsic values in everyday life to coalesce.

I have argued that the experience of the parents and children who lived and developed on these new estates was translated into a reinforced commitment to a collective, and at the least, a social democratic response to life's problems, a way to manage social relations.

I have discussed the role of several key figures in these developments from the mid-nineteenth century to the 1920s, all of whom were focused on the issue of planning, design and housing, and bringing to these deliberations their own particular values and practices. There was certainly a high value placed on the vernacular approach to house design, insisting on the particularity of local styles and materials, and craft skills. This was linked to an insistence that buildings of all kinds should 'fit' with the local physical environment, placing a high value on regional tradition and continuity. It was invariably the case that function dictated form, with for example a strong emphasis placed on designing buildings from the inside-out. What were the core needs of the users, and how could this then be efficiently and effectively (and always economically) delivered?

As I have mentioned in my study, the debates about whether to include a parlour in the design of houses for working class families is an interesting example here. There was a view expressed by many house designers that the provision of a rarely used parlour was primarily an attempt to ape the middle class household, a waste of valuable space needed for everyday family life.

The debates between the so-called Rationalists and Anti-Rationalists of the modern era reflect the arguments about style; and, for example, the degree to which ornament should be a core design feature for both interiors and exteriors. Most of the Arts & Crafts protagonists looked for simplicity and clarity of line, of form, and this aesthetic is reflected in their work. However, as I have argued, there were inevitably those designers who took this Arts & Crafts base into a new phase of ornament, creating intricate styling. There also developed a reaction to this 'over elaboration', which argued for an even more austere styling that contributed a good deal to the notion of buildings as 'machines for living in'.

One other aspect of this design complexity that I have discussed concerns the international nature of late-nineteenth and early-twentieth century theory and practice. Arts & Crafts ideas were taken up and developed in Continental Europe and North America, and invariably reflected local design cultures, always reflecting the residual and emergent cultures of particular people in specific places. *These* values were then fed back into the debates and practices of designers in Britain, and so on. As I have suggested, the rapid growth of design literature: books, journals, magazines (and often the outcomes of exhibitions), kept practitioners and consumers in touch with developments and contributed to a continuous cross-fertilisation of creative ideas and practice.

I have come to understand this complex process much more over the period of my research, and this has hopefully resulted in my shying away from hasty judgements about design development, and the use to which these designs were put.

One of the aims set out in my Introduction concerned the value of historical practice, and in particular whether what my, and countless other, examinations of the past, contribute to our understanding of the housing crisis today. It is commonplace to argue that History is written for a contemporary audience, not for the benefit of those described and discussed. It may be the case, of course, that historical enquiry might seek to promote the role of a person or group located in a past, or perhaps to rehabilitate the reputation of someone through a reassessment of their life. But, what will have become clear to the reader of my enquiry is that I do want to argue now, in the contemporary domain of the early twenty-first century, that understanding what took place a hundred or so years ago could, or should, encourage reflection and action today.

For example, most academic and mass media coverage of housing need, policy and provision today confirms that there is a real crisis, and indeed one that is on a par with the situation in Britain in 1918. The surface appearance of why and how people are housed might look different now, but the situation for many individuals and families is already desperate, and likely to worsen in the next year or so. There have been several government pledges and initiatives, but very little has been achieved that could benefit young people and increasingly so numbers of working class families. The provision of public sector housing has virtually ceased, and despite the worthy attempts of not-for-profit housing associations and the like, this social action is akin to emptying the ocean with a spoon.

I recently looked back at the 2007 Hills report on Social Housing (Ends and Means: the future roles of social housing in England), signed off by another of yesterday's politicians, Ruth Kelly, while she was parked at the Department for Communities and Local Government. In a lengthy report, Hills frontlines the point that: "…it is not hard to make a strong argument for social housing at sub-market rents to be a significant part of how we try to meet overall housing and distributional needs." (p.5.)

In their response to Hills' report, Shelter the housing charity proposed a twelve-point plan, the three main themes of which were:

❑ Build homes: without affordable housing many people have no realistic hope of accessing a decent secure home.

❑ Protect people: people who are badly housed, or at risk of homelessness because of high housing costs, need robust protection from eviction, repossession and homelessness.

❑ End the housing divide: the gap between housing haves and have-nots is widening, and there is a danger of this inequality becoming entrenched for generations.

John Wheatley would easily recognise all three of these key issues; indeed, I suspect that he would be bitterly disappointed, but not altogether surprised, that we are here again, eighty-eight years after his Act.

A further similarity between the 'then' of my study and now that I would mention is the social inequality context of housing need, of need not being met. For example, Jeremy Seabrook in his evidence to the 2009 Joseph Rowntree 'Social Evils' report, emphasised that the fundamental inequality due to the chaos of global capitalism is where our focus should be, rather than 'just' considering the consequences of this malaise, namely, poverty. How much more true this is now given the most recent crisis of 'the markets'. The Rowntree report ('Contemporary Social Evils') addresses what constitutes a social evil in contemporary

Britain, and certainly the lack of adequate housing is there. What would William Beveridge have made of this current crisis? His 1942 report addressed the need for a universal insurance scheme to invest national income in to a series of support mechanisms to protect ordinary working people against the vagaries of constantly shifting industrial capitalism.

As I have argued in this book, Beveridge was an old-style Liberal, who espoused the necessity of capitalism, but 'with a human face'; and he was closely aligned with many of the key players discussed in this book.

One of his 'evils' was squalor, and we are there again. In many parts of Britain today, what is left of council housing is used as 'welfare housing', the housing of last resort. The current debate about welfare housing focuses on the fact that this resource is the bottom of the pile, the end of a downward cycle that sees people become incapable of accessing any other form of tenure, who 'have' to be put somewhere. Many local government voices refer to this current process as 'the race to the bottom'.

There is also here the evident confusion of 'welfare', a benefit or service that is given, and can therefore be taken away again or denied to the undeserving, rather than housing as a right. The result of current attitudes and policy seems to me to be a system of dispersed 'workhouses', poor law in most respects, but dispersed because that is the nature of the housing stock spread among council estates increasingly fallen on hard times.

I hope that the reader is convinced by my argument that a concern with the design and housing provision issues at the centre of my book is still worthwhile. The concern here is not only address the value of these design cultures, their origins and practical applications; but also to use these approaches as a springboard for social action now for a better future. We have to start somewhere, and I have argued that the ideals and values that are discussed in this study can illuminate our thinking and action.

In spite of the banal and vulgar normality of most media-driven contemporary culture, there are, as always, some 'green shoots' of creative and imaginative solutions to the current crisis of housing provision and quality.

My wish is that the issues and ideas addressed in my study can add to other resources for hope.

Bibliography

ACKROYD, Peter: *Albion: The Origins of the English Imagination.* Chatto & Windus London, 2002

ABRAHAM, Ian *et al* (Eds): *The Book of Bitterne.* Halsgrove Wellington, 2007

ALEXANDER, Christopher: *The Timeless Way of Building.* Oxford University Press, New York 1979

APPADURAI, Arjun (Ed): *The Social Life of Things: commodities in cultural perspective.* Cambridge University Press, 1986

ASTLEY, John: *Secularism and the Working Class in London* 1860-1880 (unpublished dissertation). Oxford1969

ASTLEY, John: *Culture and Creativity.* The Company of Writers Exmouth, 2006 (Including three chapters on William Morris)

ASTLEY, John: *Herbivores & Carnivores: The Struggle for Democratic Cultural Values in post-War Britain.* Information Architects, Exmouth, 2008

BAILLIE SCOTT, M.H. *Houses and Gardens: Arts & Crafts Interiors.* Antique Collectors' Club Ltd, 1999

BANHAM, Reyner. *Theory and Design in the First Machine Age.* The Architectural Press, London, 1960

BANHAM, Reyner. *The Architecture of the Well-tempered Environment.* The Architectural Press, London, 1969

BAUMAN, Zygmunt: *Liquid Times: Living in an age of uncertainty.* Polity Press Cambridge, 2007

BEAUMONT, Matthew: *Utopia Ltd. Ideologies of Social Dreaming in England 1870-1900.* Brill, Leiden and Boston, 2005

BECKER, Howard S.: *Art Worlds.* University of California Press, 1982

BENNETT, Alan: 'Back-to-back to the future'. *The Guardian,* 16 December, 1989

BENTON Tim and Charlotte & SHARP, Dennis (Eds): *Form and Function.* Open University Press, 1975

BENTON Tim and BAKER Geoffrey: *Tradition and Continuity in the History of Architecture.* Open University Press, 1975

BERNSTEIN Basil: 'Education cannot compensate for society' in
    Stoneman C. & Rubinstein D. (eds) *Education for Democracy.*
    Penguin, Harmondsworth, 1970
BERTRAM, Anthony: *Design.* Penguin Books, Harmondsworth, 1938
BLAKE, Peter: *Mies van der Rohe: Architecture and Structure.*
    Pelican Books, Harmondsworth, 1960
BRIGGS, Asa: *Victorian Things.* Penguin, Harmondsworth, 1990
BROME, Vincent: *Six Studies in Quarrelling.* House of Stratus,
    London, 2001 (originally published in 1958)
BRUNSKILL, R.W.: *Traditional Buildings of Britain: An
    Introduction to Vernacular Architecture.* Cassell, 2004
BUDER, Stanley: *Visionaries and Planners: The Garden City
    Movement and the Modern Community.* Oxford University Press,
    1990
CALDER, Alan: *James Maclaren: Arts & Crafts Pioneer.* Shaun Tyas
    publications, Donnington, 2003
CHAPMAN, Stanley D.(Ed) *The History of Working-Class Housing.*
    David and Charles, 1971
CHERRY Gordon E.: *Town Planning in Britain since 1900.*
    Blackwell, Oxford, 1996
CLARK, Kenneth: *The Gothic Revival.* Penguin, Harmondsworth,
    (orig. 1928), 1962
COLLINI, Stefan: *English Pasts: Essays in History and Culture.*
    Oxford University Press, 1999
COLLINS, Michael: *The Likes of Us: A Biography of the White
    Working Class.* Granta Books, London, 2004
COLLINS, Michael: *Towards Post-Modernism: Design since 1851.*
    British Museum Press, London, 1994
COLLINS, Peter: *Changing Ideal in Modern Architecture.* Faber,
    London, 1965
COLEMAN, Alice, *Utopia on Trial.* Hilary Shipman, London, 1985
COLLINS, George R. and COLLINS Christiane Crassman: *Camillo
    Sitte and the Birth of Modern City Planning.* Phaidon Press,
    London, 1965
COLLS, Robert and DODD, Philip (Editors): *Englishness: Politics
    and Culture 1880-1920.* Croom Helm, London, 1988

CREESE, Walter L.: *The Search for Environment.* The Garden *City before and after,* Yale University Press, London,1966

CREESE, Walter L. (Ed): *The Legacy of Raymond Unwin.,* MIT Press, Cambridge Mass., 1967

CROOK, J.Morduant: *The Dilemma of Style: architectural ideas from the picturesque to the post-modern.* John Murray, London, 1987

DAVEY, Peter: *Arts & Crafts Architecture.* Phaidon Press London, 1995

DAY LEWIS, Cecil (Ed) *The Mind in Chains: Socialism and the Cultural Revolution.* Frederick Muller Ltd., London, 1937

DICKENS, Charles: *Hard Times.* Chapman & Hall, London

DICKENS, Peter, with Simon Duncan, Mark Goodwin and Fred Gray: *Housing, States and Localities.* Methuen, London, 1985

DOWSE, Robert E.: *The Independent Labour Party 1893-1940.* Longmans, London 1966

DRURY, Michael, *Wandering Architects.* Shaun Tyas, Stamford, Lincs, 2000

EAGLETON, Terry: *A Merrie State of Mind.* Book review in *The Guardian,* 14 Dec. 1993

EASTHOPE, Gary: *Community, hierarchy and open education.* Routledge K. Paul, London, 1975

EDWARDS, Arthur M.: *The Design Of Suburbia: A critical study in environmental history.* Pembridge Press, London, 1981

ELTON, Godfrey: *England Arise! A study of the pioneering days of the Labour Movement..* Jonathan Cape, London, 1931

FIELDING, Steven, Peter Thompson and Nick Tiratsoo: *England Arise! The Labour Party and Popular Politics in 1940s Britain.* Manchester University Press, 1995

GAVENTA,.Sarah: 'Keep Alive Our Lost Elysium: The Importance of the Suburban Public Realm'. In the report, *Housing and Suburban Growth* (Ed) Paul Hackett, The Smith Institute, London, 2009

GEOGHEGAN, Vincent: *Utopianism and Marxism.* Methuen, London, 1987

GERVAIS, David: *Literary Englands: versions of Englishness in modern writing.* Cambridge University Press 1993

GOMBRICH, Ernst H.: *In Search of Cultural History.* Clarendon Press, Oxford, 1969

GOODWIN, Jeff & JASPER, James M. (Eds): *The Social Movements Reader.* Blackwell, Oxford, 2003

GORDON, James E.: *Structures; or why things don't fall down.* Pelican/Penguin Books, Harmondsworth, 1978

HAAR, Charles M. (Ed): *The End of Innocence: A Suburban Reader,* Scott-Fresman, Ilinois, 1972

HALL, Peter: *Utopian Thought: a framework for Social, Economic and Physical Planning* in *Utopias,* Peter Armstrong & Roger Gill (Eds.). Duckworth, London 1984

HALSEY, A.H.: *Change in British Society.* Oxford University Press, 1978

HANNAN, John: *The Life of John Wheatley,* Spokesman Books, Nottingham, 1988

HARRISON, J.F.C.: *Late Victorian Britain 1875-1901,* Routledge, London, 1991

HEALTH, Ministry of: *Housing. The journal of the Housing Dept.* Volumes 1 & 2 for 1919 to 1921

HEBBERT, Michael: *The British Garden City: Metamorphosis.* In Stephen V. Ward (Ed) The Garden City: Past, Present and Future. E & F.N.Spon, London, 1992

HELLER, Agnes: *The Theory of Need in Marx.* Allison and Busby, London, 1976

HITCHMOUGH, Wendy: *C.F.A.Voysey.* Phaidon Press, London, 1995

HITCHMOUGH, Wendy: *The Arts & Crafts Home.* Pavilion Books, London, 2000

HOGGART, Richard: *The Uses of Literacy.* Penguin, Harmondsworth, 1958

HOLLOWAY, Mark: *The Necessity of Utopia* in Alexander & Gill. (see Hall)

HOSKINS, W.G.: *The Making of the English Landscape.* Pelican Books, Harmondsworth, 1970

HOUGH, Graham: *The Last Romantics: Ruskin to Yeats.* Duckworth, London, 1961 (first published in 1949)

HUNT, Tristram: *Building Jerusalem: The Rise and Fall of the Victorian City.* Weidenfeld & Nicolson, London, 2004

INEICHEN, Bernard: 'Council Housing and Disadvantage' in Brown, Muriel (Ed) T*he Structure of Disadvantage.* Heinemann, London, 1983

JACKSON, Brian: *Working Class Community.* Penguin, 1972

JACKSON, Frank: *Sir Raymond Unwin: architect, planner, visionar.* Zwemmer, London, 1985

JEVONS, R & MADGE J. *Housing Estates.* University of Bristol, 1946

JORDAN, Robert Furneaux: *Victorian Architecture.* Penguin, Harmondsworth, 1966

KENWARD, James: *The Suburban Child.* Cambridge University Press, UK, 1955

KILLINGBACK, Neil: 'Limits to Mutuality' in *New Views of Co-operation* Ed. by Stephen Yeo. Routledge, London, 1988

KIMBER, Sidney: *Thirty-eight years of public life in Southampton 1910-48.* Privately published autobiography, 1949

KIRK, Sheila: *Philip Webb: Pioneer of Arts and Crafts Architecture.* Wiley-Academy, London, 2005

KORNWOLF, James D.: *M.H.Baillie Scott and the Arts & Crafts Movement.* The John Hopkins Press, Baltimore and London, 1972

KUMAR, Krishan: *Prophecy and Progress: The Sociology of Industrial and post-Industrial Society.* Penguin. Harmondsworth, 1978

LAMBERT, Camilla and WEIR, David: (Eds.) *Cities in Modern Britain.* Fontana/Collins, London, 1975

LEWIS, Michael J.: *The Gothic Revival.* Thames & Hudson, London 2002

LINSLEY, Barbara: Homes for Heroes:Local Authority Housing in Rural Norfolk 1918-1923 in *Housing the Twentieth Century Nation* edited by Elain Harwood and Alan Powers. Published by the Twentieth Century Society in collaboration with English Heritage, 2008

LYALL, Sutherland: *The State of British Architecture.* The Architectural Press, London, 1980

LYMAN, Richard W.: *The First Labour Government 1924.* Chapman & Hall, London, 1958

MacCARTHY, Fiona: *William Morris: A Life for Our Time.* Faber & Faber, London, 1994

MacCARTHY, Fiona: 'The Old Romantics' article in *The Guardian,* 5 March 2005

MACLEOD, Robert: *Style and Society: Architectural ideology in Britain 1835-1914.* RIBA publications, London, 1971

McINTYRE, Anthony: *The Shell Book of British Buildings.* David & Charles, Newton Abbot, 1984

MARKUS, Thomas A.: *Buildings and Power: Freedom and control in the origin of modern building types.* Routledge, London, 1993

MASTERMAN, Charles: *England After War: A Study.* Hodder and Stoughton, London, 1921

MEACHAM, Standish: *Regaining Paradise: Englishness and the Early Garden City Movement.* Yale University Press, 1999

MELLERS, Wilfred: *Vaughan Williams and the Vision of Albion.* Barrie & Jenkins, London, 1989

MELLING, Joseph (Ed).: *Housing, Social Policy and the State.* Croom Helm, London, 1980

MICHELSON, William H.: *Man and His Urban Environment: A Sociological Approach.* Addison-Wesley Publishing Co., London, 1970

MILLER, Mervyn: *Raymond Unwin: Garden Cities and Town Planning.* Leicester University Press, 1992

MINTON, Anna: *Ground Control: Fear and happiness in the twenty-fist-century city.* Penguin, London, 2009

MOORE, Niamh & WHELAN Yvonne (Eds): *Heritage, Memory and the Politics of Identity.* Ashgate, Aldershot, 2007

MORTON, A.L.: *The English Utopia.* Lawrence & Wishart London, 1952

MULHEARN, Francis: *Culture/Metaculture.* Routledge, 2000

MURPHY, James: *Church, State and Schools in Britain, 1800-1970.* Routledge & Kegan Paul, London, 1971

NOWELL-SMITH, Simon (Ed): *Edwardian England 1901-1914.* Oxford University Press, 1964

NUTTGENS, Patrick: *The Landscape of Ideas.* Faber & Faber, London, 1972

OLIVER, Paul et al: *Dunroamin: The Suburban Semi and its Enemies.* Pimlico, 1994 (original in 1981)

OLECHNOWICZ, Andrzy: *Working-Class Housing in England Between the Wars.* (A study of the Becontree Estate in London in the 1930s). Oxford Historical Monographs, Clarenden Press, 1997

OVERY, Paul: *Light, Air and Openness: Modern Architecture Between the Wars.* Thames & Hudson, London, 2007

PAHL, Ray: *Whose City?* Longmans, London, 1970

PAWLEY, Martin: 'All the history that fits' article in *The Guardian* 1 Dec. 1986.

PEARSON, Lynn F.: *The Architectural and Social History of Cooperative Living.* MacMillan, London, 1988

PEDERSEN, Susan & MANDLER, Peter (Eds) *After the Victorians: Private conscience and public duty in modern Britain.* Routledge 1994

PEVSNER, Nikolaus: *Pioneers of Modern Design.* Penguin Books, Harmonsworth, 1960

PEVSNER, Nikolaus: *The Sources of Modern Architecture and Design.* Thames & Hudson, London, 1968

PEVSNER, Nikolaus: *Some architectural writers of the nineteenth century.* Clarendon Press, Oxford, 1972

PICOT, Edward: *Outcasts from Eden.* Liverpool University Press, 1997

POULSON Christine (Ed): *William Morris on Art & Design.* Academic Press, Sheffield, 1996

PRETTY David & HACKETT, Paul: *Mind the Gap: housing in a cold climate.* A report for the Smith Institute and published by the Town and Country Planning Association, London, 2009

PURDOM, Charles B.: *The Garden City.* Dent, London, 1913

PYE, David: *The Nature of Design.* Studio Vista, London, 1964

RATTENBURY, Arnold: 'Come and Stay' a review of several books about Clough Williams-Ellis in the *London Review of Books* Vol. 19 No.23 27 Nov. 1997

READ, Herbert: *The English Vision.* Eyre & Spottiswoode, London, 1933

REID, Richard: *Cottages (The Shell Book of).* Michael Joseph Ltd., London, 1977

REILLY, C.H.: *Representative British Architects of the Present Day.* Batsford, London, 1931

REINER, Thomas A.: *The Place of the Ideal Community in Urban Planning.* University of Pennsylvania Press, Philadelphia, 1963

RICHARDS, J.M.: *Modern Architecture,* Penguin Books, Harmondsworth, 1940

ROLFE, Joan: *Memories of Merry Oak (1930-1950): The Garden Estate.* Bitterne Local History Society, Southampton, 2001

ROWBOTHAM, Sheila: *Edward Carpenter 1844-1929: A Very Modern Victorian* in *Key Words 7 (A Journal of Cultural Materialism).* The Raymond Williams Society, 2009

RUBENS, Godfrey, *William R. Lethaby: his Life and Work.* Architectural Press, London, 1986

RUNINSTEIN, David and STONEMAN, Colin (Eds), *Education for Democracy.* enguin, Harmondsworth, 1970

SALER, Michael T.: *The Avant-Garde in Interwar England.* Oxford University Press, 1999

SAINT, Andrew: 'I had to refrain' a review in the *London Review of Books* Vol.27 No.23 1 Dec. 2005 (of Sheila Kirk's book cited above)

SCHAMA, Simon: *Landscape and Memory.* HarperCollins, London, 1995

SCHAFFER, Frank: *The New Town Story,* MacGibbon & Kee, London, 1970

SCOTT, Geoffrey: *The Architecture of Humanism: A Study in the History of Taste.* W.W. Norton, London, 1999 Edition (of the 1914 original)

SEABROOK, Jeremy and BLACKWELL, Trevor: *The Revolt Against Change.* Vintage, London, 1993

SEARLE, G.R.: *A New England? Peace and War 1886-1914.* Oxford University Press, 2004

SENNETT, A.R.: *Garden Cities in Theory and Practice.* Benrose London,1905

SENNETT, Richard: *The Craftsman.* Allen Lane, London, 2008

SERVICE, Alastair: *Edwardian Architecture: A Handbook to Building Design in Britain 1890-1914.* Thames & Hudson, London, 1977

SHARP, Dennis: (Ed) *The Anti-Rationalists* and *The Rationalists.* Two separate collections of essays: the first, on 'anti-modernists' edited by Pevsner and J.M.Richards and published by The Architectural Press in 1973; the Rationalists, on the Modernists, edited by Dennis Sharp and published in 1978. I read a combined version of these essays published in 2000.

SHARP, Thomas: *Town and Countryside: some aspects of urban and rural development.* Oxford University Press, 1932

STAMP, Gavin and GOULANCOURT, Andre: *The English House 1860-1914: The Flowering of English Domestic Architecture.* Faber and Faber, London, 1986

STANTON, S.G.: *HOUSING: County Borough of Southampton. Housing schemes carried out in Southampton.* Borough Engineer's Department, Southampton, 1931

STRONG, Roy: *Country Life 1897-1997: The English Arcadia.,* Country Life Books and Boxtree, London, 1996

SWENARTON, Mark: *'Pugin's Law' a* multi-book review in *The London Review of Books* Vol.2, No.23 4 Dec. 1980

SWENARTON, Mark: *Building the New Jerusalem: Architecture, housing and politics 1900-1930.* IHS Press, Watford, 2008

SWENARTON, Mark: *Homes Fit for Heroes: The politics and architecture of early state housing in Britain.* Heinemann, London, 1981

TAYLOR, Nicholas: *The Village in the City.* Temple Smith in association with *New Society* (Towards a New Society series), London, 1973

TAWNEY, R.H.: *Equality.* Unwin Books, London, 1931

THOMPSON, E.P.: *The Making of the English Working Class.* Gollancz, London, 1963

TINNISWOOD,Adrian: *The Arts & Crafts House*. Mitchell Beazley, London, 1999

TIRATSOO, Nick: 'New Vista: the Labour Party, citizenship and the built environment in the 1940s' in Richard Weight and Abigail Beach (Eds) *The Right To Belong: Citizenship and National Identity in Britain, 1930-1960*. I.B.Tauris, London, 1998

TOYE, Richard: *Lloyd George and Churchill: Rivals for Greatness*. MacMillan, London, 2007

WALVIN, James: *Victorian Values*. Sphere, London, 1987

WARD, Colin: '*They did it their way'*. A Review in *New Society,* 30 May 1986

WARD, Colin: *Influences: Voices of creative dissent*. Green Books Bideford, Devon, 1991

WARD, Stephen: *Planning and Urban Change*. Sage, London, 2004

WATKIN, David: *Morality and Architecture*. Clarendon Press, Oxford, 1977

WATKIN, David: *The English Vision: The Picturesque in Architecture, Landscape and Garden Design*. John Murray, London, 1982

WHITE, L.E.: *Community or Chaos: New housing estates and their social problems*. The National Council of Social Service, London, 1950

WILLIAMS, Ralph Vaughan: *National Music and Other Essays*. Clarendon Press Oxford, 1996

WILLIAMS, Ursula Vaughan & HOLST, Imogen (Eds): *Heirs and Rebels: Letters written to each other and occasional writings on music by Ralph Vaughan Williams and Gustav Holst*. Oxford University Press, 1959

WILLMOTT, Peter: *Friendship Networks and Social Support*. Policy Studies Institute, London 1987

WOODCOCK, Peter: *This Enchanted Isle*. Gothic Image Publications, Glastonbury, 2000.

WORPOLE, Ken: *Here Comes the Sun: architecture and public space in twentieth century European culture*. Reaktion Books, London, 2000

WRIGHT, Patrick: 'Brideshead and the Towerblocks'. A book review
    in the *London Review of Books* Vol.10 No.11 2 June 1988 of
    Home: A Short History of an Idea by Witold Rybczynski (1988)
YEO, Stephen: 'Socialism, the state and some oppositional
    Englishness' in COLLIS and DODD, 1988
ZIMMERMAN, Don and POLLNER, Melvin: 'The Everyday World
as a Phenomenon'. In DOUGLAS, Jack (Ed) *Understanding Everyday
Life*. Routledge & Kegan Paul, London, 1974

Index

Abercrombie, Patrick, 130

Acquisition of Land Act (1919), 169

Addison, Chistopher, 139, 143, 153, 160, *165-166, 168-169*, 171, 176, 183, 205, *218-219*, 220, 222, 225, *228-229*, 237, 276

Aesthetic movement, *31-32*, 57, 226

Aldridge, Henry, 213

Althusser, Louis, 247

Ancient Monuments Protection Act (1882), 94

Anti-Rationalists, 67

Arcadia, 48-49, 94

Arnold, Matthew, 64

Art Nouvea, 67

Art Nouveau, 67, 81, 83, 95

Arts & Crafts Exhibition (1885), 141

Arts & Crafts Exhibition Society (1888), 53, 92, 100

Banham, Reyner, 97

The Barn (Exmouth): *arch.* William Lethaby, 86

Baroque, the, 37, 56, 100

Bauhaus, 54, 68, 95

Beardsley, Aubrey, 67

Bedford Park, 82, *85-86*, 138, 225

Beeching Report, 138

Bell, Daniel, 223

Bennett, Alan, 108

Benson, William, 100

Bernstein, Basil, 239

Betjeman, John, 44, 81, 94, 101, 218

Bevan, Aneurin, 147, 175, 257

Beveridge, William, 167, 169, 175, *188-189*, 193, 195, 234, 256, 270, 305

Blake, William, 53, 110, 262, 283

Booth, William ('In Darkest England, 1890'), 113

Bournville, i, *132-34*, 137, 139, 215

Buchanan, Sir Colin: 'Traffic in Towns' report (1963), 138

Buildings Materials Research Committee, 228

Burne-Jones, Ned, 32, 60, 92, 100

Cadburys, The, 135, 139, 213

Camden Society, 38

Carlyle, Thomas, 38, 42
Carpenter, Edward, 65, 141, *199-200*, 207, 209, 223, 255, 258
Castells, Manuel, 248
Central School of Arts & Crafts (*est.* 1896), 63
Chadwick, Edwin, 114
Chamberlain, Neville, iii, 139, 143, *146-149*, *152-153*, 156, 159-160, 165, *170-171*, 176, *183-184*, 228
Chartists, The, 117, 132, 255
Cheap Train Act, The (1883), 138
Cohen, Anthony, 241
Cole, Henry, 48
Collins, Michael, 54, 69, 218, 281
Community Association movement, 282
company housing, i
Comte, Auguste, 209
Conran, Terence, 95, 213
Continental European Modernism, 8
Cosmopolitan: magazine, 294
Crane, Walter, 53, 67, 85, 141, 245
Creese, Walter, 123, 127, 141, 201, 204, 216, 296
Critical Theory (CT), 11
Cromwell, Oliver, 255, 261
de Morgan, William, 85

Design and Industries Association (DIA), 47, 63
Dickens, Charles, 106, *112-114*, 176, 192
Diggers, The, 237, 254, 255
Dresser, Christopher, 67
Durkheim, Emile, 241
Easthope, Gary: 'Community' study (1975), 239
Ecclesiological Group, The, 61
Edwards, Arthur: *The Design of Suburbia* (1981), 6
Eliot, George, 209
Emerson, Ralph Waldo, 196, 199, 209
Engels, F., 18, 39, 136, 190, 256; 'The Condition of the Working Class in England' (1844), 136
English Domestic Revival, 55
Errington family (Bitterne, Southampton), 266
Fabian Society, 88, 124, 190, 210, 212, 214, 229
First World War (The Great War), ii
Forster, E.M., 47
Frankfurt School, The, 11, 54, 248, 251, 290, 293

Garden Cities and Town
  Planning Association, 139,
  165, 220
Garden Cities of Tomorrow
  (*pub.* 1898 & 1902):
  Ebenezer Howard, **119-
  137**
Garden City movement,
  104, 110, 119, 160, 223, 235,
  300
Garden City Pioneer Co.
  Ltd, 139
Gardner, Benjamin, 156
Geddes, Patrick, 88, *128-
  130*, 181, 198, 204, 233
George, Henry, 123
George, Lloyd, 9, 51, 61, 63,
  76, 124, *132-133*, 139, 166,
  186, 209, 218, 225, 227, 276
Gloag, John, *23-24*, 80
Godwin, Edward William,
  67
Goldsmith, Oliver, 44
Gombrich, Ernst, 27
Gothic architecture, 37
Great Exhibition (1851), 22,
  24-25
Green, T.H., 189
Greenwood, Arthur, *148-
  149*, *172-173*, 175, 261, 282
Gropius, Walter, 95
Guild of Handicraft (*est.*
  1888), 65
Habermas, Jurgen, 248

Halsey, A.H., 281
Hampstead Garden, 140,
  192, 208, 216, 227, 233
Hampstead Garden
  Institute, 140
Hardy, Thomas, 51
Harmsworth, Cecil, 6, 135,
  136
Harris, Alexandra, 8
Harvey, Alexander, 134
Hills Report on Social
  Housing (2007), 303
Hobsbawm, Eric, 39, 115,
  293
Hoffman Kiln (c. 1858), 3
Hoggart, Richard (*The Uses
  of Literacy*, 1957), 116, 244,
  251, 289
Holst, Gustav, i, 61, 109,
  110, 208, 259, *261-262*
Hoskins, W. G., 201
Hough, Graham, 40
Housing Act (1923), 149,
  159, 170, *180-181*, *183-184*,
  207-208
Housing: (journal of the
  MOH), 220
Housing Act 1924 (1924), 2,
  16, 112, 144, 146, 148, 154,
  275
Housing and Town
  Planning Act (1909), 123,
  135

Howard, Ebenezer, i, 4, 26, 47, 85, 91, 104, 111-112, 118, **119-145**, *163-164*, 192, 199, 207, 236, 242, 264, 300

Hulme, T.E., 17

International Congre0ss of Modern Architecture, 232

Jekyll, Gertrude, 272

Joseph Rowntree 'Social Evils' report (2009), 304

Journal of the Institute of Municipal and County Engineers, 275

Joyce, James, 287

Kahn, Louis, 268

Kaye, Harvey, 117, *292-293*

Kelly, Ruth, 303

Kimber, Sidney: Mayor of Southampton, 276

Knight, Richard Payne, 37

Kropotkin, Peter, 123

Labour Housing Association: *est.* 1898, 221

Lancaster, Osbert, 242

Langley, Batty, 37

Le Corbusier (Charles-Edouard Jeanneret), 63, *72-73*, 95, 207, 242,

Lee, Laurie, 285

Lefebvre, Henri, *287-288*, *290-292*, 295

Letchworth, 6, 84, 123, *130-136*, *139-142*, 192, 200, *215-216*, 221, 233

Lethaby, William, 47, 55, *61-68*, *70-74*, 76, 87, 91, 94, 136, 141

Levellers, The, *254-255*

Lever, William, i, *133-135*, 137, *139-141*, 213

Liberty, Arthur, 67, 94

Local Government Act (1858), 114

Locke, John, 37

Lowenthal, David, 288

Lutyens, Edwin, 24, 79, 272

MacDonald, Ramsay, *148-149*, 151, *181-184*

MacFayden, Dugald, 121

MacKmurdo, Arthur, 81

Maclaren, James, 84

Making of the English Working Class, The (1963): Edward Thompson, 113

Marcuse, Herbert, 44, 103, 290, 293

Markus, Thomas, 75

Marx, Karl, 18, *27-29*, 30, 39, 41, 44, 102, 109, 115, 117, 192, 196, 209, 256, 287, 291, *292-293*

McKibbin, Ross, 286

Meacham, Standish, 115, 133, 193, *223-225*, *235-236*, 269

Merry Oak: Bitterne, Southampton, i, iii, iv, 9, 52-53, 69, 82, 96, 99, 103,

133, 140, 144, 153, 156, 188,
199, 204, 217, 227, 231, 234,
237, 243, 254, 258, 264,
266-298, 300
Metroland, 73
Metroland, 94
  (John Betjeman's 1973
  documentary)
Miliband, Ralph, 28
Milton Keynes, 283
Modernism, *29-30*, *46-47*,
  54, *73-74*, 94, 277, 283, 297
Moore, Henry, 30
More, Thomas (*Utopia*,
  1516), 110
Morris & Co (*est.* 1861), 76
Morris, 42
Morris, William, i, ii, 4, 8,
  18, 20, 22, **24-44**, *49-54*, 57,
  60-67, 70, *76-77*, *79-83*, 85,
  87, 91-92, 96, *100-103*, 106,
  111, 115, 117, *123-124*, 127,
  135, 141, *157-158*, *193-194*,
  198, 202, *207-209*, 213, 215,
  223, 225, 236, 245, 256, 268,
  272; 'The Housing of the
  Poor' article, 20; 'A Dream
  of John Ball' (1888), 111;
  'How I became a Socialist'
  (1894), 24; *News from
  Nowhere* (1890), 19, 29, 35,
  123, 124, 215, 245; 'Revival
  of Architecture, The'
  (1888), 33

Morrison, Arthur, 114
Morton, A. L., 123
Mumford, Lewis, *128-129*,
  263
Municipal Corporation Act,
  The (1835), 114
Nash, Paul, 8
National Housing and
  Town Planning Council:
  est. 1909, 213
National Housing Reform
  Council, 213
National Secularist Society,
  35, 193
National Trust, 51, 94, 104
Nicholls, W.H., 149
Northern Art Workers'
  Guild, 141, 209
Orwell, George, 224
Osborn, Frederic, 119, 129
Pahl, Ray, 238, 242, *248-249*
Palmer, Samuel, 46
Parker, Barry, 2, 70, 84, 127,
  140-141, **196-236**, 245
Parry, Hubert ('Jersulem'),
  110
Pater, Walter, 32
Pevsner, Nikolaus, *53-54*,
  63, *68-69*, 77, 81, *87-88*, 95,
  101, 157
Picturesque movement, *23-
  24*, 74, 233
Pollio, Vitruvius, 37

Port Sunlight, i, 82, *132-135*, 137, 139, 141

Priestley, J.B., *257-258*

Prior, Edward (1857-1932), *2-3*, 55, 61, *86-87*, 97

Public Health Act (1848), 114

Public Health Act (1870), 56

Public Health Act (1875) 114

public sector housing, i

Public Utility Societies (PUS), 221

Pugin, Augustus, 33, 36, 38, 70, 74, 99

Purdom, Charles, 132, *135-137*, *140-142*, 144, 215

'Quakers', 137, 209

Red House, The (Bexleyheath), 60, 76, 84, 100

Reform Act (1832), 57, 88, 238

Reilly, Charles (report), 9, 235

Reiss, Richard, *52-53*, *139-140*, *165-166*, 276

RIBA, 87, 206, 226, 245

Riesman, David, 263

Robertson, John, 213

Robinson, William, 272

Rolfe, Joan, 266, 271, *278-282*

Rowntrees, The, 139, 216, 304

Royal Jubilee Exhibition, Manchester (1887), 141

Ruskin, John, *24-33*, 38, 40, 42, 52, 56, 67, 70, 74, 78, 81, 85, *87-98*, 107, 111, 119, 128, 136, 223, 226

Russian Revolution (1917), 186

Saint-Simon, 18

Santayana, George, 9

Scott, George Gilbert, 51

Scott, MacKay Baillie, 51, **55-57**, **66-68**, 78, *83-84*, 96, 103

Sedding, John, 61, 70

Sharawaggi, 233; orig. Chinese, 233

Sharp, Cecil, 110

Sharp, Thomas, 69, 97, 121, 122, *260- 261*

Shaw, George Bernard, 145

Shaw, Richard Norman, 2, 42, 55, 57, 61, 69, 82, *85-87*, 100, 124, 133, 226

Simon, E.D., 150, 269

Skinner, B.F., 129, 196, 198, 207, 245

Society for the Protection of Ancient Buildings (SPAB), *50-51*, 94

Stanton, Sidney G., 143, 227, *231-232*, *275-276*

Stickley, Gustav, 54
Street, G.E., 50
Surrealists, *293-294*
Thompson, Edward, 31,
 113, 115, 251, 257
Thompson, Willliam, 213
Thoreau, Henri David, 46,
 196, 199
Tom Shaw, 149
Town and Country
 Planning Act (1932), 130
Town Planning Act (1909),
 205
Tudor Walters committee,
 168, *227-228*, 230, 245
Unwin, Raymond (1863-
 1940), i, 4, *7-9*, 62, 65, *69-
 70*, 73, 75, 84, 112, *127-128*,
 130, 134, 136, *139-141*, 163,
 166, 190, 195, **196-236**, 242,
 245-246, 255, 259, 264, 269,
 296-297
Utopia, 35, 48, 110, 207, 256
Utopia, see Thomas More
van der Rohe, Mies, 283
Voysey, Charles, 42, **54-57**,
 68, **76- 81**, **83-84**, 87, 101
'Wandering Architects', 61
Ward, Colin, 245
Watkin, David, 70
Webb, Philip, i, 2, 51, 55, 57,
 60-61, 69, 74, *76-77*, 84,
 100, 135, 141, 189, 268
Weber, Max, 161

Wells, H.G., 35, 79, 127, 140
'Wheatley' Housing Act
 (1924), *See* Housing Act of
 1924
Wheatley, John, i, ii, 1, 2, 7,
 12, 99, *112-114*, **143-160**,
 165-166, 171-172, 175-176,
 178-188, 205, 228, *230-231*,
 237, 257, 259, 276, 282, 299,
 304
White, L.E., 201
Whitman, Walt, 65, 141,
 196, 205, 208
Wilde, Oscar, 114
Williams, Raymond, i, 11,
 61, 64, *104-105*, 107, 113,
 132, 199, 208, 237, 243, 246,
 250-252, 259, *260-262, 288-
 289*
Winstanley, Gerard, 254
Workers' Educational
 Association (WEA), 34,
 193
Workmen's National
 Housing Council, 221
Wright, Frank Lloyd, 54, 65,
 79, *88-89*, 107, 198, 214,
 253, 284
Yates, Richard, 263
Yeo, Stephen, 28, 29
Young, Hilton, *174-175*, 192,
 240
Zola, Emile, 114

NOTES

N OTES

NOTES